Romantic Irony in French Literature
From Diderot to Beckett

Romantic Irony
in French Literature
From Diderot
to Beckett

Lloyd Bishop

VANDERBILT UNIVERSITY PRESS
Nashville, Tennessee
1989

Acknowledgments

I gratefully acknowledge the helpful suggestions and the encouragement of several colleagues, especially Professor Philip Mellen of Virginia Tech, Professor Robert T. Denommé of the University of Virginia, and Professor L. Ross Chambers of the University of Michigan. Special thanks are owed to Angie Harvey for her expert typing of the manuscript.

In another form, parts of this book have appeared in earlier studies. I wish to thank the copyright holders for permission to reprint passages from "Michaux's Clown," © 1962 by *The French Review,* 36 (1962), 153–157; "Romantic Irony in Musset's *Namouna,*" © 1979 by *Nineteenth-Century French Studies,* 7 (1979), 81–91; "Romantic Irony in *Le Rouge et le Noir:* Julien as Lover and Thinker," in *In Search of Style: Essays in French Literary Stylistics,* © The University Press of Virginia, 1982, pp. 46–63; *The Romantic Hero and His Heirs in French Literature* (New York: Peter Lang Publishing, 1984), pp. 122–137; "Musset's Poetic World: A Trembling Universe in Perpetual Motion," in *The Poetry of Alfred de Musset* (New York: Peter Lang Publishing, 1987), pp. 65–79; all rights reserved.

Copyright © 1989 by Lloyd Bishop
Published in 1989 by the Vanderbilt University Press
Printed in the United States of America

Library of Congress Cataloging-in-Publication Data

Bishop, Lloyd, 1933-
    Romantic irony in French literature from Diderot to Beckett /
Lloyd Bishop
        p. cm.
    Bibliography: p.
    Includes index.
    ISBN 0-8265-1233-X:
    1. French literature—19th century—History and criticism. 2. French
literature—History and criticism. 3. Irony in literature.
4. Romanticism—France. I. Title.
PQ287.B58 1989   89–35563
840.9′18—dc20   CIP

This book is dedicated to the memory of Jeffrey Carre, one of my very best teachers, and Ken Stites, one of my very best friends.

Contents

Preface

I HAVE been fascinated with romantic irony since the mid-1970s when I was struck by its presence in Musset and Stendhal. This book allows me to describe a phenomenon that has been the subject of lively discussion and debate for almost two centuries now (a debate largely monopolized by German scholars) and to explore it in works of nine important French writers. The group of authors selected is meant to be exemplary, not exhaustive. In general the sequence of chapters follows the chronology of French literary history. I have placed the discussion of Musset ahead of the chapter on Stendhal and have placed Michaux before Queneau and Beckett in the interests of the general exposition.

Ingrid Strohschneider-Kohrs's *Die romantische Ironie,* while a superb piece of scholarship and the best single study we have on the subject of romantic irony, is not a definitive work as has been claimed. Indeed it is ironic that such an epithet should be used in connection with a phenomenon one of whose philosophical assumptions (and artistic effects) is that no interpretation, theoretical or artistic, can be definitive. The present work is designed not to compete with but to complement the work of Strohschneider-Kohrs and also that of Lilian Furst, who has given us (in *Fictions of Romantic Irony*) the best discussion in English since Douglas Muecke's lucid account *(The Compass of Irony).* The most detailed discussion of romantic irony written in French, René Bourgeois's *L'Ironie romantique* suffers from a certain vagueness that permeates the entire book, a vagueness attributable to his initial reductive definition of romantic irony as *la conscience du jeu.*

Romantic irony cannot be captured in simple formulas such as "an ironic stance whereby an author playfully distances himself from his own work within the work itself." In the first place, the romantic ironist's attitude toward his material is always ambivalent, and it is only by teasing out the various strands of the ambivalence—the positive as well as the negative, the serious as well as the playful—that any meaningful discussion can proceed. In the second place, romantic irony is a philosophical irony, and its true significance resides not in the distancing effects employed but in their implications. In the third place, a definition based solely on specific strategies, structures, and formal devices will not capture romantic irony in all its impressively varied manifestations because, as Beda Allemann has noted, literary irony is all the more ironic as it dispenses with overt ironic signals. The subtlest form of irony is an irony not of *signifiants* but of *signifiés,* what Allemann, Robert Musil, and Hugo van Hofmannsthal call an "irony of things"—an ironic incompatibility of referents. This irony of things is often at work in Flaubert, Michaux, Queneau, and Beckett. The range of romantic irony is vast; it extends from the most obvious of overt devices—the Pirandellian parabasis and the destruction-of-illusion effect—to the self-conscious texts of Mann and Nabokov and to the subtlest forms of unsignaled irony. In the fourth place, romantic irony, by its very nature, resists clear-cut, univocal readings, and often its best interpretation is to be found in its very resistance to interpretation. It often partakes of what Wayne Booth calls "unstable-infinite" irony and what Roland Barthes calls "uncertain irony"—ironies that lead to paradoxical or polyvalent meanings and even to the conclusion that any definitive meaning is impossible. Stuart Sperry's definition of romantic irony in English literature is based strictly on the notion of indeterminacy.

A purely theoretical discussion of romantic irony should serve mainly as a point of departure. At least that is the premise and the plan of this book. The main justification for studying romantic irony, in my view, is to see how it illuminates particular literary works. On the other hand, we cannot study romantic irony in any work until we know rather precisely what we are talking about. The initial chapter serves as a theoretical springboard, but it is not until the chapter on Baudelaire that the general description is fairly complete and supported by sufficient examples. I use the word *description* instead of *definition* for the reasons outlined above and to suggest, as Lilian Furst has wisely done, that the goal here is to afford the reader a robust understanding of a complex subject rather than portable definitions that may be handy but are not watertight.

Friedrich von Schlegel saw in romantic irony a "progressive," everexpanding, upward-striving consciousness that moves ever closer to (but never reaches) the infinite (God). In our own century Georg Lukács has claimed that irony, or the ironic consciousness, is "the highest freedom that can be achieved in a world without God." The very extravagance of such claims is enough to indicate the great importance that has been attached to irony in general and romantic irony in particular in modern (here meaning romantic and postromantic) literature. My hope is that I have done justice to a subject that is both intrinsically interesting and unquestionably crucial for a full understanding of modern literature and the modern sensibility.

1

What Is Romantic Irony?

S INCE romantic irony has been studied chiefly by German scholars, and since the German scholars themselves have disagreed radically about the precise nature of the phenomenon, a working definition seems appropriate at the outset. In *A Dictionary of Literary Terms* we are told that "the romantic ironist detaches himself from his own artistic creation, treating it playfully or objectively, thus presumably showing his complete freedom."[1] This ironic detachment comes not after but during the creative performance itself and is imposed upon a material that is fundamentally, or at least in large measure, *serious*— hence the irony. We are dealing with a complex and highly paradoxical form of irony. The author presents us with a theme or a hero that he takes seriously to a significant degree, but he nonetheless cannot take his work as a whole with total seriousness, nor can he relate to his hero with total sympathy. A dictionary definition cannot begin to suggest the many specific stylistic strategies used to produce romantic irony, even less to indicate its important implications. The best single introduction to romantic irony is the theoretical work of the German critic and aesthetician Friedrich von Schlegel. For Schlegel, the universe as experienced by man is "an infinitude which cannot be reduced to rational order, a chaos, a complex of contradiction and incongruity, for our *limited* intellects cannot fathom the order of the *absolute*. We may at times catch a glimpse of this order, but once we try to realize it for ourselves or express it to others we are involved in contradiction and paradox" (Immerwahr, "Subjectivity or Objectivity of Schlegel's Irony," p. 177). René Wellek defines Schlegelian irony as "the recognition of the fact that the world in its essence is paradoxical and that an ambivalent attitude alone can grasp its contradictory totality" (*History of Modern Criticism* 2:14). Irony for

Schlegel, as it was for Tieck, Solger, and Adam Müller, is not simply a stylistic or rhetorical device but a vision of the universe at large. He speaks of "philosophical irony" and defines it as "klares Bewusstsein der ewigen Agilität, des unendlich vollen Chaos" (clear consciousness of eternal mobility, of the infinite fullness of chaos).[2]

Ingrid Strohschneider-Kohrs (*Die romantische Ironie,* pp. 59–63; "Zur Poetik," p. 77) claims that in this important statement Schlegel is not joining the concepts of mobility and chaos, is not creating a synonymous expression, but that he is speaking of two different things: the mobility *(Beweglichkeit)* of the ironist's mind *and* the outer chaos, which the mind attempts to grasp. But if Schlegel, in this particular fragment, were indeed speaking of both the outer chaos and the perceiving mind, he would have said so—and as he usually does—with the (often underlined) coordinating conjunction *und.* The use of the comma, rather than the conjunction, and the possessive construction—the double genitive—indicate that we are dealing not with an additive phrase but with an amplification. Eternal mobility—eternal becoming—is an essential aspect of chaos. (Other essential aspects are its infinite fullness and its creative capacity.)

Strohschneider-Kohrs is misinterpreting this fragment, but she does not misinterpret Schlegel's view of the ironist's mind, which he *does* perceive, but in other passages, not this one, as characterized by a vivacious mobility, constantly shifting from subjectivity to objectivity, from the particular to the universal, from realism to idealism, from earnestness to jest, and from what he calls self-creation *(Selbstschöpfung)* to self-destruction *(Selbstvernichtung).* This mobility of the artist's mind and subsequently the mobility *produced* in (and by) the mind of the reader will become clearer as we proceed through this chapter and through the book.

The true ironist, according to Schlegel, is not discouraged by this eternal mobility of chaos; irony is simultaneously a mode of perceiving and of transcending the paradoxes of existence. The ironic consciousness is a stage in a dialectical progression toward an ideal, "transcendental" poetry in which the poet, although he can never resolve the inherent contradictions and logical antinomies of existence (and of art), can rise above them by acknowledging and confronting them in the work itself. Many of Schlegel's commentators have not fully realized that there is a difference between rising above or beyond paradox and dissolving it, a difference between transcendence and resolution. The Schlegelian dialectic admits of no final synthesis; it is an endless process leading to higher and higher consciousness but not to an infinite or absolute consciousness.[3] Schlegel frequently states his conviction that the essence of romantic poetry is that it can only eternally "become"; it can never be completed. The centrality of irony in German romantic poetry cannot be overstressed since this poetry tended to be defined by German aestheticians like Adam Müller as a union of opposites. For Solger, irony is the defining principle of *all* poetry and all art.

Schlegel is aware of the irreducible contradiction involved in attempting to represent a dynamic universe in terms of a static representation, to represent the infinite (the artist's ultimate goal) in finite terms: "While art is bounded on every side, nature, on the contrary, is everywhere vast, illimitable and inexhaustible" ("On the Limits of the Beautiful," AMW, p. 418). Any theoretical or artistic representation of reality can never be complete but only an approximation. And language itself, being both a rational system and a mediating, approximate instrument, cannot capture the unsystematic chaos and infinite fullness of the cosmos. Anticipating Samuel Beckett, Schlegel insists on the paradoxocal situation of the writer, who is aware of both "the impossibility and the necessity of total communication" *(Lycaeum, 108)*. Another Schlegelian paradox catches the spirit of romantic irony: "It is equally deadly for the mind to have a system or to have none. It will simply have to decide to combine both" *(Athenaeum, 53)*.

In his *Literary Notebooks* Schlegel defined romantic irony as a "tension of opposites." Douglas Muecke (*Irony,* p. 20) has well described this tension and the "ironic position" of the romantic ironist as seen by Schlegel.

> The artist is in an ironic position for several reasons: in order to write well he must be both creative and critical, subjective and objective, enthusiastic and realistic, emotional and rational, unconsciously inspired and a conscious artist; his work purports to be about the world and yet is fiction; he feels an obligation to give a true or complete account of reality but he knows this is impossible, reality being incomprehensibly vast, full of contradictions, and in a continual state of becoming, so that even a true account would be immediately falsified as soon as it was completed. The only possibility open for a real artist is to stand apart from his work and at the same time incorporate this aware-

ness of his ironic position into the work itself and so create something which will, if a novel, not simply be a story but rather the telling of a story complete with the author and the narrating, the reader and the reading, the style and the choosing of the style, the fiction and its distance from fact, so that we shall regard it as being ambivalently both art and life.

The ironist's healthy skepticism, his acute awareness of his limitations and of the impossibility of doing full artistic justice to the task he has set himself, does not dampen his "romantic" enthusiasm. He enjoys representing, however imperfectly and incompletely, the fertile, abundant, and "creative" chaos of life. Philosophical irony, in criticizing one's own enthusiastic commitment to the theories and fictions of one's mind (this is part of what Schlegel means by self-destruction), enables the thinker and the artist (and especially the artist-as-thinker) to maintain contact with the infinitely variegated abundance of reality. Moreover the artist delights in his godlike creativity, in his freedom and superiority over his creation, and tends to sport with it playfully. He sports with it for another reason as well: he is self-consciously aware of art as illusion and feels both an obligation to puncture the illusion and a keen pleasure in doing so (this is another aspect of self-destruction)—and at the very moment of creation, confident that he can re-create what he has playfully deconstructed. Schlegel was influenced by the ideas of Kant and Schiller on the importance of the free "play" of the imagination in true and noble art. The caprice of the poet, says Schlegel, suffers no law above itself. Friedrich von Schelling, whose ideas on irony coincided in several respects with those of Schlegel, spoke of the "beauty of caprice."

Romantic art for Schlegel, as it was for Schelling, is *ein ernster Scherz,* a paradoxical mixture of playfulness and earnestness. To produce such art, to play such a game, the artist himself must be in a paradoxical frame of mind, tempering the self-intoxication of genius and inspiration with self-critical detachment and self-restraint.

> In order to write well about something, one must have ceased to be interested in it. *(Lycaeum,* 37)

> We must rise above what we love and be able to destroy in our thoughts what we adore; otherwise, we lack—regardless of any other abilities we may have—the feeling for the universe. (*Über Goethes Meister*, KA 2:131)

> All the greatest truths of every sort are completely trivial and hence nothing is more important than to express them forever in a new way and, wherever possible, forever more paradoxically, so that we won't forget that they still exist and that they can never be expressed in their entirety. ("On Incomprehensibility," LF, p. 263)

Part of the "play" in romantic irony is a game of mirrors or a *mise en abyme*. D. C. Muecke *(Compass of Irony,* p. 201) has observed that "once a man has become self-conscious he can hardly not take the next step and become conscious of being self-conscious and conscious of being conscious of being self-conscious." As Albert Béguin *(L'Ame romantique et le rêve,* p. 33) puts it, the romantic ironist makes of himself a spectator of himself and the spectator of that spectator. And Irving Babbitt *(Rousseau and Romanticism,* p. 241) has noted that there is something in the romantic ironist that stands aloof even from his aloofness and so on indefinitely.[4]

The playful side of romantic irony has led critics like Babbitt and J. B. Priestley *(Literature and Western Man)* to see in it a sign of immaturity. Whereas Nietzsche *(Beyond Good and Evil)* saw in such irony a sign of health, Babbitt saw "psychic weakness" and pathology. But for A. W. Schlegel, Friedrich's elder brother, and for Tieck, romantic irony was a sign and a *source* of maturity, of mental equilibrium and equipoise. Tieck insisted on the positive value of irony, its power to preserve the artist from a unilateral conception of things and from the tendency to idealize what one loves.[5] And A. W. Schlegel asserted that "irony . . . is a sort of confession interwoven into the representation itself, and more or less distinctly expressed, of its overcharged one-sidedness in matters of fancy and feeling, and by means of which the equipoise is again restored."[6]

In our own century I. A. Richards, too, defined irony in terms of equipoise, "the bringing in of the opposite, the complementary impulses, in order to achieve a balanced poise" *(Literary Criticism,* p. 250). This view led to the broad definition of irony proposed by Cleanth Brooks and the New Critics. Brooks ("Irony as a Principle of Structure," p. 732) defined irony as "the recognition of incongruities" and insisted that it was an essential ingredient of "mature" poetry, "a poetry which does not leave out what is apparently hostile to its dominant tone and which, because it is able to fuse the irrelevant and discordant, has come to terms with itself and is invulnerable to irony."

In *Lycaeum,* fragment 108, Schlegel celebrates the "continuous self-parody" of Socratic irony, which "contains and incites a feeling of insoluble conflict of the absolute and the relative, of the impossibility and the necessity of total communication." He called the authorial consciousness that simultaneously affirms and mocks its own creation "transcendental buffoonery": "There are ancient and modern poems that are pervaded by the divine breath of irony throughout and informed by a truly transcendental buffoonery. Internally: the mood that surveys everything and rises infinitely above all limitations, even above its own art, virtue or genius; externally: in its execution, the mimic style of an averagely gifted Italian *buffo*" *(Lycaeum,* 42). Elsewhere *(Philosophische Fragmente,* KA 18:85) he speaks of irony as a "permanent parabasis." In Greek Old Comedy the parabasis was an interruption of the action in which the author's spokesman addressed the audience directly, much like the *buffo* of the *commedia dell'arte* who in his ludic improvisations visibly controlled the action and mocked the play in progress. The fictional equivalents of the theatrical parabasis are the self-conscious narrator and the intrusive author who disrupt the fictional illusion.[7]

The term *parabasis* must be handled with some care. Schlegel obviously approved of the device in its literal meaning since he approved of the "outward manifestation" of an ironic work resembling the manner of the *buffo*. But the tauntingly terse aphorism, "Irony is a permanent parabasis," must be taken metaphorically since, as Bernhard Heimrich points out *(Fiktion und Fiktionsironie,* p. 62), a literally *permanent* parabasis, in the sense of an actor or an author stepping out of his role, would no longer be a parabasis. The term must be understood as a structuring principle informing the whole work, more precisely as a deliberate dialectical tension between artistic illusion and an expressed awareness of the illusion, and especially between affirmation and self-contradiction: "Jeder Satz, jedes Buch, das sich nicht selbst widerspricht, ist unvollständig" (Any sentence, any book, that does not contradict itself, is incomplete).[8] In its broadest sense, parabasis can be understood as an expressed awareness of the limits of the work in progress. Jonathan Culler's definition of romantic irony coincides with this broader view: "The posture of a work which contains within itself an awareness of the fact that while pretending to give a true account of reality it is in fact fiction and that one must view with an ironic smile the act of writing a novel in the first place."[9] Culler's definition of romantic irony is more acceptable than that of Ingrid Strohschneider-Kohrs *(Die romantische*

Ironie, p. 70): "Mittel der Selbstrepräsentation der Kunst" (Art's means of self-representation); the latter is better applied to parabasis in particular than to the entire spectrum of romantic irony, which involves more than a work's self-representation. A less reductive definition would have to include a work's ambivalence toward its material and toward itself. Such ambivalence may be so subtle at times that a critic can find it only through deconstructive reading strategies.

René Wellek *(History of Modern Criticism* 2:15) claims that there is no evidence that Schlegel found irony in the constant interference of the author in his work, but there are three pieces of evidence indicating clearly that Schlegel did approve of such interference: the reference to the *buffo*[10] and to the importance of both the internal "mood" and the external "buffoonery"; the reference to parabasis—there are no fewer than ten references to it in the *Literary Notebooks;* and, most conclusively, Schlegel's admiration for works like Sterne's *Tristram Shandy,* Diderot's *Jacques le fataliste,* and Tieck's *Der gestiefelte Kater.* Early, "subjective" definitions of romantic irony were based on the authorial intrusions of writers like Tieck, Jean-Paul, Brentano, and E. T. A. Hoffmann and the subsequent "destruction of artistic illusion." "Objective" definitions stressed the author's almost invisible and godlike condescension toward his work, a condescension expressed not so much through overt interruptive devices as by an intangible ironic spirit hovering over the whole work. In the *Literary Notebooks* Schlegel urges that parabasis in the novel be veiled *(verhüllt),* not obvious as in the Old Comedy. In the objective type of romantic irony a particular mood is produced that conveys two distinct impressions to the reader: (1) that all of creation is ironic, paradoxical, or incomprehensible, as in Shakespearean *Welthumor,* and (2) that the author himself is not unreservedly committed to his own creation but is partially (i.e., ambivalently) detached from and critical of it.

Raymond Immerwahr ("Subjectivity or Objectivity of Schlegel's Irony," pp. 173–91) has cogently argued and ably demonstrated that both the subjective and the objective forms of romantic irony were advocated by Schlegel and that the long and heated debate (now pretty much of a dead issue thanks to Immerwahr) reflects the irresolvable conflict inherent in romantic irony itself. In other words, both contradictory interpretations are right! Through his constant recourse to fragments and aphorisms, Schlegel was forced to stress now one, now the other aspect, but it is clear that he approved of the author's godlike transcendence to *and* immanence in his creation, his possession of what St. Paul called God's visible invisibility.[11]

Schlegel admired the subjective-objective irony that Goethe aimed at the very hero of *Wilhelm Meister* and at the entire work itself: "The author himself seems to take the characters and incidents so lightly and humorously, almost never mentioning his hero without irony and smiling down upon his masterpiece itself from the height of his genius" *(Über Goethes Meister,* KA 2:133). Like Schlegel, Schelling saw irony as the guarantor of aesthetic distance between hero and author: "The novelist . . . must not become too involved with his hero, even less subordinate everything in the book to him. Indifference can reach the point of changing into irony against the hero."[12] Stendhal will apply this principle of composition to *Le Rouge et le Noir.*

Schlegel said that an ironic work should be "an artfully ordered confusion," a charming symmetry of contradiction, "a wonderfully perennial alternation of enthusiasm and irony, which lives even in the smallest part of the whole" *(Dialogue on Poetry,* p. 86). It rejects the classical genres, which strictly separated different moods and modes, presenting itself rather as an "arabesque," capriciously blending disparate motifs in a curvilinear and labyrinthine structure, but offering in reality a balance of caprice and purposefulness, of apparent chaos and underlying order, and reflecting two essential aspects of the universe: its infinite plenitude *(unendliche Fülle)* and its infinite unity *(unendliche Einheit).* Hans Eichner *(Friedrich Schlegel,* p. 69) summarizes Schlegel's position thus: "Chaos and eros, fantastic form and sentimental content, seeming confusion and underlying order, infinite variety in infinite unity are formulae both for the ideal work of art and for the universe as a manifestation of the Godhead."

Schlegel thought that the novel was the most appropriate form for the philosophical ironist. But his romantic *Roman* was in reality an ideal, unrealizable form that was to embrace all genres, including poetry, so as to present a truly comprehensive view of the world. He saw intimations of this ideal *Roman* not in the traditional novel of sentimental romance but in ironic works like *Don Quixote, Tristram Shandy, Jacques le fataliste,* and *Wilhelm Meister.* Such novels, he asserted, were "the Socratic dialogues of our time" *(Lycaeum,* 26). Schlegel's own novel, *Lucinde,* with its deliberately chaotic structure, its self-proclaimed "charming confusion," was written in this ironic tradition. Another form appropriate to the expression of philosophical irony was the "fragment" or aphorism, which allowed an author to express ideas without incorporating them into a rigid system and which best expressed the "fragmentary genius" of "wit"; the latter was defined by Schlegel as the uniting of dissociated concepts and by Jean-Paul as the discovery of similarities between incommensurables.

The irony of the German romantics does not have the pessimistic implications of modern irony, such as that of a Thomas Mann, a Franz Kafka, or a Samuel Beckett. Schlegel, again, viewed irony as the expression of a positive philosophical stance. It allows the artist both to participate in the fullness of reality and to enlarge his awareness. By playfully de-creating the forms and myths he has just created and then re-creating ever new forms and myths, he is involved in a process of ever-expanding consciousness. In the *Lycaeum* Schlegel insisted that romantic irony "raises the author above himself," meaning that the "self-destruction" of self-irony leads to self-enhancement—an original development of the Fichtean view of self-consciousness. And the ironic work, by the very fact that it points to its own limitations, serves as sign and symbol of the Infinite. But there is in romantic irony what Beda Allemann calls a "dunkle Kerseite,"[13] a dark other side; if such irony does *not* lead to transcendence, as Schlegel thought, certain negative and nihilistic tendencies could be foregrounded. Schlegel seems to have been blissfully unaware of the potential negative charge of romantic irony, whereas Hegel and later Kierkegaard were to see in it a "principle of absolute negativity." For Kierkegaard, who accepted Solger and Hegel's negative assessment of Schlegelian irony, romantic irony so capriciously, so frivolously, and so cynically ironized everything out of existence that nothing was left in the writer's imaginative world except the bored self-consciousness and nihilism of the ironist himself. In the twentieth century this charge has been repeated by Babbitt, by Priestley, and more eloquently by Vladimir Jankélévitch, who speaks (*L'Ironie*, p. 17) of the irresponsible "license" of Schlegelian irony.

French authors of the romantic period—Musset, Stendhal, Gautier—while they did not theorize about it or even label it, used romantic irony in large measure for its negative charge. Stressing the opposition between pleasant appearances and harsh realities, they often tinged their irony with bitterness or melancholy.[14] French romantic

irony involves the perception and artistic expression of unresolved ambivalence, contradiction, and paradox in human nature (including the
hero and the author), of relativism in the realm of human values, and of
a radical agnosticism in epistemological and metaphysical matters. It is a
consciousness that is conscious of its own predicaments. In its original
form, French romantic irony reflects a tragicomic view of life. While
dealing with matters of serious and tragic import, and while often col-
ored with sadness, it is a rejection of the tragic mode and register. It is
the expression of the irreducible and tragicomic paradoxicality of existence without that certainty of transcendence enjoyed by many German
writers. This deep-rooted skepticism, however, cohabits (ironically) with
genuine enthusiasm, producing a more profound ambivalence even
than that found in Schlegelian irony, the latter being "progressive,"
forward-moving and upward-striving and thus heavily weighted in favor
of the positive side of the ambivalence.

The book attempts to describe what romantic irony is and how it
informs specific French works, but it is appropriate to ask at this point
why it developed in French literature. One obvious "cause" was the
influence of non-French ironists, that of Sterne on Diderot for example,
that of Byron on Musset, that of both Schlegel and Byron on Stendhal,
that of Hoffmann and Jean-Paul on Gautier and Baudelaire, and more
generally the widespread mixture of genres and styles in German
romantic literature, which preceded and no doubt encouraged the
mélange des genres of the French romantics. The question of "influence"
can be studied by future biographers, by intertextualist critics, and even
by latter-day adherents of old-fashioned source criticism. What I should
like to sketch briefly in the following pages are some of the reasons, both
historical and personal, why French authors had recourse to romantic
irony, why it flourished precisely during the romantic period, and why
the French version, as opposed to the German, tends to be tinged with
melancholy.

There may well be as many reasons for an author to have recourse
to romantic irony as there are authors. One impetus to romantic irony
was the desire to avoid the embarrassing sentimentality, bathos, and
hyperbole that marred so much preromantic literature and the self-
conscious author's painful awareness of *his own* excessive sentimentality.
According to Georges Palante, it is chiefly among sentimentalists that

ironists are recruited. Schlegel claimed that even Petrarch displays romantic irony during those moments when he smiles at his own sentimentality and parodies himself. One antidote administered by the romantic ironist is the sudden passage from one mood to another *(Stimmungsbrechnung),* for example, having hot baths of sentiment followed by cold douches of irony, as Jean-Paul expressed it. Another is to break the spell of poetic enthusiasm by a cumbersome intrusion of the author's presence ("subjective irony"). Or the hero can be placed in an embarrassing or demeaning situation ("objective irony"). Or the author can apologize to the reader for the weakness of the poem or novel in progress ("naive irony"). Or an actor can step out of his role and remind the audience that this is only a play. A well-known example of "objective" romantic irony is the passage in Byron's *Don Juan* in which the hero indulges in blatant hyperbole and sentimentality when taking leave of his mistress and Spain, then suddenly, and anticlimactically, becomes seasick.

> And oh! if e'er I should forget, I swear—
>   But that's impossible, and cannot be—
> Sooner shall this blue Ocean melt to air,
>   Sooner shall Earth resolve itself to sea,
> Than I resign thine image, oh, my fair!
>   Or think of anything, excepting thee;
> A mind diseased no remedy can physic—
>   (Here the ship gave a lurch, and he grew sea-sick.)
>
> Sooner shall Heaven kiss earth—(here he fell sicker).
>   Oh, Julia! What is every other woe?—
> (For God's sake let me have a glass of liquor;
>   Pedro, Battista, help me down below.)
> Julia, my love—(you rascal, Pedro, quicker)—
>   Oh, Julia—(this curst vessel pitches so)—
> Belovèd Julia, Hear me still beseeching!
>   (Here he grew inarticulate with retching.)
>
>   (*Don Juan,* Canto 2, ll. 145–160)

Similar passages are frequently found in the poetry of Heine and of Musset as well.

A second impetus to romantic irony was the tendency of the romantic imagination to view history as a mixture of grandeur and farce or, as

Edmund Burke expressed it, a "monstrous tragi-comic scene."[15] This view of history precludes on the author's part an attitude of total seriousness toward what he is trying to accomplish.

A third impetus arose from the fact that the romantic age was, among many other things (e.g., ingenuousness and enthusiasm), an age of disingenuousness and irony: "Feeling is dead, the mind dry: one jokes about the most respectable things which were, formerly, respected."[16]

A fourth source of romantic irony was the tension between the romantic author's search for the Ideal or the Absolute and the *simultaneous* awareness of the search's futility.

A fifth source was the romantic ironist's tendency to distrust his own convictions, what Amiel called "the law of irony" based on self-contradiction. It is the tendency, in a consciousness paralyzed by the contradictions it observes, to suspend judgment (aporia), action, and even feeling. It is difficult, Jankélévitch reminds us, to be both analytical and ardent. *The romantic ironist may well believe what he says,* but at the same time he does not totally trust what he sincerely believes. He is ever distrustful of appearances; what may seem to be true worth or true love may be a sham, or it may prove to be ephemeral. The romantic ironist, says Peter Szondi ("Schlegel und die romantische Ironie," pp. 406–11), sees reality as something tentative, which produces in his work of art a tentative style and a tentative content. And so he will institute a critical analysis at the very moment an emotion or a dramatic action reaches its peak of intensity. The work's center of gravity is thus displaced. Here is Alfred de Musset on the subject:

> I place Scribe very high, but he has one fault, *he never gets angry with himself.* . . . I mean that when Scribe begins a play, an act, or a scene, he always goes directly from his starting point to his finish. Hence, no doubt, a *meritorious straight line,* which gives solidity to what he writes. He is too logical; he never loses his head. I, on the contrary, during a scene or a passage of poetry, often change routes, upset my own plan, turn against my favorite character, and have him beaten by the person to whom he is speaking. . . . I had started out for Madrid but end up going to Constantinople.[17]

A sixth source was the ambivalence of iconoclasts who adored the idols they broke. One recalls Schlegel's injunction to destroy in one's mind what one adores. Here is Paul Bourget speaking of Heine and Musset:

Whether they realize it or not, they, like all of us, are the products of an era of inexorable criticism, of methodical reflection, of fierce and meticulous analysis, in short of Science. . . . That this iconoclast has kept at the same time the naive fervor of faith, that he cannot restrain himself from adoring the idol while breaking it, from loving with frenzy what he dissects with ferocity, that the exaltations of desire and tenderness are united in him with all the lucidity of disenchantment—what misery! What an anomaly! This is the daily lot of modern man, however, and this was the destiny of Musset as well as of Heine. *(Sociologie et littérature,* p. 267)

A seventh source was an instinctive defense mechanism that prompted writers like Musset and Stendhal to hide and protect their real identity under a kaleidoscope of masks.

Far from offering himself directly to the public, far from singing of his loves, his political faith, his religion, his place in society, Musset displays himself only facetiously, and if he draws his own portrait, it is as a caricaturist; he wants to give of himself only an amusing and contradictory image that allows him to escape the grasp of readers and to safeguard the fundamental integrity of his heart. (Van Tieghem, *Musset,* p. 21)

Indeed, Musset presents to his fellow creatures several successive and contingent characters each of whom suggests a world that is in reality nonexistent, deceiving others in this way and preventing them from divining the inner being and attacking it. (Dolder, *L'Être et le paraître,* p. 39)

An eighth impetus was the modern tendency to see man not as the classical *homme absolu* but as a paradoxical animal who can be accurately depicted only in terms of paradox. Man, according to this view, is a complex network of contradictory impulses, wavering between idealism and cynicism, between altruism and solipsism, between reason and emotion, and, for the orthodox, between good and evil.

Victor Hugo first asked his fellow romantics in France to ponder the aesthetic implications of man's dualism. One can therefore take 1827 and the *Préface de Cromwell* not as the actual starting point (for reasons that will be discussed immediately) but as the initial springboard of, or "call for," romantic irony in France. Alfred de Musset was its first important practitioner in romantic poetry and drama; Mérimée and especially

Nerval, Nodier, Stendhal, and Gautier were the first important French writers of the romantic period to put it to use in fiction.[18]

In his influential *Préface* Hugo argues for a Shakespearean mixture of the comic and tragic because such a mixture is found in the very heart and soul of man and therefore at the center of the human experience. Robert Penn Warren ("Pure and Impure Poetry," p. 252), explaining how Mercutio can use coarse humor within the tragic atmosphere of *Romeo and Juliet* and how Othello can pun when about to kill his wife, says that "the poet wishes to indicate that his vision has been earned, that it can survive reference to the complexities and contradictions of experience." However, Shakespeare's vision is "earned" not simply through this rather facile structural device but chiefly through the density of his characterization and style. Hugo, rather naively, thought that the mere juxtaposition of the comic and tragic, the sublime and the grotesque, would guarantee that the romantic drama would achieve this earned vision and that it would capture life in all its complexity. But Hugo's *mélange des genres* is mere antithesis, not ambivalence or paradox. No romantic irony is to be found in the Hugoesque hero. He may rub elbows with buffoons in comic scenes tacked on to the main business at hand, but his attitude toward himself remains essentially simple: he takes himself seriously and even tragically. So does the author.

Alfred de Musset's heroes, on the other hand, often give off a sense of romantic irony, not just because one can feel *within the same character* a tension between opposite impulses, but especially because the author's attitude toward his protagonists as well as their attitude toward themselves seems ambivalent. The heroes of Musset, like the personae of Heine, tend to laugh at their own distress. "Who can say whether I am sad or happy?" asks Fantasio. He is not sure himself. The cynical frivolousness of Musset's heroes is presented initially as the only appropriate life-style in view of their weltschmerz. But at the same time they do not take their cynicism too seriously. They tend to see themselves, rather, as sad clowns—a type of hero to which we have become accustomed in the twentieth century since it is one of the chief heroes of our literature and of our painting. Fantasio, for example, remains unemployed because, he says, people don't hire teachers of melancholy; and so, to escape his creditors, he gaily dons the jester's togs. Octave, in *Les Caprices de Marianne,* another instructor in melancholy, carries as his sword Harlequin's wooden bat. But just as we are getting used to interpreting Octave and Fantasio as silly, flippant clowns, they turn out to be, in their role as friends, both steadfast and courageous. One effect of romantic irony is immediately evident; it tends to keep the reader either off balance or very much on his or her toes.

As Schlegel had insisted, romantic irony is more than a stylistic device used in the service of a limited context; it is a mode of vision with psychological and philosophical implications. The French author's ambivalent attitude (alienation-identification; antipathy-sympathy) toward the hero of his story stems from a moral agnosticism informed by a view of the human psyche as fundamentally unstable, contradictory, and unpredictable or, as Montaigne and Gide would put it, *ondoyant et divers*. The pseudoscientific foresight of an earlier generation of *idéologues* and, for that matter, the more modest hindsight of our own generation's *caractérologues* are summarily dismissed by a skeptical irony directed not only outward at the incomprehensible Other but also at the elusive, slippery Self. This instability, this multiple ego or, if you prefer, this existential freedom will be studied extensively in the twentieth century by writers as different as Proust, Pirandello, Eugene O'Neill, and Nathalie Sarraute. For writers like Musset, romantic irony is based on the ambiguity of feelings ("Gaiety is sometimes sad, and melancholy has a smile on its lips" [*André del Sarto*]), the ambiguity of knowledge ("No doubt; what you say there is perfectly true and perfectly false, like everything in the world" [*Lorenzaccio*]), the ambiguity of morals ("This mixture of mud and sky" [letter from Musset to Paul Foucher]), and the ambiguity and inadequacy of language ("What human word will ever express the weakest caress?" [*Confession d'un enfant du siècle*]; "How cold and insignificant are words, how miserable is speech when one tries to say how one loves" [*Bettine*]).[19]

What is "romantic" about romantic irony? The epithet is appropriate since it was logical, almost inevitable, for such irony to flower during the heyday of romanticism, which was an explosion of subjectivism and self-consciousness in literature, art, and philosophy; which believed in the transcendental nature of art and in the artist's quasi-divine genius and creativity; which viewed the universe as infinite, as a dynamic and creatively chaotic process of change, becoming, and organic growth; which developed an "open ideology" (Muecke) that "tolerated—indeed welcomed—disorder, flux, mystery and fragmentariness as the elements of that creative chaos from which a better world could be shaped."[20]

Ingrid Strohschneider-Kohrs considers romantic irony to be basically a historical phenomenon linked to the romantic period. But Lilian Furst (*Fictions of Romantic Irony*, p. 237) points out that "the sporadic occurrence of an irony akin to romantic irony before the Romantic period and its frequent recurrence thereafter vitiates the argument that it is predominantly a historical phenomenon." She admits that there is "a certain aptness" in the term "romantic irony" but quarrels with it because it has resulted in a failure to appreciate fully the importance of romantic irony beyond the romantic period. Her point is well taken, but while preromantics such as Sterne and Diderot developed many of the specific strategies and even many of the philosophical underpinnings of romantic irony, it is the romantic period that deserves credit for giving the phenomenon its biggest push. In addition to more than a half-dozen theoreticians in Germany, one could name some twenty creative writers of the romantic period in Germany, France, England (Byron especially but also Coleridge, Keats, and Carlyle), and Russia (Pushkin). The number would more than triple if we added the many imitators of Sterne, Diderot, and Byron in the first half of the nineteenth century.

The negative or melancholy side of French romantic irony is linked with the *mal du siècle*, which itself derives in part from that legacy of skepticism concerning all traditional values bequeathed by the Enlightenment and in part from the confusion of values brought on by political instability, social anarchy, and the very acceleration of history ("Events raced faster than my pen," wrote Chateaubriand in his memoirs). During the very brief period between 1789 and 1815, France experienced absolute monarchy, a violent revolution, a Directorate, a Consulate, an Empire, and a restored but constitutionalized or "charterized" monarchy criticized by the *ultras* as being too liberal—from extreme absolutism to extreme revolution to extreme reaction. Political and religious opinions were so diverse that France was becoming, nay, had already become, a centrifugal civilization. By 1820 young men did not know where to turn for faith, hope, or ideals. The glorious emperor was gone and was already the victim of revisionism. The Restoration offered its youth no lofty ideals and produced no inspiring leaders. A mercantile-industrial society was founding a new order and a new moral code built, as Balzac has so vividly shown us, upon Money.

It is a fact of literary history that the *mal du siècle* did not die out with the romantic period. Paul Bourget, writing at the end of the century, speaks of the *mal de fin de siècle,* and Henri Peyre noted as late as 1954 that the phrase "le mal du demi-siècle" had recently been coined to characterize the literature of the mid-twentieth century.

*

Looked at from a technical point of view, romantic irony is a complex phenomenon. It is, again, not simply a local device (e.g., antiphrasis). It is a structural principle, in fact a combination, often, of several different structural principles: the self-conscious, unreliable, or nescient narrator; the intrusive author; the multiple point of view; the deflation of a hero who is ambivalently admired and ridiculed; the fragmentation of time into a series of discrete, independent, isolated moments; the eschewal of closure in favor of an open-ended dénouement; textual self-reflexiveness with metafiction often overtaking the fiction; frequent recourse to oxymoron, paradox, parabasis, parataxis, montage, or other staccato effects such as sudden changes of mood, theme, or stylistic register. And when it pervades an entire text, as it usually does, it becomes, again, the expression of a philosophical stance, either ethical (e.g., ambivalence or skepticism regarding traditional values), ontological (intimating that paradox is inherent in human nature and even in the "nature of things"), and/or epistemological (often stating and always implying the question: "What can we really know for sure?").

It is fascinating to observe the great extent to which other ironies partake of romantic irony. Douglas Muecke distinguishes verbal or specific irony from "general irony" (subspecies of which are world irony, cosmic irony, and metaphysical irony), the latter tending to raise "historical and ideological questions" *(Compass of Irony,* pp. 50–51) and to include the ironic observer not as a detached consciousness but as an involved victim of irony along with the rest of mankind. The distinction is between the irony of limited and specific moments and what Kierkegaard called "essential irony," an irony that the true ironist, looking at the totality of existence *sub specie ironiae,* possesses "all day long." A. E. Dyson, in *The Crazy Fabric,* distinguishes between irony as a rhetorical technique and "irony as a vision of the universe itself" (pp. 220–23). The second type stems, he says, from the perception of cross-purposes, of absurdity, or of tragic suffering, the enigma of events that happen to us. As the title of C. I. Glicksberg's *Ironic Vision in Modern Literature* indicates, modern irony is seen in terms of awareness, the ironic awareness of "the irreconcilable contradictions of existence" (p. 257). Wayne Booth (*A Rhetoric of Irony*) distinguishes between "stable" ironies, readily reconstructible, and "unstable" ironies, which elude definitive interpretation.

Alan Wilde (*Horizons of Assent: Modernism, Postmodernism and the Ironic Imagination*) distinguishes between "mediate irony," "disjunctive irony," and "suspensive irony." Mediate or traditional irony, what Wayne Booth calls normative irony, conveys a fundamentally satiric vision and imagines a world lapsed from a recoverable norm. Disjunctive irony, which Wilde also calls "absolute irony," and which he sees as the characteristic form of modernism, "strives, however reluctantly, toward a condition of paradox. The ironist, far more basically adrift, confronts a world that appears inherently disconnected and fragmented. . . . Disjunctive irony both recognizes the disconnections and seeks to control them . . . and so the confusions of the world are shaped into an *equal poise* of opposites: the form of an unresolvable paradox" (p. 10; emphasis added). Suspensive irony, which Wilde connects with postmodernism, with "its yet more radical vision of multiplicity, randomness, contingency, and even absurdity, abandons the quest for paradise altogether—the world in all its disorder is simply (or not so simply) accepted" (p. 10). *Acceptance* is the key word in Wilde's definition of contemporary irony, just as it was for Solger and Tieck: a "smiling acceptance of incessant change."[21] General irony, world irony, cosmic irony, metaphysical irony, suspensive irony, disjunctive irony, unstable irony—each label stresses a facet or phase of what can generically (and economically) be called romantic irony. Douglas Muecke has aptly said (*Compass of Irony*, p. 182) that "to study Romantic Irony is to discover how modern Romanticism could be, or if you like, how Romantic Modernism is." The irony of a Samuel Beckett, for example, provides a brilliant illustration of Schlegel's definition of romantic irony: "clear consciousness of eternal mobility, of the infinite fullness of chaos." The main difference in outlook is that Beckett sees and offers little hope for transcendence.

Many critics have failed to see the filiations between "modern irony" and romantic irony because as the latter changed in progressing through the nineteenth and twentieth centuries—mainly in the direction of increased shrillness and tragic overtones—it was not recognized as such but was given other names. Romantic irony did not die out; it branched out. It developed into the demonic laughter of Baudelaire and Lautréamont, the "black humor" of Charles Cros, the "yellow laughter" of Corbière and Laforgue, the perverse laughter of the Decadents, the bittersweet laughter of the *poètes fantaisistes,* and the mirthless, "dianoetic laughter" of Samuel Beckett, which laughs at the laughter and at what is unhappy and in which is heard the gnashing of teeth. It is the predecessor of all forms of black humor in this century, of the modern tragic farce and the antihero (e.g., the passive hero and the hero as clown), of the unreliable and imperceptive narrator of contemporary fiction, of the postmodern novel's urge to dispel representational illusion and to question its own strategies and presuppositions, of the sad clown in modern painting, even the Satie-like autoparody in contemporary music. It has been termed a prelude to the philosophical notion of the Absurd. I believe it is one of the chief legacies of romanticism. It is certainly one of the most significant literary expressions of the modern sensibility.

2

Eternal Mobility:
Diderot's *Jacques le fataliste*

There is always in poetry a bit of deceit. The philosophical
spirit accustoms us to discern it: and goodbye to the illusion
and the effect.

(Diderot, *Salon de 1767*)

IT was in part upon the work of Diderot that Friedrich von Schlegel
constructed his theory of irony. In his "Letter about the Novel"
(Dialogue on Poetry, p. 96) Schlegel praised *Jacques le fataliste* for its
"abundance of wit" and its freedom (as opposed to Sterne's fiction) from
"sentimental admixtures." He judged it to be a true work of art, not of
high rank, "but only an arabesque. But for that reason it has in my eyes
no small merit; for I consider the arabesque a very definite and essential
form or mode of expression of poetry" (p. 96). Schlegel, as we saw
earlier, used the image of the arabesque as his emblem of the successful
ironic work: a capricious blending of disparate and even discordant
motifs that replaces the linear by the curvilinear, the straightforward by
the labyrinthine, that exhibits unity within complication and confusing
diversity, order and pattern within apparent chaos.

Schlegel conceived of the novel in particular as a *mélange des genres,* a
mixture of storytelling, poetry, song, and other forms. The best novels,
he thought, combine the objective with the subjective, high seriousness
with playful humor: "Nothing is more contrary to the epic style than
when the influence of the subjective mood becomes in the least visible,
not to speak of one's ability to give himself up to his humor and play with
it, as it often happens in the most excellent novels" (p. 102). Novels based
on such a model "would be true arabesques which, together with confes-

sions . . . are the only romantic products of our age" (p. 103). Despite its apparent formlessness and disorder, *Jacques* was praised by Schlegel as being a work "designed with understanding and executed with a firm hand" (p. 96). Whoever has an appreciation of Diderot's work, he said, "has a better start on the way to learning to appreciate the divine wit, the imagination of an Ariosto, Cervantes, Shakespeare" (p. 97).

Jacques le fataliste was indeed a model for future romantic ironists fond of sporting with their literary creation and of flaunting their artistic freedom over the text precisely as they were creating it. The opening paragraph sets the tone:

> How had they met? By chance, like everyone. What were their names? Of what importance is that to you? Where were they coming from? From the nearest place. Where were they going? Does anyone know where one is going? What were they saying? The master wasn't saying anything; and Jacques was saying that everything good and bad that happens to us here below was written up there.[1]

The novel's first sentence—a query—and four of the six interrogative sentences that follow are uttered not by the narrator but by the contrived reader, whose natural inquisitiveness is rudely rebuffed. The real reader, like the contrived reader, is immediately warned that the normal conventions and contractual obligations of traditional fiction (e.g., an informative exposition) are not going to be respected. The "plot" is structured around a voyage, but neither its motivation nor its destination is ever revealed. Neither Jacques nor his master is ever fully named. The novel's major unifying element—the story of Jacques's amours—is constantly short-circuited by interruptive and disruptive devices. The narrator is evasive rather than informative, and instead of ingratiating himself with the reader, he assaults him—not only here but throughout the novel—accusing him especially of enjoying only conventional fiction, that is, the fiction of romance and adventure. The relations between the narrator and his hero are also problematic from the start; the hero's fatalistic and deterministic philosophy, expressed in the paragraph's last sentence, seems countered or challenged by the narrator's philosophy of chance, expressed in the second sentence.

A few pages later the narrator expresses his impatience with the reader's questions: "Always questions. Don't you want Jacques to continue the narration of his love affairs? Once and for all, explain yourself" (p. 478). At another point the narrator warns the importunate reader that he will tell his story with or without him: "Listen to me, or don't listen to me, I'll talk all by myself" (p. 529).

Not only do we witness a narrator who constantly interrupts his narration to admonish the reader, on several occasions it is the reader who interrupts the narrator! "What shocked Jacques and his master the most all the while they were walking. . . — THEY WERE WALKING, THEN? — That's all they did, when they weren't sitting or lying down" (p. 492; emphasis added). At another point the contrived reader not only interrupts the narrator but becomes childishly petulant.

> But if you interrupt me, reader, and if I interrupt myself at every turn, what will become of Jacques's love affairs? Believe me, let's leave the poet there. . . The host and hostess withdraw. . . NO, NO, THE STORY ABOUT THE POET FROM PONDICHÉRY, — The surgeon approached Jacques's bed. . . — THE STORY ABOUT THE POET FROM PONDICHÉRY, THE STORY ABOUT THE POET FROM PONDICHÉRY. (P. 504; emphasis added)

In two other passages the reader even has the audacity to upbraid the narrator for pretending to be omnipresent as well as omniscient ("How do *you* know? You weren't there!").

Thus the relationship between the narrator and his reader is, as often as not, adversarial. The climax of this aspect of the novel occurs in a passage in which the narrator and the reader swap insults.

> And your *Jacques* is nothing but an insipid rhapsody of facts, some real, others imagined, written without grace and distributed without order. — So much the better, my *Jacques* will be all the less read for that. Whichever way you turn, you're wrong. If my work is good, it will please you; if it is bad, it won't do any harm. No book is more innocent than a bad book. I amuse myself by describing, under borrowed names, the foolish things you do; your foolish actions make me laugh; my writing puts you in a bad mood. Reader, to be frank with you, I think the more wicked of the two of us is not I. How gratified I would be if it were as easy to protect myself from your black deeds, as it is for you to protect yourself from the boredom or the danger of my book! Vile hypocrites, leave me alone. F—— like rabbits; but allow me to say f——; I allow you the act, allow me the word. (P. 656)

Of course the narrator has the upper hand and usually manages to keep his composure. Throughout the novel he playfully flaunts his creative freedom.

You see, reader, that I am on the right path, and that it is purely up
to me whether I make you wait one year, two years, three years, for the
narration of Jacques's love affairs, by separating him from his master
and making each one of them run all the risks that would please me.
What would prevent me from getting the master married, and then
making him a cuckold? of embarking Jacques for the islands? of taking
his master there? of bringing them both back to France on the same
boat? How easy it is to write stories! (P. 476)

. . .it's purely up to me whether all that happens. (P. 484)

On more than one occasion (e.g., pp. 494, 607) the narrator offers the
reader several optional outcomes to choose from. And he warns the
reader (pp. 494–95) that he is fond of certain terms borrowed from
geometry (e.g., direct ratio, inverse ratio) and uses them in this story
whenever he likes.

Schlegel found in *Jacques le fataliste* a paradigm of the "eternal mobility" so characteristic of romantic irony, the main sources of which are
stories embedded in other stories, digressions superimposed on earlier
digressions and even on digressions in progress, the constant interruptions and resumptions, and the constant rotation of narrative point of
view. We move from an omniscient to a nescient narrator, from a merely
addressed and passive reader to an active reader who comments on the
narrator's strategy and on the events themselves ("Cela est beau!"; "Hor-
reur!"), from Jacques's point of view to that of his master or to that of
some minor character.

And Schlegel, who saw paradox as the main stylistic ingredient of
romantic irony, could not but appreciate the importance accorded to
paradox in *Jacques*. Diderot greatly admired the paradoxes he found in
the writings of Richardson, Helvétius, and Rousseau. Of the last two he
says, "There is always something to learn in works based on paradox
such as his and Rousseau's, and I prefer their false reasoning which
forces me to think to the commonplace truths that have no interest for
me."[2] Indeed Schlegel seems almost to be paraphrasing Diderot when he
writes, in his essay "On Incomprehensibility," that "all the greatest truths
of every sort are completely trivial and hence nothing is more important
than to express them forever in a new way and, wherever possible,
forever more paradoxically" (LF, p. 263). In *Jacques* paradox is found in
a variety of forms: the unexpected and strange twists that so many of the
stories take; the paradoxical treatment of the major theme, fatalism, and

of the hero; the paradoxical relations between the hero and his master, between the hero and the narrator, between the narrator and the reader. The hero is aware that paradox lies at the very heart of human existence; so, too, does his master.

> JACQUES. — A paradox is not always a falsehood.
> THE MASTER. — That is true. (Pp. 517–18)

Jacques is a creature of paradox. His morals tend to be on the loose side; he is a bit of a drunkard; he is stubborn; he is an unmitigated chatterbox who likes a good story but mainly when he is telling it; he is insolent to his master. But this same Jacques is essentially honest and unswervingly loyal. There is also in him a paradoxical blend of (occasional) stoicism—passive acceptance of predestination, especially on the abstract and theoretical levels—and of an earthy epicureanism. A proletarian with some education—another paradox until recent times—he is his master's master in both intellectual and practical matters.

The supreme paradox in *Jacques le fataliste* is the irony that the text aims at itself. The fictional illusion constantly self-destructs. The author insists on several occasions that this story is not a genuine novel and suggests that anyone with a modicum of imagination can write in such a facile genre. As Schlegel writes *(Literary Notebooks,* fragment 1459): "Jacques von Diderot ist night sowohl ein Roman als eine Persiflage dagegen" (Diderot's *Jacques* is not so much a novel as a persiflage directed against it). Not only does the narrator spare the reader certain details but informs the reader of the fact (e.g., p. 486). He admits to the reader that he is not above telling a falsehood if he has to or if he finds it useful to his purpose (p. 254). He admits to having forgotten to offer more descriptive details in one episode (p. 580), and so forth. We are dealing here not simply with irony *in* fiction but with what Lilian Furst, after Bernhard Heimrich, calls "irony *of* fiction," and what Walter Benjamin calls "ironization of form." Schlegel was correct in noting that this ironization of form expressed a philosophical stance, but what he did not fully perceive was the potential subversiveness of the stance. Neither the hero nor the narrator-author of *Jacques le fataliste* rises above or resolves the many paradoxes and incongruities of existence that are incessantly presented during the course of the narration.

Fatalism can be taken as the novel's overt thesis. For one thing, in any opposition, as Derrida asserts, there is a hierarchical order. For another, the doctrine of fatalism is not only formulated by the prestigious though invisible captain and espoused by the hero, but also conceded on several occasions by his vacillating master who at times presents weak and conventional arguments in favor of free will; it is also conceded on at least three occasions (pp. 499, 572, 708) by the vacillating narrator. On another occasion (p. 621) the narrator tells us that he challenged Jacques on his philosophy but without winning the argument. But the text deconstructs its overt thesis at every turn. Instead of a coherent universe governed by a rigid and logical chain of cause and effect, a world of uncertainty and unpredictability is presented. To state baldly that the novel is a satire on fatalism is to do an injustice to the complexity of the presentation. Fatalism (which Diderot himself espoused in the form of materialistic determinism) is an object not of wholehearted satire but of ambivalence. This ambivalence and the sense of uncertainty that pervades the novel are produced not only by the constant interruptions and the kaleidoscopic points of view mentioned earlier; within a single point of view—of the narrator, of the hero, or of the master—there is a high degree of instability.

Jacques, for example, declares himself to be a card-carrying fatalist but relies on his own resourcefulness in every particular situation in which he finds himself. And instead of developing a consistent stoic response to events over which neither he nor anyone supposedly has any control, he usually reacts the way nonfatalists do: with laughter, tears, hopes, fears, moral indignation, etc. Furthermore, as William Ray ("A Writer of Our Times," p. 76) writes, "Jacques's obsession with recounting past events suggests a confidence in former experience as a guide to current situations and character traits. This is inconsistent with a fatalistic posture: were the course of events truly predetermined, historical knowledge would be of little use." Diderot, in a statement that combines a generalized irony with self-irony, has noted that such a contradiction is typical of all fatalists, even fatalistic authors (like himself): "One is a fatalist, and yet at every moment one thinks, one speaks, ONE WRITES as if one persevered in the bias of free will."[3] Diderot is as perplexed as his hero by the paradoxes of human life and by the paradoxes of the human psyche.

Jacques's main assertion is not so much that every event is preordained by what is "written up yonder on the great scroll" but that we are all ignorant of what is written up there and of what impels us to do the things we do. We walk in the dark, he says, below what is written up there.

> THE MASTER. — And if you want to save time, why do you walk slowly as you do?
>
> JACQUES. — It is because, for lack of knowing what is written up there, one knows neither what one wants nor what one is doing, and because one follows one's fantasy, which people call reason, or one's reason, which is often only a dangerous fantasy that turns out sometimes well sometimes badly. (Pp. 482–83)

Our hero acknowledges (p. 561) that it is "annoying" never to know where one is going in life or why. "Who knows?" is one of his most frequent responses to his master's questions, even to questions concerning fatalism.

> JACQUES. — My captain used to say that each bullet that left a rifle had a note with a name on it.
>
> THE MASTER. — And he was right.
>
> JACQUES. — Who knows? (Pp. 475–76)

Even more unsettling is his agnosticism with regard to the authorship of the great scroll.

> THE MASTER. — And who up there wrote down happiness and unhappiness?
>
> JACQUES. — And who made the great scroll on which everything is written? A captain, a friend of my captain, would have gladly given a small gold piece to know that; as for him, he wouldn't have given a farthing, nor would I; for what good would that do me? Would I avoid because of that the hole in which I am bound to go break my neck? (P. 483)

The world seems to be governed not by an omniscient deity but by blind chance; even heaven may not know what it wants: "One never knows what heaven wants or doesn't want, and maybe it doesn't know anything about it itself" (p. 552). Jacques, who prays each night "à tout hasard," that is, on the off chance that someone may be listening "up there," addresses his prayer not to a clearly perceived personal God or heavenly Father but to "Quel que tu sois"—to Whom it may concern.

Jacques's metaphysical and epistemological agnosticism is reflected in the equivocal expressions he utters from one end of the novel to the other.

So much the better or so much the worse. (P. 491)

Maybe so, maybe not; who knows? (P. 546)

Maybe yes, maybe no. (P. 554)

Sometimes yes, sometimes no. (P. 637)

I neither believe it nor disbelieve it. (P. 481)

Maybe it was true, maybe it was false; what does one know? (P. 509)

He is painfully conscious of the subjectivity and changeability of human judgment and sentiment: "Each person appreciates an insult or a benefit in his own way; and perhaps we don't have the same opinion in any two instants of our life" (p. 520). The often confused narrator says that he is not sure whether the following reflections are those of Jacques or of his master or of himself; what is certain is that they are part of the novel's central theme:

> The first oath that two creatures of flesh made to each other was at the foot of a rock that was crumbling into dust; they called to witness for their constancy a heaven that is never the same; everything was changing in them and around them, and yet they believed their hearts free of vicissitudes. Oh children! always children! (P. 567)

Alfred de Musset remembers this passage in *Souvenir*. It expresses a central theme of his opus. The sudden shifts of mood of the romantic ironist reflect his awareness of the eternal mobility and instability of the human psyche.

Jacques's ambivalent, ambiguous, paradoxical, and generally unstable behavior is echoed by that of the minor characters, for example, the ambivalence of the two captains toward each other, and the moral ambivalence of Gausse, who generously gives all his money to two young people in love but neglects his own family, and is not above adding a zero to an eighty to get himself paid ten times more than he is owed. Similarly, the reader is left to decide between two contradictory points of view regarding the behavior of Mme de la Pommeraye, that of Jacques (for whom she is a despicable creature) and that of the narrator (for whom she is at least partially justified in her brutal act of vengeance).

The instability of the characters is also matched by that of the narrator. As mentioned earlier, the latter's attitude toward fatalism is ambiguous and ambivalent, vague and vacillating. In several passages he seems to accept the doctrine, but on one occasion he admits having fruitlessly challenged Jacques on the issue. In another passage he says that theologians have been arguing about fatalism for millennia without resolving the issue. The prideful "It's purely up to me . . ." is a contradiction of the predestination and predetermination implied in fatalism. The statement itself, however, is contradicted in another passage in which the narrator confesses that he does *not* have the power to prevent a character from reentering the scene. And the narrator's godlike omniscience, like that of his omnipotence, often fails him.

> *I don't know* whether he started by putting the petticoats back down or by freeing the foot. (P. 477; emphasis added)

> *I don't know* what happened in the inn after their departure. (P. 484; emphasis added)

Both Aram Vartanian and Otis Fellows have shown that Diderot exploits semantically the ambiguity of the word *fatalism*. Vartanian ("Ramifications of a Dilemma," p. 332) points out that the term can pertain "either to a necessary concatenation of events, hence implying their predictability, or contrariwise, to a fortuitous series of events, with the suggestion of their unpredictability." Fellows *(Diderot,* p. 137) has shown that Jacques presents his ill-defined fatalism in three different forms:

> (1) as a mechanistic materialism whereby he sees the principles of cause and effect leading to an inevitable result in the future; (2) his religious fatalism in which he imagines the future incontrovertibly written in the heaven above . . . ; (3) his acceptance of the indisputable role of chance and caprice, perhaps the most dangerous of all fatalistic credos.

Fellows uncovers (p. 136) four distinct narrative points of view regarding the already multiple ambiguities surrounding fatalism: "(1) that of Jacques, the determined supporter of an unrelenting pseudo-Spinozism; (2) that of Jacques, who, unconsciously, by word and action, revolts against his adopted doctrine; (3) the position of the master, one of oscillation, of fluctuation; (4) that of the third person, the narrator, who addresses the reader and calls attention to the inconsistencies in the first three points of view"—and, as we have shown, in his own.

*

All the formal devices in *Jacques* contribute to a conceptual irony similar to that of Sterne's *Tristram Shandy*. At the end of the novel Diderot playfully alludes to *Tristram,* and in a letter to Sophie Volland he says of it: "This book, so mad, so wise, so gay, is the Rabelais of the English."[4] In another passage of his correspondence he speaks of *Tristram* in superlatives: "the wisest, the maddest, the gayest."[5]

Both books present a self-conscious narrator who abruptly interrupts his narration to comment on it or to address the reader or to digress. "Digressions, incontestably, are the sunshine; they are the life, the soul of reading," says Sterne's narrator. During the very course of the novel's progress, Sterne informs the reader of the technical difficulties confronting him and of the strategies he will use to overcome them, thus puncturing the very fictional illusion he is supposed to be constructing. He deliberately leaves the reader in a state of perpetual uncertainty by a comic abuse of long dashes and asterisks, by blank, black, or marbled pages, by aposiopesis, by dropping hints that are left dangling, and by an obstinate refusal to answer pertinent questions. There is a misplaced dedication and a misplaced preface; there is a blank chapter, an omitted chapter, and a misplaced chapter; the narrator advises the reader to "skip over the remaining part" of his first chapter, at another point to reread a preceding chapter and, near the end, feeling his "want of powers," invites the reader to finish the story himself.

As Lilian Furst has pointed out *(Fictions of Romantic Irony,* pp. 204, 217) linear thought processes and linear plotting are abandoned in *Tristram* in favor of a frustrating (and amusing) circularity, and whatever is posited in one phrase is restricted, modified, or amended in the next: "Sterne relativizes every position he assumes by envisaging its opposite." Raymond Queneau, one of the many intellectual heirs of Sterne and Diderot, will write *(Entretiens avec Georges Charbonnier,* p. 12): "Whenever I set forth an assertion, I realize immediately that the opposite assertion is just about as interesting, to the point that it is becoming a superstition with me."

Diderot uses many (but by no means all) of the devices employed by Sterne to produce a similar sense of uncertainty, relativity, and unpredictability, but there is in Diderot's work a degree of seriousness not found in Sterne, who writes not as a *philosophe* but chiefly as an entertainer (though a provocative one). In *Tristram* the problem of predestination, for example, is dropped almost as soon as it is broached. Sterne's satire is much gentler than that found in Diderot and in French romantic irony in general. As A. E. Dyson *(The Crazy Fabric,* p. 47) has noted,

Sterne manages to convey the rich mixture of motives—sincere and insincere, conscious and unconscious, self-centered and disinterested, tainted and yet still human and honest—of his good-natured and good-hearted characters: "We are confronted with complexity and eccentricity, and challenged to find behind it [sic] the simple decency of the uncorrupted heart" (p. 49).

Diderot's irony has a more negative charge because the ambivalences are not tilted in the direction of implicit praise, the tensions and contradictions do not resolve themselves into a warm glow of good cheer. Jacques is at once generous *and* self-centered, loyal *and* impudent, good-hearted *and* roguish, stoic *and* hedonistic—and that's where things remain. We are not invited to find beneath the contradictions a more important substratum of goodness and decency. The goodness and decency are there, but they are not given privileged status. As Bergen Evans has noted,[6] Sterne's satire is too gentle and affectionate to be really satirical; the serious evils of life are never attacked in *Tristram Shandy,* Sterne's domain being that of innocuous eccentricities. Sterne's gentler irony is reflected not only in the narrator's relationship with the characters but also in his relationship with his readers. He teases his "gentle reader" gently; his manner is more deferential than adversarial: "As you proceed farther with me, the slight acquaintance which is now beginning betwixt us will grow into familiarity; and that, unless one of us is in fault, will terminate in friendship."

Sterne's irony is at times subtler and at times funnier than Diderot's, but the latter's is closer to the true spirit of romantic irony, or at least the general run of that irony as it developed in the nineteenth and twentieth centuries, in that it suggests nothing to relieve the tensions and paradoxes that assault us on every page. Sterne tells us that man is a paradoxical but basically decent animal. Diderot's vision begins and ends with the paradoxical. As Lilian Furst has pointed out, Sterne's universe is freakish but essentially stable and static. Diderot's universe is a dynamic, constantly changing cosmos of chaos. What Furst *(Fictions of Romantic Irony,* p. 100) has said of Sterne can be said even more of Diderot: "Irony becomes not a matter of reconstructing a covert intended meaning but of confronting a bewildering multiplicity of possible meanings." Truth is seen as elusive and perhaps unattainable.

In Diderot, as Leo Spitzer has commented ("Style of Diderot," p. 135), nervous system, philosophical system, and "stylistic system" are exceptionally well attuned. Spitzer has shown the correspondences between the "mobility" of Diderot's mind and that of his style. The literary paradoxes can be traced to a psychological propensity mentioned often by the author in the Volland correspondence and also by the partially autobiographical hero of *Jacques*, namely, that "there is perhaps under the skies no other head that contains so many paradoxes." Diderot's digressions have often been explained as the result of his impulsiveness, his inveterate spontaneity, and his tendency toward disorderliness, which he has frequently acknowledged: "I throw my ideas onto the paper, and they become what they can."[7] Laurence Sterne made the same "confession"; he set down his first sentence as best he could, he tells us, "and trusted to Almighty God for the second." The digressions have been explained more recently as the result of Diderot's "claustrophobic scriptural behavior" (Jack Undank). More to the point is the view of David Berry ("Literary Digression in Diderot," pp. 232–61), who sees the digressions as mimetic expressions of Diderot's "hectic vision" of the universe. Not only the digressions per se, but what they introduce into the text: the startling juxtapositions of widely different types of events and the rapid shifts between diametrically opposed themes and moods, from the bawdy to the lyrico-poetic, which produce an effect of perpetual motion, of eternal and ubiquitous flux, and of capricious chance. Diderot tells us in *Jacques* that life is a journey and that no one knows where the journey leads. This particular weltanschauung justified and encouraged an aesthetics based not on classical notions of unity, simplicity, compression, and succinctness, but on a preromantic diffuseness and inclusiveness. In a review of a poem by Le Mierre that Diderot wrote in 1769, just a few years before *Jacques*, he explicitly praises digression as a structural principle: "Nothing is more appropriate for a poem than digressions . . . the image of a man who wanders off the beaten path while taking a stroll at the bidding of the places and objects he encounters, stopping here, there hastening his step, interests me much more than a traveler bent over his luggage."[8]

Stephen Mautner ("Compromised Author," pp. 21–32) has linked Diderot's coming forward and unmasking himself before the reading audience of *Jacques* to that of the ironic author of Schlegel's essay "On Incomprehensibility" and has shown that both are new forms of

parabasis. Schlegel had commented on the parabasic quality of *Jacques:*
"Whenever Diderot in his *Jacob* has done something ingenious, he usually comes right out himself and rejoices at how ingenious it has become"
(Lycaeum, 3). Otis Fellows has remarked that if Diderot were a playwright
we might well imagine him calling out to the audience over the
footlights—which is precisely what he did in the 1964 stage version of
Jacques.

All the manifestations of romantic irony in *Jacques* are intimately
connected to Diderot's philosophy, especially his vision of a universe in
perpetual movement, ferment, and fermentation (Lester Crocker has
pointed out that Diderot uses the word *fermentation* in both senses) and
his dual philosophical commitment to freedom and, paradoxically, to its
archenemy, determinism.

As early as 1746, with the *Pensées philosophiques,* Diderot, under the
influence of Lucretius's *De Rerum Natura,* had broken with the deism of
his youth and had conceived of a universe produced not by some outside
unmoved Mover but by the autonomous and random movement of
atoms. In *Pensée* 21 the atheist, in rebuttal to the deist's vision of a divine
intelligence giving the world its marvelous order ("this order that as-
tounds you"), claims that such order results from the simple mechanical
motions of particles arranging themselves not according to divine design, but strictly according to chance and the calculus of probability.[9]

The *Lettre sur les aveugles* (1749) describes man as a product of
chance in a sort of cosmic lottery; he is a fortuitous collocation of atoms
in constant motion and constant *fermentation.* The randomness of atomic
motion is not contradictory to causal determinism. J. M. Jauch, a contemporary physicist, has explained *(Are Quanta Real?)* that deterministic
cause and the randomness of chance coexist in all dynamically unstable
systems.[10] For Diderot, every part of the universe and every creature in
it are subject to constant movement and change. Absolute rest, he says
(OEuvres philosophiques, p. 395), is an abstract notion that does not exist
in nature.[11] Not only is each creature different from every other, but
each individual is different from itself at different times and under
different circumstances. *Moi* says of *Lui* in *Le Neveu de Rameau:* "Nothing
is more dissimilar to him than himself." As late as the *Eléments de
physiologie* (1778) Diderot persisted in the view that the most constant of
humans is simply the person who changes the least.

The *Lettre sur les aveugles* presents eternal change and becoming not only in the form of new molecular constructions but as a result of inexorable entropy.

> What is this world, Mr. Holmes? A compound subject to revolutions, all of which indicate a continual tendency toward destruction; a rapid succession of creatures that follow each other, push each other and disappear; a momentary order. (OPH, p. 123)

As Lester Crocker has shown (*Diderot's Chaotic Order*, pp. 10, 30), Diderot's

> eternal ontological law is the struggle of every form of existence to persist in organized form in the face of inevitable and increasing entropy: This law alone is as eternal as matter itself: the disorderly efforts to construct and to maintain an order, and the inevitable destruction of the precarious stability. . . . The same propulsive forces which constitute the very nature of matter . . . create a chaotic universe in which all order is transient.

In the *Eléments de physiologie* Diderot sees every member of the plant and animal kingdom as a coordination of infinitely active molecules, which everything works to break up. And in *Le Rêve de D'Alembert* (1769) he expresses the notion of entropy quite explicitly: "Who knows whether everything doesn't tend to be reduced to a grand inert and motionless sediment?" (OPH, p. 302).

Diderot sees chemical forces as the prime mover of matter; life is a series of actions and reactions. Schlegel's "eternal mobility" is inherent in and essential to all matter: "What is a being? The sum of a certain number of tendencies. . . . And life? Life is a series of actions and reactions. Living, I live and react *en masse* . . . dead, I act and react as molecules. . . . To be born, to live, to die, is to change form" (OPH, p. 313). Give Diderot matter and movement and, like Descartes and Hobbes, he will create a world—which he does ever so slyly and surreptitiously in his article "Chaos" for the *Encyclopédie*.

In the beginning was matter, and matter was eternally endowed with movement and sensitivity. Put sensitive matter in the place of God and one has an explanation for everything that has happened in the universe from the stone to man. Life can arise from spontaneous generation within the cosmic fermentation; entire species can evolve from a single molecule. The whole universe is in a state of flux, all boundaries overlap: "Every animal is more or less man; every mineral is more or less plant; every plant is more or less animal. There is nothing precise in nature" (OPH, p. 311).

The *Principes philosophiques sur la matière et le mouvement* (1771) restate the main theme of the *Rêve de D'Alembert:* "I see everything in action and reaction . . . whence arises the movement or rather the general fermentation of the universe" (OPH, p. 398). In such a universe of "creative chaos" things are constantly transforming into their very opposites, life into death and death into life, a molecule into an elephant, a virtuous man into a scoundrel or the reverse.

At least as early as 1753–54, with the publication of *De l'interprétation de la nature,* Diderot wrestled with one of the grave implications of his materialist philosophy: the problem of free will within a rigid and universal determinism of cause and effect. Diderot the scientific and philosophic determinist had to do battle with Diderot the libertarian, the staunch defender of freedom of thought, of conscience, of religion, of the press, and of economic activity, a dilemma and a paradox he shared with La Mettrie and D'Holbach, among others. His letter to Landois (June 29, 1756) summarizes his deterministic philosophy:

> Look at the matter closely and you will see that the word *freedom* is a word empty of meaning; that there is not and there cannot be free beings; that we are only what is suitable to the general order, to the organization . . . and to the chain of events. That is what governs us invincibly. . . . What deceives us is the prodigious variety of our actions, joined with the habit we have taken since birth of confusing the voluntary with the free. . . . But if there is no free will, there is no action deserving of praise or blame; there is neither vice nor virtue, nothing that must be rewarded or punished. *(Correspondance* 1:213–14)

Diderot rejected Spinoza's divine Substance but adopted Spinoza's position that our sense of freedom is an illusion caused by our ignorance of the innumerable secret causes that dictate our every thought, mood, and action. An act can be voluntary but still not free. For Diderot, the malefactor is a man not to be "punished" with moral indignation but to be neutrally "destroyed" for the safety of the community. Diderot's determinism, like Skinner's behaviorism, led to the concept of behavior modification: "But although man, be he benefactor or malefactor, is not free, man is nonetheless a being that can be modified" *(Correspondance* 1:214). In the *Rêve de D'Alembert* as in the Landois letter the notions of innate or absolute virtue and vice are replaced by notions of social utility:

bienfaisance and *malfaisance*. People are not good or bad; they are "happily or unhappily born." Rewards and punishments are simply means of correcting *l'être modifiable*.

In presenting his views on determinism (disguised as fatalism) the author of *Jacques le fataliste* has his hero lift several sentences directly from the Landois letter as well as from the *Rêve*:

> Jacques recognized neither the name of vice nor the name of virtue; he claimed that one was happily or unhappily born. Whenever he heard the words *rewards* or *punishments*, he would shrug his shoulders. According to him, reward was the encouragement of the good; punishment the frightening of the wicked. What else is it, he would say, if there is no free will and if our destiny is written up there? (P. 620)

But again, the author's deterministic ontology did not satisfy the humanitarian and libertarian ethic that he espoused at the very same time. His painful paradox is expressed in his confession to Sophie Volland: "I fume at being entangled in a devilish philosophy that my mind cannot keep from approving and my heart from denying."[12] Diderot's philosophical ambivalence is signaled by the very structure of *Jacques le fataliste*: the ironic tension between the *écriture là-haut*, "metaphor of the preordained" (Vartanian) and, on the other hand, the fortuitousness that marks the hero's journey through life and the fortuitousness of the digressions whose causal links with the main thread of the story are more or less haphazard and whose time frames disrupt the chronology of the hero's "story." And the narrator's dogged insistence on artistic freedom, even arbitrariness, runs directly counter to the hero's vision of preordination, predestination, and the intransigence of fate.

To put the matter another way, Diderot is exploring in *Jacques* the embarrassing gaps that exist between his theory of reality and his existential experience of reality. The "Grand Rouleau" can be taken as a symbol for the incontrovertible laws of "Nature"—that well-oiled, smoothly running "machine" of Newtonian physics seen as the totality of an objective, ordered, physical reality existing independently of mind but obeying permanent, systematic, and logical laws of cause and effect. These laws were capable of being known by human reason and expressed, as in the *Encyclopédie*, by human language. The following two descriptions of the link between Newtonian physics and deterministic philosophy apply perfectly to the central thesis of *Jacques le fataliste*.

A mechanical philosophy was appearing. It became popular to regard both the physical world and the nonphysical world as mechanical.
For every effect, there had to be a known cause. For every cause, there
had to be an accountable effect. The future, therefore, became a conse-
quence of the past. It seemed there was little anyone could do to alter
the world. Even our thoughts were to be explained somehow by New-
ton's machine. The "hand of God" had set the machine in motion eons
ago, and no one could stop it. (Fred A. Wolf, *Taking the Quantum Leap,* p.
42)

If we are to accept the mechanistic determination of Newtonian
physics—if the universe really is a great machine—then from the moment that the universe was created and set into motion, everything that
was to happen in it already was determined.

According to this philosophy, we may seem to have a will of our
own and the ability to alter the course of events in our lives, but we do
not. Everything, from the beginning of time, has been predetermined,
including our illusion of having a free will. The universe is a *prerecorded
tape* [cf. le grand rouleau] playing itself out in the only way that it can.
(Gary Zukav, *The Dancing Wu Li Masters,* p. 26; emphasis added)

But as David Highnam points out in a recent and important paper
("Narrative Structure and New Physics," pp. 15–26), Diderot does everything possible to disrupt the syntagmatic, linear structure of the novel
that would valorize logical causality, and he even prefigures many of the
discoveries of anti-Newtonian "new physics" (i.e., the conjunction of relativity theory and quantum mechanics). Jean-Paul Sartre said that the
theory of relativity has serious implications for the novelist: there can no
longer be any justification for an absolute, omniscient point of view
determining the ultimate meaning of a novel; a novel is an action presented from various points of view, no single one of which represents
absolute, objective truth. *Jacques le fataliste,* of course, could be taken as a
paradigm for such a conception of the novel. And just as Diderot shows
us that people are not good *or* bad, but good *and* bad, faithful *and*
insolent, etc., quantum theory states that something can be, paradoxically, both a wave *and* a particle. Just as Diderot developed in *Jacques* his
own Uncertainty Principle, questioning man's ability to know ultimate
reality, the new physics has discovered that on the level of subatomic
particles things move without following laws of mechanical motion, that
there is no such thing as an imperturbable machine that can be objectively measured and known since the very act of measuring electrons

changes their state and the state of the universe. Reality as seen by the new physics is not really a state but a dynamic process of interactions and collisions (sometimes between *opposites*). The "building blocks" of matter exist not in a smooth flow or continuum but in "contiguous discontinuity."

> One could search indefinitely before finding a more apt description of the structure of *Jacques le fataliste* than the term "contiguous discontinuity"; radical juxtapositioning of different spatial and temporal planes, multiple interruptions of story lines, the predominance of paradigmatic axes, all of these are aspects of the contiguous discontinuity which reigns in this novel. (Highnam, "Narrative Structure and New Physics," p. 22)

Ultimately, the only "reality" we know, both for Diderot and for many theoreticians of the new physics, is our own consciousness; the order of the universe, as physicist Fred A. Wolf has said, may be the order of our mind.

One of the theories emanating from the new physics and compatible with the Grand Rouleau view of the universe is that of *superdeterminism*, which goes far beyond ordinary determinism.

> Ordinary determinism states that once the initial situation of a system is established, the future of the system also is established since it must develop according to inexorable laws of cause and effect. This type of determinism was the basis of the Great Machine view of the universe. According to this view, however, if the initial situation of a system, like the universe, is changed, then the future of the system also is changed.
>
> According to superdeterminism, *not even the initial situation of the universe could be changed.* Not only is it impossible for things to be other than they are, it is even impossible that the initial situation of the universe could have been other than what it was. (Zukav, *The Dancing Wu Li Masters*, pp. 303–4)

Contemporary physicists and astronomers have confirmed Diderot's theories concerning the mutability of matter and what Fritjof Capra *(The Tao of Physics)* calls the "restlessness" of matter. Subatomic particles are never at rest but always in a state of motion. A similar restlessness is observed in the vast world of stars and galaxies, from the formation of stars out of rapidly rotating clouds of hydrogen gas to their expansion, subsequent contraction, and final collapse. All the galaxies are spinning rapidly around their center and moving away from each other at speeds approaching that of light. The entire restless universe has been expanding ever since the Big Bang.

Particle physics in the 1950s and early 1960s replaced what had seemed to be the apparent underlying simplicity of atomic structure (i.e., proton, neutron, and electron) with what physicist James Trefil *(From Atoms to Quarks,* p. 149) calls the confusing "chaos" of elementary particles numbering in the hundreds—a chaos only recently reduced by the quark model. But even more recent discoveries in particle physics (e.g., "charm" and "color") suggest the possibility of a disquieting proliferation of quarks and "subquarks."

> Either the quarks are themselves manifestations of some yet more fundamental entities, or our search for ultimate simplicity is a chimera.... Even if we do wind up with a unified field theory showing that the fundamental interactions are identical, we shall still be left with the problem of finding some underlying simplicity in the suddenly complex world of quarks. (Trefil, pp. 190, 217)

By the late 1970s quarks were coming in six "flavors," each of which could have three "colors." Furthermore, quarks may ultimately have no more physical reality than a "wave" of water (Trefil, p. 170).

Thus, Diderot's philosophical intuitions about the nature of matter—indeed the intuitions of all romantic ironists concerning the eternal mobility, restlessness, and seeming chaos of the universe—have been remarkably consistent with developments in modern theoretical physics.

There is also an interesting and significant parallel, I think, between those romantic ironists who treat playfully what they earnestly believe or desire and those (many) contemporary physicists who, because of the radical implications of quantum logic and quantum theory (e.g., Bell's theorem), find themselves seriously "discussing types of phenomena which, ironically, they do not believe exist" (Zukav, *The Dancing Wu Li Masters,* p. 298).

*

Thomas Kavanaugh ("Encyclopedia of the Novel," p. 153) stresses the tension between the overt theme of *Jacques* as stated by the hero and the experience of the reader.

On the one hand, the novel's main character, Jacques, repeatedly
insists that all actions are bound together by strict relations of cause and
effect corresponding to the irresistible dictates of the Great Scroll. On
the other hand, everything about the way we as readers come to experience these stories, our access to them only through a second and always
unpredictable level of authorial discourse, consolidates an opposite impression of total indetermination, of a chaos absolutely alien to the
operation of any didactic principle.

And he concludes (p. 161), "What the reader finally takes away from the
novel is an unfettered vision of chaos and indetermination, of a world
which is fundamentally recalcitrant to man's attempts to impose upon it
his various systems of reasons, laws and predictability."

Man cannot understand the workings of the universe at large nor
even his fellowman. In the first place, men are too different from each
other, and in the second, even if they were alike, language is an inadequate tool to express our feelings and ideas with any kind of precision.

Even in the most energetic, the most limpid, the most precise writer, words can never be the absolute signs of an idea, a sentiment, or a
thought.[13]

We always use in our own way an inherently defective instrument,
the idiom that always expresses too much or too little.[14]

We never understand precisely, we are never precisely understood;
there is more or less in everything: our discourse always falls short or
goes beyond the sensation.[15]

As Jacques tells his master (p. 518), the message is always inexact, and it is
always misinterpreted by its receiver.

Marxist critics have attempted to find in Diderot's thought an incipient dialectic. But throughout the opus in general and in *Jacques le
fataliste* in particular we are presented not with a dialectic but with a
dilemma. As Lester Crocker has pointed out *(Diderot's Chaotic Order,* pp.
10, 46), Diderot's thought is not a dialectic on the cosmic level since there
is no solution of the endless antagonisms and antitheses, no unity of
contraries producing a new synthesis. Crocker goes on to say of *Jacques:*

These passages contain intimations of man's alienation in a meaningless universe. "It was written up there" is in itself indicative of a
directing force, though whether its nature is that of a plan or of utter

caprice is unknowable. This suprahuman reality is not meaningful in human terms. It strikes us in any case as a disorder, whatever it may be. Jacques's motto thus has a high symbolic value. "Direction," or law, and disorder are coexisting contraries. (P. 50)

The relevance of this statement to my purpose can be found in Maurice Boucher's definition ("L'ironie romantique," p. 29) of romantic irony: "the consciousness of the coexistence of contraries."

Also germane is the following remark by Crocker (*Diderot's Chaotic Order*, p. 44): "The implicit contradiction is not in Diderot, but in man, who is both determined and self-directing, both a physical and a moral being. It turns out that the acme of the cosmic ordering process is a creature who is an element of disorder, by his nature. This is indeed cosmic irony."

For Diderot and the French romantic ironists who followed him, man is indeed a source of disorder and the locus of many paradoxes from which there is no escape. But the romantic ironist is also conscious—playfully and painfully conscious—of the fact that *he, too,* is embroiled in all the paradoxes of the human condition as well as all the paradoxes that Schlegel was to find in the complex process of literary creation. Among many other things, the dense and rich text of *Jacques le fataliste* is an exercise in self-parody. Diderot pokes fun at his own philosophy, lampoons his own ambivalences and self-contradictions, and mocks the very art form he has espoused.

3

Self-Reflexive Irony in Musset's *Namouna*

O my friend! The world incessantly moves
Around us, within us. . . .
(Suzon)

What agitation, what noise in the city!
What a restless monster this humanity!
(La Coupe et les lèvres)

Do I know, at the moment when I leave you,
Where my wandering star is dragging me?
However, my sweet, I go
Very far, very fast. Always running.
("Adieux à Suzon")

ALFRED DE MUSSET's deep-rooted tendency toward romantic irony can be seen in two of his earliest works, *Les Marrons du feu* and *Mardoche*. Both narrative poems, completed in 1829, appeared in Musset's first collection, *Les Contes d'Espagne et d'Italie* (1830).

Rafaël, of *Les Marrons du feu*, is a Byronic hero in the Don Juan mold: flippant, callous, caddish. Love to him is a short-lived affair that leads inevitably to boredom. Despite the implied author's obvious identification with him, he is the first of Musset's antiheroes; from the beginning of the poem to the end he is identified with the clown. We first see him carrying a broken guitar and wearing a wet and tattered coat. The clown topos is made explicit in scene 2 when Rafaël presents La Camargo with a fan that, he says, is the very portrait of himself; among other things it is covered with the silver spangles of Harlequin. This motif is echoed later in a song that Rafaël sings of Trivelin and Scaramouche and more significantly at the end of the poem when the dying hero's last request is that all his worldly goods be bequeathed to his jester, Bippo. Rafaël's self-image is that of a buffoon.

41

> I am called Lord Emptypurse, breaker
> Of jars; in English, Blockhead, master killer
> Of priests. . . .
> . . . .
> What do you expect? I have given my life
> To that lazy god called Fantasy.
> It is he who—sad or insane—from front or side,
> Pulls me like a puppet on a string.[1]

He does not try to hide a sense of emptiness. He calls himself "a shallow brain" and says that he is "more vain than the smoke / Of my pipe." He is a hollow man, emptier than a tin soldier, as a later hero, Lorenzaccio, will describe himself.

We are dealing here with a modern type of antihero: the sad clown endowed with (or beset by) self-consciousness—the clown who *knows* he's a clown. Rafaël's clowning not only expresses his feelings of self-worth but also serves, like the great amount of alcohol he consumes, to drown his sorrow.

> As for melancholy, it smacks too much of holes
> In one's stockings, of the fifth floor, and old pennies.
> They say that she has people who drown themselves for her.
> —As for me, I drown her.

Mardoche is a lively, deliberately disjointed and humorous narrative that pokes fun at certain aspects of French romanticism (including Anglophilia, melancholy, and the macabre of "bas romantisme") and treats its hero (who, for instance, sprains his ankle while escaping from an enraged husband) with the same disrespect.

Despite the poem's comic tonality, there are serious implications that the poet might have developed more fully. For example, the theme of love's evanescence—one of the major themes of Musset's opus and already an important leitmotif in the *Contes*—appears in *Mardoche,* although presented in a lighthearted vein.

>   But everything wears out.
> A honeymoon does not have thirty quarterings
> Like a Saxon baron.—And beware of the last ones!
> Love (alas! nature is so strange and false!)
> Lives on inanition and dies from nourishment.

And then, what is one to do? A day is very long.—
                                    And tomorrow?
And always?—Boredom wins.—Of what shall one dream
                                    in one's bath?

But the reader of the *Contes* is aware of having encountered this theme repeatedly in earlier pieces and in more serious contexts. The theme is used again as the finale. Mardoche's beloved Rosine is sent to a convent. His reaction?

And what did Mardoche do?—To change
Loves, it took him six months of travels.

Mardoche's cynical *désinvolture* is given a serious explanation in a passage at the beginning of the poem.

Perhaps having, to relieve boredom,
Only one book (by that I mean the human heart),
He had learned to read in it too soon and too far;
It's a great misfortune to have a precocious mind. . . .

Mardoche is Musset's first presentation of a basic type of romantic hero who will become prominent in his work, the *puer senex,* the disillusioned and cynical young man who is old before his time.[2]

While lacking the serious side of romantic irony, *Mardoche* displays several of its most typical devices. For one, *interventionnisme.* The narrative is constantly interrupted by apostrophes to the reader that inform the latter about the author's intentions and techniques; for example, not only does the poet abridge an episode, he informs the reader of the abridgment.

I do not plan in any way, reader, to write
Here what in Paris is called a novel.
An author, who makes his way step by step, almost
Has you sleep with his heroine.
That is not my style; and, if you permit,
It's two full weeks we shall have skipped.

Then there is the mock-heroic tonality.

O silent woods!—O guarded walls!
Balconies left so late! so quickly scaled!
. . . .

> And you, silver lamp, pale and cool light
> Who make the sweet nights whiter than milk!
> —Sustain my inspiration in this divine verse!
>
> I want to sing of that eternally memorable day
> When, his supper finished, before it grew dark,
> Our hero, his nose hidden under his cloak,
> Got in his carriage at least an hour too soon!

The poet even pokes fun at his own poem by pointing out, in a rhymed footnote, the weakness of the plot's ending.

> This ending is hackneyed; and we offer it as such,
> A great change from the new fashion.

It is clear that the narrator does not take seriously what he is narrating.

In *Namouna* such devices are used not just to create one-dimensional humor as here but to produce a tonality and thematics of ambivalence. *Mardoche* is charming but thin; *Namouna* gives off more meaningful vibrations.

*

Irony in Musset is basically a tendency to deflate, often at the expense of his fellow romantics, often at his own expense. Irony directed at certain tendencies of the romantic movement is *not* romantic irony since the author is not identifying in the least with what he is mocking. For example, when Musset irreverently likens the moon shining over a belfry to a trivial dot over an *i,* or a Byronic hero perched on the Jungfrau to a fly on a sugar loaf, he is deflating not his own style but the clichés of his contemporaries. Similarly, when Musset in *Namouna* (1.23–24) apologizes for the lack of local color in this "oriental tale," because, he says, he has never been to the Orient and has "never stolen anything from a library," this is not true romantic irony either since it is really directed at the superficial local color of Hugo's *Orientales.* In a passage such as the following, from the dedication page of *La Coupe et les lèvres*—

> You ask me if I love my fatherland.
> Yes; —I love very much Spain and Turkey too.
> . . . .
> You ask me if I am Catholic.
> Yes; —I also love the gods Lath and Nésu.
> . . . .

> You ask me if I love wisdom.
> Yes; —I also like very much smoking tobacco.

—the last line, on first reading, may seem to be deflating the author's own ego, but the context and the parallel structure of the couplets make it clear that the irony is still being directed outward at conventional wisdom, just as it is against patriotism and Catholicism rather than the author's supposed hedonism and anti-intellectualism. It is conventional life, not the poet himself, that is not being taken seriously, just as in Byron's lines:

> I say—the future is a serious matter—
> And so—for God's sake—hock and soda water.[3]

However, in *Namouna* we witness a curious mixture of irony-at-the-expense-of-romanticism and romantic irony, the latter directed against Hassan, the very hero of Musset's poem. Consider the following passage:

> He had neither parents, nor monkey, nor mistress.
> Nothing ordinary about him, —nothing that linked him
> To the common run of martyrs, —not one dog, not one cat.
> I must, however, interest you
> In my poor hero. —To say that he is a pasha,
> That's a worn-out device, a clumsy trick.
> To say that he is peevish, somber, mysterious,
> That's not true first of all, and is even more trite.

> (1.27–28)

Musset is poking fun at the hackneyed hero of romanticism: the orphan; the outcast; the pariah, solitary both in his *état civil* and in his moral-intellectual superiority; the *beau ténébreux*, somber, mysterious, moody, misanthropic, and melancholy. But at the same time he is deflating his own hero. First, he dashes the reader's hopes of encountering a more flamboyant hero, and more important, he abruptly halts the narrative to ponder the technical problem of enlisting the reader's sympathy. Throughout the entire poem, as here, the narration of Hassan's story is interrupted thematically by the intrusions of the author and structurally by the intrusion of the present tense upon the regular narrative tenses. The reader is constantly shuttled between the past exploits of the hero and the present preoccupations of the author.

This intrusion of the present tense begins as early as the poem's second stanza:

> Hassan had, moreover, a very noble pose,
> He was as naked as Eve during her first sin.
> What! stark naked! had he no shame?
> Naked, as early as the second word! —What will we have
>   at the end?
> Sir, excuse me, —I begin this tale
> Just when my hero is leaving his bath.
>
>   (1.1–2)

The description of Hassan's *entrée en scène*—deflating in itself—is interrupted first by the anticipated exclamations of the scandalized reader, this contrived reader using the future tense, and later by the vocative and imperative of the penultimate line. Then the narrative completely breaks down as Musset switches to the present of the narrative act: "I begin this tale / Just when. . . ."

Musset constantly uses the present tense to express his independence from his hero:

> In fact, if he acts badly, one could think of worse.—
> My word, so much the worse for him:—I don't see why
> The foolish actions of Hassan should fall back on me.
>
>   (1.30)

> —I remind the reader that here as well as above
> It's my hero speaking, and I would die of shame
> If you believed for one moment that what I relate,
> Here more than ever, does not revolt me.
>
>   (1.39)

In his brilliant analysis of a passage from Rousseau's *Confessions* Jean Starobinski *(L'Oeil vivant* 2:115) has shown how the author achieves subtle ironic effects by shifting from the narrative past to the present as "qualitatively privileged tense," or what other critics have called "the ethical present." The present of the narrative act conveys not only a foreknowledge of what is going to be related (and is thus invested with Sophoclean irony) but also the superior wisdom and experience of the writer writing *now*, so that the relation of author to character (or, in Rousseau's case, of author-past versus author-present) is one of amused condescension. We are dealing with romantic irony here because Musset, like Rousseau, does identify with the character he is mocking. It must be borne in mind that *romantic irony is a double irony;* it works in two opposite directions at once. The poet declares himself alienated from his hero, but this alienation itself is also ironic—it masks the author's limited but genuinely sympathetic identification. *Romantic irony commits itself to what it criticizes at the same time it criticizes what it affirms.* Despite his many (ironic) declarations of independence and detachment, Musset offers Hassan, as we shall see, as an important incarnation of a serious, or partly serious, worldview. The role of Hassan, like that of Rolla, Octave, Fantasio, Frank, or Lorenzaccio, has serious implications that have been consistently overlooked by the critics.

By stanza 32 the romantic irony shifts from the hero to the poet himself who despairs of being able to finish his rambling poem; that is, there is a shift from subjective and objective irony to naive irony. In stanza 61 Musset's narrator, speaking as implied author, admits having digressed so long that he has forgotten where he has left his story. Then he apologizes to the reader for a hiatus here, a barbarism there, and so forth. What we really have here is romantic irony in triplicate: first, the poet pokes fun at his hero; then at himself and his poem; and finally the reader is constantly discouraged from identifying with Hassan by being made self-conscious through the many vocatives directed at him by the poet. The hero is constantly wedged between the reader and the writer:

> You see, reader, how far my frankness goes,
> My hero is stark naked, —and I am in my nightshirt.

> (1.75)

Another source of romantic irony in *Namouna* is the poem's overall structure. The narrator keeps promising the reader to get on with the story but keeps putting it off. The narrative proper does not begin until the third and final canto—a mere fourteen stanzas compared to the fifty-five stanzas of the second canto and the seventy-eight stanzas of the first. The poet even devotes the first four of the final fourteen stanzas to still another apology for rambling off the subject, leaving only the last sixty lines (out of a total 882) to the actual plot of this narrative poem, this "oriental tale." Thus the hero of the story and the story itself are treated with ironic detachment and are deconstructed from beginning to end.[4] The obvious fact is that we are dealing not with narrative poetry at all—even to mock the heroic would require more narrative than we are given—but with the poetry of ideas. The poem must be read not only on its comic level (brilliantly done in itself) but on a deeper one.

The second canto is a digression (i.e., another instance of structural irony) and is devoted not to Hassan at all, but to Musset's idea of the perfect Don Juan. Musset's Don Juan has none of the vulgarity, the gratuitous cruelty, the hatred of both God and man found in many of his illustrious predecessors:

> It's because with all their horrors, their doubt and blasphemy
> Not one loved thee, Don Juan; and I do love thee.
>
> (2.39)

He is rather the "innocent corrupter," loving and leaving three thousand women in his search for the ideal one. The hyperbolic figure, tripling the usual number of Don Juan's conquests, is serious rather than comic in effect. Although his thirst—which is of a moral and aesthetic as well as erotic nature—is never satisfactorily quenched, Don Juan never gives up hope:

> you died full of hope.
> You lost your beauty, your glory and your genius
> For an impossible being and who did not exist.
>
> (2.53)

There is no sadism in Don Juan's dealings with women, only a fierce optimism urging him on in his quest.

The relationship between this idealized Don Juan and Hassan is crucial for an appreciation of the poem's total impact. The relationship is expressed in the last two lines of the canto:

> What Don Juan loved, Hassan loved too perhaps.
> What Don Juan sought, Hassan did not believe in.

Thus, Don Juan goes from woman to woman because of an impossible dream, a quixotic quest, whereas Hassan goes from woman to woman since, knowing such a quest is hopeless, one woman is as good as another.[5] Although Musset is stressing the difference between the two types of Don Juan in the lines quoted above, they are nevertheless linked not only by the anaphora and the parallel syntax but also by the tentative "perhaps," suggesting a latent idealism in Hassan; he would gladly remain faithful to a perfect woman if such a woman existed. Hassan's doubt is linked to that of the implied author ("an impossible being and who did not exist"). In fact, there can be no doubt that Hassan, no less than Musset's other heroes, is a projection of the poet himself, a significant point to keep in mind when assessing the causes and effects of romantic irony.

On the deepest level the poem, despite its comic surface, must be read as a somber meditation on the ethical implications of a world devoid of a perfect being in heaven as well as on earth and denied self-delusion by virtue of its newfound skepticism. The only response to such a bleak situation is Hassan's quantitative ethic. Since the spiritual longings of man will never be satisfied, the modern Don Juan (Hassan) must live within the confines of the senses, deriving what consolation from them he can and prolonging his transient pleasures as long as he can.

One of the curious effects of the second canto is that, though Hassan does not even figure in it, sympathy is indirectly built up for him. We have mentioned the latent idealism; it is only Hassan's superior lucidity (Voltaire's men have by now been born) that prevents him from being as naively idealistic as Don Juan. There is also the suggestion of a certain courage, for Hassan as well as for Don Juan, to live in the face of ugly reality. And the absence of self-pity, automatically precluded by the romantic irony, makes Hassan more sympathetic than many another romantic hero.

But the romantic irony also prevents Hassan from being inflated into an idealized creation. The chief source of irony directed against him is that he must compete with and be overshadowed by the Don Juan of the canto-long digression. Don Juan, too, is a victim of romantic irony: he is treated seriously but is wedged between the Hassan of the first and final cantos that are, furthermore, written basically in a comic vein. The final irony is that neither hero is given the title role, which belongs to an inconsequential servant girl whose plight is described in less than thirty lines. The total effect of the poem—and this seems to have escaped all the critics—is an irony directed at modern man. With our disabused cynicism and scientism, our unredeemed sensualism, Hassan is the only Don Juan figure we deserve.

A significant passage at the beginning of *Namouna* throws light on the poem's romantic irony and on the particular kind of vision that impels the poet to use it.

> Do you remember, reader, that serenade
> That Don Juan, disguised, sings under a balcony?
> —A melancholy and pitiful song,
> Expressing pain, love and sadness.

But the accompaniment speaks in another tone.
How lively and joyous it is! With what nimbleness
It leaps!— One would say that the song caresses
And covers with languor the perfidious instrument,
While the mocking air of the accompaniment
Turns to derision the song itself,
And seems to be mocking its sad air.
All that, however, gives extreme pleasure.

(1.13–14)

This "extreme" aesthetic pleasure, produced by the ironic counterpoint in *Don Giovanni,* is based on the spectator's recognition of a psychological and moral truth:

It's because everything about it is true, —it's because
    one deceives and one loves;
It's because one cries while laughing; —it's because
    one is innocent
And guilty at the same time; it's because one thinks
    oneself deceitful
When one is only deceived; it's because one sheds blood
With spotless hands, and because our mother Nature
Has molded her creature with both good and evil:
Such is the world, alas! and such was Hassan.

(1.15–16)

Thus, more succinctly than the *Préface de Cromwell,* this minimanifesto urges a *mélange des genres* based on a view of man not as a smooth monolith but as a creature of ambivalence and paradox, what Laforgue will call "l'innombrable clavier humain." Musset's description of Hassan, which immediately precedes this passage, provides an illustration.

He was very joyous, and yet very sullen.
A detestable neighbor, —excellent comrade.
Extremely frivolous, —and yet very sedate.
Shamefully naive, —and yet very blasé.
Horribly sincere, —and yet very sly.

With *Les Marrons du feu, Mardoche,* and especially *Namouna,* nineteenth-century French literature is given a new kind of comic vision, tinged with sadness and seriousness but not taking the seriousness too seriously. It started with Musset in poetry and in drama and with Stendhal in the novel and will have distinguished variations performed by Gautier, Flaubert, Baudelaire, Corbière, Cros, and Laforgue. The twentieth century will take romantic irony and turn it into *humour noir;* the playfulness will still be there, but the tragic overtones will be emphasized. With early forms of French romantic irony we are dealing with skepticism and disillusionment leading to a delicately balanced ambivalence, a tragicomic sense of life in which the tragic dimension does not overshadow or overwhelm the comic.

*

In Alfred de Musset, as in Diderot, nervous system, philosophical system (which does not mean systematic philosophy), and stylistic system are exceptionally well attuned. And as in Diderot, and romantic ironists in general, the key concept linking the three systems is mobility.

Musset was a man of unstable temperament, of quicksilver moods, of fickle fancies and contradictory impulses, a man divided and always on the run. Wavering constantly between idealism and cynicism, he yearned for true love and for an enduring faith, but just as constant were his mistrust and his unbelief. Vague religiosity and anguished incredulity were to follow him throughout his life. Changeability was his essence; nothing could hold his attention for long. The frightful vulture, Boredom, he said, had early marked him as its prey. Epicurean delights, the excitements of wine, women, song, and gambling, even the blessed moments of poetic inspiration—all were quickly and inevitably followed by periods of dejection. His "instinct for unhappiness," as he called it, caused the sweetest honey that touched his lips to change to bitter brew.

Musset was painfully aware of the contradictions in his nature. He speaks in his correspondence of the two totally different men inhabiting him. In one passage it is the man of action and the passive observer; in another it is the idealist and the cynic, Coelio and Octave. His biographers have spoken of the Chérubin–Don Juan antinomy and of Jekyll and Hyde. Mme Allan-Despréaux says of him: "I have never seen a more striking contrast than the two beings contained in this one person. One is good, gentle, tender, enthusiastic, full of wit and common sense, naive. . . . If you turn the page and look on the other side, you find a man possessed by a sort of devil. . . . His nature consists of extremes, both of good and bad."[6] A psychoanalytically oriented biographer, Pierre Odoul (*Le Drame intime,* pp. 76–77, 175), speaks of Musset's strong id, especially the dominance of the pleasure principle, constantly countered by a strong superego (unconscious emulation of his highly moral parents). Morality and libertinage, modesty and impertinence, sociability and solitariness, gaiety and moroseness, cohabited in him and fought for dominance. They were all unsuccessful, the battle being internecine.

The inner conflict troubling him most was that between his yearning for ideal, pure love and his incapacity to achieve it or even believe in it fully. Odoul, somewhat gratuitously, finds the trouble in a mother fixation (Sand being six years older, Mme Jaubert being the *marraine* [the stepmother], etc.) that becomes a sister fixation. Others have pointed to his inveterate masochism. Here the internal evidence of Musset's literary work is convincing, as a small sampling illustrates.

> And yet my heart took bitter pleasure
> In feeling that it was in love and was going to suffer!
>
> ("Idylle")

> Nothing is good except loving, nothing true but suffering.
>
> (*A la Malibran*)

> And how sweet it is to suffer for love of you!
> . . . .
> And how torment itself is a wild passion!
>
> ("A Ninon")

Love is called a "cherished sorrow" in "A Ninon," a "delicious suffering" in *Carmosine.* Then there is the medallion bearing the portrait of his mistress that the autobiographical Octave of the *Confession d'un enfant du siècle* turns into an instrument of masochistic pleasure.

> I used to wear it on my heart, a thing that is done by many men; but one day, having found in a curiosity shop an iron scourge, at the end of which was a metallic plate bristling with sharp nails, I had the medallion attached to the plate and wore it thus. Those nails, which entered my chest with every movement, caused me such a strange sensual pleasure that sometimes I would press down with my hand in order to feel them more deeply. (*OEuvres complètes,* p. 564)

Whatever the unconscious springs of his amorous behavior and misbehavior, his conscious efforts to achieve a lasting love were always frustrated.

His brother Paul has spoken of the "mobility" of Musset's mind;

Sainte-Beuve, who knew him well, has said: "With Musset everything was conducted quickly, at a furious pace" *(Causeries* 13:370); and Mme Jaubert, who knew him even better, says of him: "There is no stormy, multicolored sky, lighted by a March sun, whose mobility can be compared to that of his moods."[7] Both Sainte-Beuve and Maurice Toesca have noticed the acceleration of seasons in Musset's life.

> Why could he not be patient? Everything would have come in its season. But he was eager to condense and devour the seasons.[8]

> There was in Musset a constant displacement in the seasons of his life: as a child, he sees himself as an adolescent, and in truth he is because of his culture; toward his fifteenth year . . . he has already read so many books that he is overbrimming with poetry, dreams, adventures, and desires that are those of an adult. *(L'Amour de la mort,* p. 41)

Musset's precocity and impatience made of him a romantic *puer senex,* older (but not wiser) than his years. Jean Pommier has distinguished between normal human time and "le temps de Musset": "Everything is swept along at a different pace from ours" *(Musset,* p. 8).

To observe Musset's psyche is to observe restless, rapid movements.

> I go and come, advance and withdraw: a strange instinct pushes and attracts me. I don't know if it is out of fear or pleasure that I quiver. *(Correspondance,* p. 72)

> Where then am I being led by that invisible hand that does not want me to stop? *(Correspondance,* p. 67)

> Wriggling, twisting, in total disarray . . . that is my perfect image. *(Correspondance,* p. 184)

> Do I know, at the moment when I leave you,
> Where my wandering star is dragging me?
> However, my sweet, I go
> Very far, very fast. Always running.

> ("Adieux à Suzon")

There are movements of impulsiveness, impetuousness, and impatience; movements, too, of excited anticipation and movements of remorse. Other movements arise from his near manic-depressive swings in mood, his constant shuttlings between contradictory patterns of behavior—

jerky movements, then, caused by unstable equilibrium. His well-documented masochism is a voluntary return to the scene of the pain; here the movement is cyclical: "His ideal cycle: to escape from boredom through amorous conquests, to suffer from them, to sing of his grief to free himself from them, and then finally to fall back again into boredom" (Toesca, *L'Amour de la mort*, pp. 199–200). There are centrifugal movements away from the norm and toward the extremes: "I need excess in whatever form" *(Correspondance*, p. 15). There are movements away from the real and toward the impossible; George Sand has spoken in *Elle et Lui* of Musset's love of what does not exist. This is the constant movement of the eternal questor, which in the poetry is expressed by a variety of analogous images: the eagle flying toward (but not reaching) the high mountaintop, the miner digging furiously for diamonds in the bowels of the earth, the diver sinking deeper and deeper in the unplumbed depths, the traveler who feels the ground beneath him collapse as soon as he arrives, Don Juan on his "infinite road" seeking an "impossible being," Frank pushing ever forward toward an ever-receding goal.

> Everything carries him, drags him, toward his ideal goal,
> A brilliance always fleeing him, always pursued.[9]

There are movements of aversion, even from happiness: "At a formal ball, at festive gatherings, whenever he encountered pleasure, he could not stand it, he sought through reflection to draw sadness, bitterness from it" (Sainte-Beuve, *Causeries* 13:366). This strange gift, or handicap, of seeing the worm the moment he bites into the fruit, of seeing the slip 'twixt the cup and the lip *(La Coupe et les lèvres* is his most philosophical play), has led Pierre Gastinel to speak of his contractile movements, his *contractilité*. Other critics, Charlotte Dolder *(L'Être et le paraître*, pp. 21, 135) and Jean-Pierre Richard, have seen oscillating and undulating movements as both the poet and the man shuttle between opposite moods and impulses: "He constantly swings back and forth, moving abruptly from one opinion to the opposite opinion. . . . hesitation, procrastination, unexpected reversals: that is the law of this uncompassed universe" (Richard, *Etudes sur le romantisme*, p. 209). Philippe Soupault has summed him up well as the poet of vertigo.

The mobility of his temperament no doubt influenced his general outlook on life, which is characterized by the mobility and changeability he sees in all things animate and inanimate. His *summum bonum* was love, *l'amour-passion*. But love, like all of Nature's creations, is subject to her first law, the law of impermanence, inconstancy, and inevitable change. Man is a creature inherently incapable of sustaining the intensity of a deep passion. He is both the victim and the agent of change. Musset's cynical Don Juans—Rafaël, Mardoche, Hassan—change mistresses nearly as often as they change their clothes. His idealistic Don Juans are also subject to the law of impermanence. The Don Juan of *Namouna* goes from woman to woman in search of what Drieu la Rochelle's Gille calls "that perfect creature." He sacrifices his physical and spiritual energy in search of an impossible dream. Musset's other idealistic Don Juan, the hero of *La Matinée de Don Juan,* asks himself: "And what do you have left for having tried to slake your thirst so many times? —O my God, an ardent thirst!" *(OEuvres complètes,* p. 496). The movements of all his Don Juans, then, resemble those found in all the great myths of frustration—Sisyphus, the Danaides, Tantalus—the movements of an eternal treadmill.

Love can arise from the ashes through the persistence of memory; privileged moments live on in memory, in poetry, and in the soul's immortal consciousness *(Lettre à Lamartine; Souvenir)*. But privileged moments are fleeting by nature and rare by definition. It is the law of change that remains primary in Musset's view of reality. The inexorability of change governs not only love but friendship, worldly glory, politics, and history. The death of a celebrated singer (La Malibran) becomes a forgotten story in a fortnight. Politicians change with the wind, and their conflicting ideas are quickly adopted and abandoned by a fickle populace. It is the latter who is blamed, in "Sur la Naissance du Conte de Paris," for the confusing acceleration of history since 1789.

To the law of impermanence and change must be added the second law of emotional dynamics in Musset's "uncompassed universe": entropy. Change moves in one direction only: from a higher order to a lower one; from paroxysm to apathy and boredom. All the good things in life—hopes, dreams, love—wear down and wear out.

> The first experience, Aimée, consists in suffering, it consists in discovering and feeling that absolute dreams are almost never realized; or if realized, they wither and die upon contact with the things of this world. *(Lettres d'amour,* p. 59)

> The things that bind in this world, even the strongest ones, become undone most of the time. *(OEuvres complètes,* p. 715)

That black torrent that leads everything to nothing. ("Sur la paresse")

Everything, of necessity, fades away. ("Sylvia")

Everything vanishes like smoke. *(Le Saule)*

Everything dies. *(Souvenir)*

Everything wears down. *(Mardoche)*

Musset's universe is in constant flux, too, because it is ruled not by providential Necessity,

> At least we do not have that silly thought
> Of believing that the world was made for us.
>
> ("Brandel")

but by Chance, "l'inconstant hasard." "Providence provides chance" is the epigraph, from Schiller, that he gives to *Portia*. In the "Réponse à M. Charles Nodier" the poet describes himself as a "child adopted and spoiled by Chance." In his early youth he did indeed pose as the spoiled and insouciant dandy who was quite willing to let Chance dictate his whims.

> Going out at random, singing some refrain.
>
> ("Après une lecture")

> Then I would go by chance to the theater, smoking a cigar.
>
> ("Une bonne fortune")

But in his maturity he came to curse "the instability of things here below and the pitiless caprices of chance" *(OEuvres complètes,* p. 730). It is with bitterness that Frank, Musset's most philosophical hero, calls himself the "son of chance." The word *hasard* (chance) occurs much too frequently in Musset's work to be dismissed as a facile filler.

> Chance willed it that this place
> Be on the slope of a prairie.
>
> ("Simone")

> . . . Those whose birth was crowned by chance.
>
> ("Au Roi")

> An almost unknown verse, an unfinished refrain,
> Fresh as chance.
>
> ("Une soirée perdue")

Chance can do anything.

(Namouna)

There, from evening to morning, rolls the great *perhaps,*
Chance, the black torch of these centuries of ennui.
The only one that still floats in today's sky.

("Une bonne fortune")

Now chance leads to the shadowy depths
The worlds awakened from their illusions.

(Rolla)

The dust belongs to God.—The rest belongs to chance.

(La Coupe et les lèvres)

Indeed Paul de Musset tells us in the *Biographie* that the vision of a universe ruled by capricious Chance had become a veritable obsession with his brother. Even in his most religious poem Musset complains: "Chance threw me into creation" *(L'Espoir en Dieu).*

This view of a universe governed by chance and change is reflected in Musset's style: the quickly changing tonalities, the contradictory moods, the sudden switching of themes, the mixing of registers, the shifting perspectives, the tendency to juxtapose fragments—in two words, romantic irony.

Musset's imagery is informed by this vision of a fragile, volatile, constantly moving and trembling world. People are compared to blades of grass (grass itself is seen as "running" in "A la Mi-Carême" and "Simone"), to thin reeds, to grains of sand, to ashes, dust, smoke, the changing tide. The verbs *agitate, shake, stagger, bend, shudder, shiver, quiver, turn, twist, stumble,* and *tremble* recur in his narrative and dramatic poetry to portray the actions and reactions of his heroes and heroines and, in his lyric poetry, of himself and his personae. His young protagonists tremble in the anticipation, the enjoyment, or the recollection of passion; or from the premonition of their partner's infidelity; or in the commission of a crime of passion; often it is from inebriation, the risks at the gambling table, or the throes or mere thought of premature death. Since the Revolution all of France "staggers," he says, from having drunk too quickly and too deeply of freedom and from the loss of its greatest man, the emperor. The cross of Christ "trembles" from the onslaught of Voltaire and his fellow *démolisseurs;* the Holy Ghost, mortally wounded dove, falls fitfully, twisting and turning, out of control, into the abyss of eternal oblivion.

> For whom were you working, stupid demolishers,
> When you dissected Christ on his altar?
> What did you want to cast on his celestial tomb
> When you threw to the wind the bleeding dove
> That falls, twisting and turning, into the eternal abyss?
>
> *(Rolla)*

The skeptical poet himself "trembles" more than once before the eternal silence of infinite space *(L'Espoir en Dieu)* and when driven by romantic escapism.

> I run from reality, trembling.
>
> ("Stances")

Another of Musset's favorite verbs is *voltiger* (to flit; to fly about) because, says Pierre Moreau ("L'ironie de Musset," p. 506), of the capricious movements it evokes. It occurs throughout his poetry but especially in the bird imagery. Musset's birds are not feathered songsters calmly and contentedly perched on a still bough but birds on the wing.[10] Whether the bird in a particular context is associated with a yearning for happiness or, as with the frequently recurring swallows, with the end of happiness, it is usually a bird in movement.

> Where does man go? Where his heart calls him.
> The swallow follows the zephyr,
> And the swallow is less light than
> The man who follows his desire.
>
> ("Chanson")

> Or, as the swallow flies off, sighing,
> Will my happiness flee away, having lasted but one evening?
>
> *(A quoi rêvent les jeunes filles?)*

> You who fly over there, light swallows,
> Tell me, tell me, why am I going to die?
>
> *(Rolla)*

> Time carries off on its wing
> Both the springtime and the swallow,
> And life and the lost days.
>
> ("A Juana")

The swallow represents swift movement, fragility, change of season and state, evanescence leading to death. These associations are traditional, but the choice of image and the frequency of the choice are significant.

Musset's use of liquid imagery and his images of light and of night derive from the same psychological impulses and philosophical biases. Michael Herschensohn, who has studied Musset's water imagery from a phenomenological viewpoint, has discovered that in all of it there appears to be motion of some kind. He concludes that "Musset's view of life can be conceived of as motion, as a wave whose curve can readily be plotted on a graph" ("Imagery in Musset," p. 66). Simon Jeune ("Aspects de la narration," p. 184) has noted that in Musset's images of light there is always something uncertain and trembling. James Hewitt ("Tropes of Self," chapter 1) has studied Musset's nocturnal imagery and found that the Mussetian night is not one of repose but a feverish, sleepless night, one of uncontrolled passion or impending fatality: "wild, mad nights," "sleepless nights," "nights of insomnia."

*

The fact that Musset's imaginative universe is a trembling one is confirmed by an examination of his fictional and theatrical work. In *La Confession d'un enfant du siècle,* in his autobiographical *nouvelles,* and in his more serious plays, his heroes and leading ladies tremble physically as well as figuratively with each new emotional experience and in every part of the body: hands, arms, feet, voice, heart, shoulders. (Musset was frequently seized with convulsive tremblings of the face and neck, tremblings that became more violent in his later years.) Often the whole body trembles. The verb *trembler* recurs with the same high frequency as in the poetry and, as in the poetry, is frequently reinforced with *frémir* (shiver), *frissonner* (shudder), *tressaillir* (shake), and half a dozen other synonyms. This stylistic tic can be attributed only in part to romantic hyperbole (or, more accurately, to a throwback to eighteenth-century *sensibilité);* more significantly it reflects the genuine hypersensitivity that Musset's protagonists share with their creator. For his fictional and dramatic heroes, disorder is the order of the day, inconstancy the only constant in their behavior. The reader or spectator can become almost dizzy from the rapidity of change in Musset's leading characters. At the end of *La Nuit vénitienne,* for example, Razetta moves from utter despair to insouciant gaiety in—literally—a matter of seconds. The dissipated Octave of *Les*

Caprices de Marianne boasts that he will not spill one drop from his cup of joy on the tightrope he walks through life, but admits he must move "faster than the wind" to keep his balance. By my count, the verb *trembler* and its synonyms are used seventy-three times in Musset's plays, eight times in *Le Chandelier* alone and fifteen times in *Lorenzaccio*.

Musset's fictional heroes are as unstable as his theatrical protagonists. They are incapable of assuming a career (e.g., Prévan, the narrator-hero of *Le Roman par lettres*, and Pippo of *Le Fils de Titien*); they often exhibit dual personalities (e.g., Valentin, hero of *Les deux maîtresses*, of whom the narrator says, "It was thus that he became double and that he lived in perpetual contradiction with himself" [*OEuvres complètes*, p. 654]); they possess inconstant tastes and desires (e.g., Prévan, Pippo, and the hero of *Le Poète déchu*, who says of himself, "My constantly moving and curious mind trembles incessantly like the compass" [*OEuvres complètes*, p. 648]).

Inconstancy and instability are often presented in Musset's fiction as the essence of his heroes and of mankind in general; they are even seen to be in the very nature of "things."

> As you are a man and thus inconstant yourself.
> > (*La Confession d'un enfant du siècle*)

> . . . Our inconstant mind
> Nourishes fantasy and feeds on change.
> > ("A la Mi-Carême")

> There is nothing stable here below.
> > ("A la Mi-Carême")

> The things that bind in this world, even the strongest ones, become undone most of the time. (*Frédéric et Bernerette*)

> The inconstancy of things. . . . (*Frédéric et Bernerette*)

> The instability of things here below. . . . (*Margot*)

Musset is the only major French dramatist of the nineteenth century to write under the modern assumption that psychological truth is elusive and unstable. Life is called a dream (*La Nuit vénitienne; Caprices*), a shadow (*Caprices*), a stormy sea, a slippery soil, and a precipice (*Lorenzaccio*), a pun (*Fantasio*), and a pantomime (*La Quenouille de Barberine*) in which the gestures have nothing to do with the thought or spoken word.

Human emotions are presented as incoherent and contradictory, ambiguous and ambivalent, constantly changing without rhyme or reason. To say that a man is good or bad, happy or unhappy, is folly.

> Gaiety is sometimes sad, and melancholy has a smile on its lips. *(André del Sarto)*
>
> Your gaiety is as sad as night. *(Lorenzaccio)*
>
> ELSBETH: You give me the impression of looking at the world through a changing prism.
> FANTASIO: Each person has his own eye glasses; but no one knows exactly of what color the lenses are made. Who can tell me exactly whether I am happy or unhappy, good or bad, sad or gay, stupid or witty?
>
> *(Fantasio)*

Human behavior is governed by neither inner nor external necessity: "Je parle beaucoup au hasard," puns Fantasio, "c'est mon plus cher confident" (I talk a good deal to [literally, by] chance; he's my dearest confidant). Capriciousness is found not only in the heroine of *Les Caprices de Marianne* but in the plot itself. In fact, at one point in the play Octave widens the application of capriciousness to metaphysical dimensions: "Celestial justice holds a pair of scales in its hands . . . but all the weights are hollow . . . and all human actions go up and down, according to these capricious weights." Pierre Gastinel has said that all of Musset's plays could be entitled *Les Caprices de. . . .*

*

At times, Musset's vision of a trembling world is truly cosmic in scope. This world, not just the terrestrial realm of human relationships but the entire physical universe, is in constant motion, and it is love, or rather the yearning for love (physical desire), that literally makes this mobile world go round.

In *La Confession* he speaks of love as a "celestial law" equal in power and incomprehensibility to the law of gravity. Then in a striking and surprising development of this thought he changes the status of the "celestial law" from the figurative to the literal. Love becomes his *explanation* of the law of gravity; it becomes the central law of celestial mechanics. Human love is now but a local manifestation of the law of universal attraction that keeps the entire cosmos in motion.

Why is the immense sky not immobile? Tell me if there ever was a moment when everything was created. By virtue of what force did they begin to move, these worlds that will never stop? . . . By eternal love. The weakest of the stars leaped toward the star it adores as its beloved; but another one loved her, and the world started out on its never-ending voyage.

This idea was so important to Musset that he expressed it both in *Le Roman par lettres* and in *Il ne faut jurer de rien*—and in exactly the same terms. The thought is also expressed in *Rolla*.

I love!—that's the word that all of nature
Shouts to the wind that carries it off, to the bird that
                                                    follows it.
Somber and last sigh that the earth will utter
When it falls into the eternal night!
Oh! you murmur it in your sacred spheres,
Morning stars, that sad and charming word!
The weakest of you, when God created you,
Tried to cross the ethereal plains
In search of the sun, her immortal lover.
She leaped to the bosom of the deep nights.
But another one loved her; and the worlds
Started on their voyage around the firmament.

Maurice Allem's comment on this passage is germane: "Alfred de Musset is fond, as one can easily see, of this symbolic interpretation of the Newtonian law of universal gravity. It is the expression of a phenomenon of attraction; attraction is the spur of desire and desire is the essence of love. Thus Eros is not only master of men and gods but is also the animator of all of nature" (in *Poésies complètes*, p. 723).

This organic philosophy is, of course, a romantic philosophy. For Musset, as for Fichte, motion is instinct; the stars and planets of his cosmos attract each other, not so much through gravitational pull as through desire; they organically strive toward each other just as Fichte's rivers "strive" toward the sea.[11]

But this universal attraction, this cosmic yearning, like Schopenhauer's Will, is never satisfied; never is anything or anyone at rest. Musset's vision is that of "a creation ever born anew and ever dying," always in the throes of a feverish cyclical movement.

The earth is dying; Herschel says that it is from cold. . . . That great law of attraction that suspends the world in its place wears it down and gnaws at it in a never ending desire; all the planets transport their miseries while groaning on their axle; they call to each other from one end of the sky to the other and, desperately hoping for rest, wonder which one of them will be the first to stop. God holds them back; assiduously and eternally, they accomplish their empty and vain labor; they turn, they suffer, they burn, they are extinguished and are kindled, they descend and rise back up, they follow each other and avoid each other; they intertwine like links; they bring to their surface thousands of constantly renewed creatures; these creatures agitate each other, cross each other too, huddle against each other for an hour, then fall, and other ones arise. *(La Confession)*

The predominance here of verbs of motion is inevitable. Musset's world is that of Heraclitus and Democritus, a world of whirl and swirl. It is one in which one never steps into the same river twice; a world in which polite society is but a collection of "disconnected whirlwinds" (the image is used in both *La Confession* and *Les Caprices)* and deviations from it such as debauchery become tightrope walking and vertigo; a cosmos whose very planets are at the mercy not of mechanical laws but of emotional laws, unstable and unpredictable, of attraction and repulsion. In this vertiginous world man gropes desperately for permanent love and happiness, but in the end he grasps for straws.

4

Pathedy: The Hero as Fool
in Stendhal's *Le Rouge et le Noir*

> If Julien had had a bit of the skill that
> he so gratuitously supposed he had. . . .
>
> The worst of it was that he saw and
> exaggerated his absurdity.
>
> I admit that the weakness that Julien
> is displaying in this monologue gives me
> a poor opinion of him.
> (*Le Rouge et le Noir*)

STENDHAL was an admirer of Schlegel's theoretical work, of Byron's *Don Juan*, and of Diderot's *Jacques le fataliste*. It should come as no surprise, then, that the hero of *Le Rouge et le Noir* is more a recipient than a dispenser of irony. However, René Bourgeois (*L'Ironie romantique*, p. 107) has noted an astonishing fact: "If Stendhal's irony has already been the object of detailed and exhaustive studies, it does not seem that anyone has ever been able to talk about romantic irony in this connection." Grahame C. Jones, for instance, examines Stendhal's ironic attitude toward Julien but concludes that it is "benign"; Julien is simply the charmingly awkward *ingénu* whose ingenuous ineptitude we are to admire: "In Stendhal's mind irony is accompanied by admiration; the hero whom he ridicules enjoys his esteem; the faults that he points out in his hero are qualities he respects" (*L'Ironie*, p. 80). And Erica Abeel ("Multiple Authors," p. 22), distinguishing between the novel's implied author and the masked author, the latter being an ironic persona whose views contradict those of the implied author, makes the somewhat rash claim that whenever the masked author says things like "Julien is a

64

presumptuous fool" the reader immediately and always reconstructs the view of the implied author, to wit: that Julien is a superior man.[1] Even René Bourgeois, in his chapter on Stendhal, discusses not the crucial issue of the author's attitude toward his protagonist but the latter's attitude toward the world. And in the three pages he devotes to *Le Rouge* he simply shows us that Julien is not an ironist in any sense of the word, correctly concluding *(L'Ironie romantique,* p. 117) that "it is the role of the ironist to let his thought be divined, to let his real thought be sufficiently detected to allow the irony to have a meaning." Julien, of course, cannot afford what H.-E. Hass has called the transparency of ironic dissimulation. We are concerned here not with the hero's ironic attitude, or lack of it, but with the author's attitude—or, better, since one must be constantly on one's guard against the infamous intentional fallacy, the author's *presentation* of his hero.

Victor Brombert has written the best work to date *(Stendhal et la voie oblique)* on Stendhal's irony but fails, like Jones and Bourgeois, to do justice to the author's use of romantic irony. In fact he does not discuss it at all. He makes only one fleeting reference to it at the end of his book, quoting Vladimir Jankélévitch's remark that romantic irony can be as ingenuous as enthusiasm. Since Brombert's theme is the "oblique way" of Stendhalian style, he must discuss mainly the affirmative value of the sarcasm directed at Julien. The "supposed criticism," we are told, is really "dissimulated admiration." When the author is condescending, patronizing, shocked, surprised, or disgusted at his hero, we are constantly advised that this is an oblique invitation to admire the young man's charming naiveté. True. But it is at the very same time an invitation to laugh at the hero's expense. It must be kept in mind that Stendhalian irony, like all romantic irony, is a double one; it moves in two opposite directions at once. The sarcasm does mask genuine enthusiasm, but it is also, and *simultaneously,* genuine sarcasm. Brombert alludes several times to the "double meaning" of nearly every stylistic device in Stendhal's repertoire but concentrates, as he must for the sake of his argument, on the positive connotations. He insists that the author's "fear of the reader" forces him to hide his enthusiasm under the mask of irony. He cannot quite bring himself even to admit that "often" or "occasionally" the sarcasm is really sarcastic: "But who can say that at the very moment he acts as judge, he has ceased to feel? Who can affirm that at the very moment he claims to break his ties with his characters, he does not feel toward them an even more tenacious and subtle sympathy than the one that tears from him exclamations of enthusiasm?" (p. 164). Epithets of blame such as "foolish," "ridiculous," "stupid act," "weakness," when applied to Julien, are interpreted as "terms of praise." This has been the traditional approach to Stendhalian irony. The approach is not wrong so much as it is incomplete.

In this chapter I am going to accentuate the negative; that is, I am going to look at the sarcasm in terms of romantic irony, not merely rhetorical irony, in hopes of restoring the balance and of doing fuller justice to the uniqueness and richness of Stendhal's ironic style. In the first place, although it is true that the author's principal attitude toward the hero of *Le Rouge* is one of enthusiasm and admiration, Julien has many *real* faults, and the author makes no attempt to conceal them. In the second place, both Jones and Brombert have very well explained the psychological bases of Stendhal's unstable point of view with regard to his hero.[2] And in the third place, it is one of Stendhal's aesthetic biases, too well established to be documented here, to abhor novels, so dear to chambermaids and the marquises who resemble them, presenting flawless heroes. Until the final section of the novel, Julien, in his role as lover and thinker, is a comic figure, ridiculed, chastised, berated, belittled— and loved.

The only real discussion of romantic irony in *Le Rouge* up to now is found in several pages of Morton Gurewitch's doctoral dissertation, "European Romantic Irony." He studies it from the point of view of Julien's ambivalent nature: the mingling of romantic and antiromantic traits, the Wertherian Don Juanism, and especially the internal warfare between innocence and experience.[3] It is a good discussion but incomplete. Gurewitch focuses on the novel's hero but neglects the novel's tone. The author's ironic attitude toward his material is presented almost parenthetically. We are told that Stendhal does cast "several" astringent glances at Julien and that he does "occasionally" reprove him. These remarks overattenuate the sarcastic texture of the novel. The war between innocence and experience is waged not so much between Julien and himself as between the young and inexperienced Julien and his mature and experienced creator, Henri Beyle alias Stendhal. Gurewitch has painted much of the picture; the following discussion should fill in the rest.

Stendhal is pitiless in his description of Julien's youthful ignorance and awkwardness at the beginning of the novel. Uneducated, inexperienced, provincial, Julien walks and talks like the country bumpkin that he is, moving from one ridiculous extreme of behavior to the opposite. His initial interviews with Mme de Rênal are filled with awkward silences interrupted only by bombastic and often unintelligible speeches.

> If, as ill luck would have it, he forced himself to speak, he would say the most ridiculous things. . . . Mme de Rênal noticed that, when alone with her, he never managed to say something well, except when, distracted by some unforeseen event, he wasn't thinking about turning a compliment well.[4]

His extreme timidity, as is often the case, leads to an equally extreme temerity. Reviled by so many nineteenth-century critics as a vile, scheming roué, Julien is in reality a comically awkward figure in his role as lover. Here, for example, is the first kiss: "Nothing could have been less well brought off, nothing less pleasant both for him and for her" (p. 294). Here is his strategy as seducer: "The day was boring for Julien, he spent it entirely in awkwardly executing his plan of seduction" (p. 294). Here he is as Don Juan: "Julien insisted obstinately in playing the role of a Don Juan, he who had never in his life had a mistress, he was deadly foolish the whole day" (p. 295). If the author speaks of Julien's cleverness, it is either an antiphrasis ("He understood that, by his *clever* conduct of the day before, he had ruined the fine impression he had made the day before that" [p. 296; emphasis added]; "This line of reasoning was very *wise*" [p. 611; emphasis added]) or a sarcastic oxymoron ("his such unskillful skill" [p. 298]). Desperately trying to act suave, he enters Mme de Rênal's bedchamber with trembling knees and voice, making a "frightful racket." During his first entry into Mathilde's bedroom, he fares no better. Here he is the victim not of a sarcastic authorial intrusion but of objective irony.[5] Armed to the teeth with daggers, pistols, in fact "every manner of weapon," he looks under the bed and in all corners of the room for imagined conspirators. When Mathilde tenderly touches his arm, he thinks it is an assassin and pulls out his dagger! At a loss for words, he calls upon his memory and recites several beautiful sentences from *La Nouvelle Héloïse*.

As thinker, as well as lover, Julien is a constant victim of romantic irony. It is his imagination especially that gets him into trouble. His greatest failing is a frequent tendency to exaggerate a danger, a triumph, or a defeat. Here, for example, is what the author says of the episode in which Julien fears that M. de Rênal will discover the portrait of Napoleon hidden in his bed: "He was pale, overwhelmed, he exaggerated the extent of the danger he had just run" (p. 272). Here is Julien bemoaning the loss of Mathilde's love: "Now he could exaggerate as much as he pleased the total atrocity of his fate" (p. 548). His awkwardness is compounded by his exaggerated awareness of it: "He was awkward and exaggerated his awkwardness" (p. 293), and "The worst of it was that he saw and exaggerated his absurdity" (p. 257). Whenever he manages to be less than awkward, he exaggerates his cleverness: "If Julien had had a bit of the skill that he so gratuitously supposed he had, he might have been able. . ." (p. 296). If he manages not to fall off a horse, he immediately sees himself as one of Napoleon's heroic officers charging a battery of cannon. In the seminary he thinks he has molded himself by now into a clever hypocrite; the narrator thinks otherwise:

> All the initial steps taken by our hero, who thought himself so prudent were, like the choice of a confessor, total blunders. Misled by the presumptuousness of a man of imagination, he mistook his intentions for deeds, and thought himself a consummate hypocrite. His folly reached the point of reproaching himself for his success in this art of weakness. (P. 383)

This reproach is repeated a few pages later: "Ever since he had been in seminary, Julien's conduct had been only one long succession of false starts" (p. 386). Or, when upbraided by Mathilde, he falls into the other extreme and exaggerates his shortcomings:

> Far from thinking in the least about defending himself, he came to despise himself. Hearing himself scorned so cruelly, and by remarks cleverly calculated to destroy any good opinion he might have of himself, he thought that Mathilde was right and that she could have said much more against him. (P. 566)

In such periods of depression, Julien's judgment is so warped that he overestimates all the mediocre and spiteful people he has met: "Thinking back on the adversaries, the enemies he had encountered in his life, he always found that he, Julien, had been in the wrong" (p. 589). These moments of exaggerated self-abasement and "excess of ridiculous modesty" (p. 589) do not preclude delusions of grandeur at other moments.

Learning that the Marquis de la Mole has just named him Monsieur Julien Sorel de la Vernaye, illegitimate son of a nobleman,

> Julien could no longer master his delight, he kissed the priest, he saw himself acknowledged as a son. . . . Could it indeed be possible, he said to himself, that I may be the illegitimate son of a great lord exiled in these mountains by the fearsome Napoleon? With each moment this idea seemed less improbable. (P. 641)

When Mme de Rênal tells him, "Be careful, I order you," the oversensitive Julien wonders whether he should take offense at the verb used: "She could tell me 'I order you' if it concerned something relative to the education of the children, but in responding to my love, she assumes equality between us. One cannot love without 'equality' . . . . and his mind was completely occupied in composing commonplaces on equality" (p. 295). The more perceptive Fabrice del Dongo, on the other hand, does *not* misinterpret these very same words, "I order you," which Clélia addresses to him in *La Chartreuse de Parme;* he knows he has every reason to be delighted. Julien has a similar defensive reaction later with Mathilde. When this beautiful and brilliant girl, perhaps the most exciting young woman in all Paris, asks him not to leave town, our touchy hero is piqued by her choice of vocabulary: "But would one ever have guessed what his second thought was. . . . He was offended by the imperious tone with which she had said: *You must*" (p. 523). His error is all the more blatant in that Mathilde says this "You must" in a trembling, almost inaudible voice. And even a third time Julien is piqued by a tender imperative: "Adieu, flee" (p. 632).

In many other passages Stendhal mentions Julien's "stupid" or "foolish" ideas; he also tells us of his hero's frequent inattention to details (p. 386), confides that he would never make a good administrator (p. 399), suggests that his aesthetic sense is neither innate nor precocious (p. 493) and that often his ideas, although original, are inappropriate to the occasion or the context (p. 451). As Albert Cook ("Ironic Interplay," p. 42) has noted, Julien is frequently "a brilliantly correct calculator in a ridiculously inappropriate situation." Just as frequently his tortuous calculations miss the mark entirely.

Julien's biggest blunder is his blindness with regard to Mme de Rênal. It is here that all his weaknesses, both as lover and as thinker, converge. His touchiness and suspiciousness lead him to underestimate a

woman worthy of his love if ever there was one. He can see in her only a
rich woman of the aristocracy, that is, someone who has been brought up
in the "enemy camp." He conceives of his relationship with her in terms
of military strategy, of victories and defeats. He draws up battle plans.
(When the "enemy" is Mathilde, he goes on a military "reconnaissance.")
Mme de Rênal's very beauty is interpreted as an ambush, her beautiful
clothes as the "vanguard" of Paris, as "feminine artillery," and so on.
This is not just an uncomfortable feeling of being in an inferior social
class; this is an inferiority *complex*. And Julien's large arsenal of defense
mechanisms is more comic than charming. It is not until the very end of
the novel and his life that Julien fully appreciates Mme de Rênal and
understands the depth of his love for her. It is not until then that he
grows up.

His seduction of Mme de Rênal is not a case of base conniving as so
many critics have complained, but the desperate and usually ludicrous
attempts of an awkward adolescent trying to prove himself to himself as
well as to this woman whom he imagines saying with a sneer: "The little
fellow didn't dare." His main motivation is to reduce the distance between himself and her. Far from being a vile seducer, Julien, in sexual
matters, is not even precocious: "Certain things that Napoleon says
about women, several discussions about the merit of those novels that
were fashionable during his reign, gave him then, *for the first time*, some
ideas that any other young man of his age would have had for a long
time" (p. 265; emphasis added). It is true that in *Le Rouge* we have all the
stages of an ordinary seduction: (1) he must hold her hand; (2) he must
tell her he loves her; (3) he must kiss her; and (4) he must enter her room
this very night. But, and this is of capital importance, each stage is
independent of the others; it is not part of an overall plan. Stage one is
motivated, as the author explicitly tells us, not by love but by "duty" (i.e.,
what Julien owes to himself): "Julien thought it was his duty to bring it
about that that hand not be withdrawn when he touched it" (p. 265). In
stage two it is not his sensuality but his pride talking:

> He had done *his duty, and a heroic duty*. Filled with happiness by this
> feeling, he locked himself in his room, and indulged, with a totally new
> pleasure, in the reading of his hero's exploits. When the bell for lunch
> was heard, he had forgotten, while reading the bulletins of the Grand
> Army, all the advantages he had won the day before. He told himself,
> lightheartedly, while going down to the drawing room: I must tell that
> woman that I love her. (P. 269; author's ironic emphasis)

In stage three it is not a question of love or seduction but of making up for a humiliation. He has just had one of his many moments of awkward silence, and as usual he overreacts:

> Julien remained deeply humiliated by the misfortune of not knowing how to reply to Mme de Rênal. A man like me owes it to himself to redeem this failure, and seizing the moment when people were passing from one room to the other, he thought it his duty to give Mme de Rênal a kiss. (P. 294)

Stage four sounds like the height of audacity, but when Julien says to Mme de Rênal, "Madame, tonight, at two o'clock, I shall go to your bedroom," the author is quick to add: "Julien trembled for fear that his request might be granted" (p. 296). And a few lines later: "Nothing, however, would have embarrassed him more than success" (p. 297). And finally as he enters Mme de Rênal's bedroom, neither he nor the author has any idea as to what he will do: "But, good Lord! what would he do there? He had no plan whatsoever" (p. 297).

This entire section of the novel, moreover, is de-eroticized by the frequent use of the indefinite pronoun *on* and by what Leo Spitzer (in connection with Racinian style) calls the "demonstrative of distance"; for example, when Julien says, "The other day, as she was leaving, *that* woman reminded me of the infinite *distance* that separates us. She treated me like the son of a working man" (p. 288; emphasis added). The demonstrative conveys not only a sense of social distance but also Julien's timidity and nervousness as he attempts to reduce that distance. The hand of Mme de Rênal is not that of a woman to be cherished; it is an inanimate object, an impersonal goal:

> *Cette* main se retira bien vite; mais Julien pensa qu'il était de son devoir d'obtenir que l'on ne retirât pas *cette* main quand il la touchait. L'idée d'un devoir à accomplir, et d'un ridicule ou plutôt d'un sentiment d'infériorité à encourir si l'on n'y parvenait pas, éloigna sur-le-champ tout plaisir de son coeur. (P. 265; emphasis added)

> *That* hand withdrew very quickly; but Julien thought it his duty to bring it about that *one* did not withdraw *that* hand when he touched it. The idea of a duty to be accomplished, and of ridicule or rather a feeling of inferiority to be incurred if *one* did not succeed, immediately removed all pleasure from his heart.

The second *on* refers, of course, not to Mme de Rênal but to Julien. His frightened attention is focused neither on her nor on himself but on *that* object, "that hand." The convergence of impersonal pronouns, demonstrative adjectives, and abstract nouns removes all sensuality from this "seduction scene."

Stendhal's use of the demonstrative is increased tenfold in this section of the novel, and the context in which it is used indicates, in nearly every case, that it is meant to convey a sense of distance rather than closeness, *cette femme-là* rather than *cette femme-ci*.

> *Cette* femme-*là* m'aime, se dit-il. (P. 289; emphasis added)

> Aux yeux de *cette* femme, moi, se disait-il, je ne suis pas bien né. (P. 289; emphasis added)

> *Cette* femme ne peut plus me mépriser. (P. 291; emphasis added)[6]

> *That* woman is in love with me, he told himself.

> In the eyes of *that* woman, he would tell himself, I am not well born.

> *That* woman can no longer scorn me.

In fact the distance is such that at one point Mme de Rênal is merely one of two possibilities: "I must have one of *those* women. He would have much preferred paying court to Mme Derville. . . . she had always seen him as a tutor honored for his knowledge . . . and not as a worker" (p. 291; emphasis added).

The attenuated demonstrative—the definite article—is also used frequently in this section of the novel and conveys the same sense of distance and impersonality.

> Quoique bien ému lui-même, il fut frappé de la froideur glaciale de *la* main qu'il prenait; il la serrait avec une force convulsive; *on* fit un dernier effort pour la lui ôter, mais enfin *cette* main lui resta. (P. 267; emphasis added)

> Julien serra fortement *la* main qu'*on* lui abandonnait. (P. 268; emphasis added)

> Julien couvrait *la* main qu'*on* lui avait laissée de baisers passionnés. (P. 278; emphasis added)

> Although very much moved himself, he was struck by the glacial coldness of *the* hand that he was taking; he squeezed it with convulsive

strength; *one* made a last effort to remove it from him, but finally *that* hand remained in his.

Julien squeezed very hard *the* hand that *one* was abandoning to him.

Julien covered *the* hand that *one* had left in his with passionate kisses.

The same effect of distance and impersonality is achieved through the use of the indefinite article:

Il voulut prendre *une* main blanche que depuis longtemps il voyait près de lui, appuyé sur le dos d'une chaise. *On* hesita un peu, mais *on* finit par la lui retirer d'une façon qui marquait de l'humeur. (P. 278; emphasis added)

He tried to take *a* white hand that he had seen for a long while near him, resting on the back of a chair. *One* hesitated a bit, but *one* finally withdrew it in such a way as to indicate anger.

Julien, too, is occasionally depersonalized by the *on* and by the personification of abstractions.

I owe it to myself all the more, continued Julien's little *vanity*, to succeed with that woman. (P. 291; emphasis added)

His *pride* did not want to leave anything to chance. (P. 293; emphasis added)

His *pessimism* made him believe that he had earned the scorn of Mme de Derville. (P. 297; emphasis added)

There now, said Julien's *conscience*. (P. 348; emphasis added)

The funniest thing about the entire seduction episode is the almost total absence of pleasure. What little there is, is the product of inflated adolescent pride.

Both as lover and as thinker Julien compares unfavorably with Fabrice del Dongo, Lucien Leuwen, and even the Octave of *Armance*. Fabrice, we are constantly told, is a truly "charming" creature; even his rival, Count Mosca, admits that he is "irresistible." Lucien is everything Julien wishes to be, but isn't. He is a dashing young second lieutenant, distinguished in appearance and manners, wealthy, educated, admired by the ladies. Unlike Julien, he has no neuroses and no ulterior motives.

He is sincere, even frank, feeling not the slightest need to hide behind the mask of hypocrisy his scorn for the many mediocre and despicable people he encounters. Although Octave, like Julien, is an imperfect lover, it is not through any fault of his but "a decree of nature" (impotence). Except for his physical handicap, Octave outshines poor Julien in most respects. He is articulate whenever he wants to be, dances with magnificent grace, is endowed with "perfect taste," physical beauty, and courage. The few times Stendhal directs any criticism at him it is felt as purely cautionary (as when the author informs his aristocratic reader that his hero's jaundiced view of Parisian high society is exaggerated), or it is attenuated by an adverb:

> He was counting *a bit* too much on his clearsightedness. (P. 62; emphasis added)

> We will admit that he went *a bit* beyond the permissible bounds of impertinence. (P. 130; emphasis added)

Or with a chiasmus the author gives back with one hand what he took away with the other: "Octave told himself out loud some things that were foolish and in bad taste, the bad taste and folly of which he observed with curiosity" (p. 115). The words "observed with curiosity" indicate a lucidity that belies the folly.

When the point of view becomes ironic and the author wants to put some distance between the protagonist and the reader, Julien becomes "our hero" (used twenty-one times in *Le Rouge* as compared to just once in *Armance),* "our provincial hero," "our plebeian in revolt," or "our young philosopher," the last when Julien's thinking is particularly weak.[7] Calling the hero "our hero" is like calling a spade a spade; it can be dangerous. The device is used frequently in *Lucien Leuwen* and *La Chartreuse* but merely as a traditional fictional license, a vestige of the oral style, and does no violence to the objective representation or to the hero's stature. But in *Le Rouge* it converges with an already sarcastic or ironic context to dispel the hero's charisma and deflate his machismo.

The reader's identification with Julien is disrupted several hundred times by the subjective irony of narrative parabasis, those famous intrusions of the author who, for instance, will remind us that this is just a novel (here the subjective irony combines with naive irony and scores a triple hit: the hero, the author, and the work) or that Julien is just an adolescent, or who will allow the present and conditional tenses to intrude upon the regular narrative tenses. Only minor intrusions are caused by the descriptive present, the generalizing present, and the digressive present; the last, like the others, is usually confined to just a few lines and does not denigrate the hero or his story. Stendhal also uses the dramatic or historic present, but that does not constitute an ironic intrusion since it is an intensification of the narrative, not an interruption. But when Stendhal first presents the theme of Julien's hypocrisy and adds, "Does this word surprise you?" (p. 238), a slightly jarring note is introduced. Not only does the present tense interrupt the narrative, but the reader is made self-conscious, thereby compounding the technical problem raised (the reader's anticipated surprise or shock). More damaging still is the present of the narrative act. Not only does Stendhal spare the reader certain details, he *informs* the reader that he is doing so.

> The reader will allow us, I trust, to give very few clear and precise facts about this period in Julien's life. It is not that we lack any of these, quite the contrary. (P. 392)

> But it is wise to suppress the description of such a degree of felicity. (P. 559)

> The monologue we have just abridged. . . . (P. 605)

The excisions and abridgments the author informs us he is obliged to make do not increase the work's stature in our eyes; they deliberately lessen it. As Georges Blin comments:

> He cannot come on stage to specify that he is effecting some excisions unless he is trying very clumsily to persuade us that the events of his narrative are extending beyond its boundaries and that he is denouncing the tale's slipshod plot. . . . Moreover, it is perilous to emphasize the fact that one is effecting omissions because that prevents the reader from disregarding the author and because by this very fact, as J.-P. Sartre has noted, the reader is being cast outside the hero's time and into that of the narrator alone. *(Les problèmes du roman,* p. 234)

Whenever Julien waxes lyrical, Stendhal counters with subjective irony and switches to the "ethical present" or what Jean Starobinski calls the "present as qualitatively privileged tense": "I admit that the weakness that Julien is displaying in this monologue gives me a poor opinion of him" (p. 438). As we have seen, Musset, another master of romantic irony, uses this ethical present to the same effect. Similarly, in *La Char-*

treuse Stendhal uses the present tense to offer his ironic plea for artistic immunity: "Why should the historian who faithfully follows the slightest details of the story he has been told be guilty? Is it his fault if the characters, seduced by passions that unfortunately he does not share himself, fall into profoundly immoral actions?"[8]

The author's attention constantly switches from his hero to his reader. Sometimes it is done indirectly.

> *One can see* that Julien had no experience of life. (P. 551; emphasis added)

> *One must* forgive him for one weakness: he burst into tears. (P. 403; emphasis added)

The reader is treated to mock-lyrical apostrophe ("oh my reader" [p. 445]), mock-heroic hyperbole ("We are afraid of tiring the reader by relating the thousand misfortunes of our hero" [p. 395]), and confidential asides. If the author gives the hero a sincere compliment, he tones it down with the present tense and the modesty of a narrator enjoying only limited omniscience: "In my opinion it is one of the finest traits of his character; a person capable of such an effort on himself can go far" (p. 463). Occasionally the narrative is halted by a hypothetical question that the author poses the reader: "Upon receiving this terrible blow, mad with love and unhappiness, Julien tried to justify himself. Nothing is more absurd. Does one justify oneself for failing to please?" (p. 565). Although the author does not launch into a digression here, the reader is invited to. The latter might very well lay down the book at this point and sketch a maxim or an essay on the subject.

Victor Brombert has given us an excellent discussion of the use of the conditional mood as part of Stendhal's strategy of *interventionnisme*, but this device, too, short-circuits the reader's identification with the hero. Not only does the conditional remove us from the hero's current activities (creating what B. F. Bart calls parastories grafted upon the main one), it measures the distance between these inept activities and those of the ideal strategist: Henri Beyle.

> Had it not been for this silly idea of making a plan, Julien's intelligence would have served him well, the element of surprise would only have added to the keenness of his insights. (P. 293)

In a word, nothing would have been lacking for our hero's happiness, not even an ardent sensitivity in the woman he had just abducted, if he had known how to enjoy it. (P. 299)

If, instead of hiding in a remote place, he had wandered about the garden or in the mansion, so as to keep within range of opportunities, he might have changed his frightful unhappiness to happiness in a single moment. (P. 549)

If he had been a little less clumsy and if he had told this woman with a little composure. . . . (P. 551)

And there are many sentences that could easily have been put into the conditional:

Julien did not possess enough genius to tell himself: I must dare. (P. 558)

He did not have the genius to see that. . . . (P. 565)

These disparaging conditionals and quasi-conditionals weaken the book's positive one: What would Julien have been like if circumstances had allowed him to serve with Napoleon, to follow the Red rather than the Black? They suggest that Julien is not a tactician, military or otherwise, that he would have been an officer of daring and energy but not of genius. The reader can well imagine our intelligent, sensitive, but thoroughly unprecocious hero stumbling up the military ladder of success through trial and many errors.

In addition to the objective and subjective irony aimed at Julien, *Le Rouge* abounds in naive irony directed at itself and its author. One instance is the famous digression—"This page is going to harm the unfortunate author in more than one way"—in which Stendhal, among many other interesting things, apologizes for the lack of verisimilitude in Mathilde's character. He also apologizes for an alleged structural flaw (p. 476) and, as he often does, for letting politics intrude into the narrative like a pistol shot at a concert (p. 570). The political details, our author ingenuously admits, were added at the insistence of his publisher to give more seriousness to a novel the latter considers "frivolous." Stendhal even apologizes for the dullness of an entire section of the novel: "All the boredom of this uninteresting life that Julien was leading is doubtless shared by the reader. These are the barren places of our voyage" (p.

610). Naive irony, although directed at the work rather than at the hero, affects him as well since it plays down the seriousness of his story and even removes us from it.

*

One of the uses of romantic irony that, to my knowledge, has never been studied is foreshadowing.[9] *Le Rouge et le Noir* offers a good example. A hero who is the object of an ambivalent point of view will probably evolve—the reader is forced to assume—in one of two possible directions: either his strengths or his weaknesses will win out in the end. The third possibility—that the hero will *not* evolve out of this ambivalence or ambiguousness—is *not* a natural expectation of the reader, who assumes that narrative instability, whether of central plot or crucial characterization, will lead to a rather definite "conclusion." This is a convention of fiction ignored only at the risk of leaving the reader dissatisfied with a dénouement that does not settle the hero's fate. Critics have carefully cataloged the ironic intrusions in the novel; they have not indicated where they *stop*. Throughout the entire ten final chapters there is only one intrusion ("It's a revolutionary speaking here" [p. 680]), which is not really directed at Julien, nor is there any irony of any kind aimed at him, not even one of those comments about "our hero" (the last one occurs in Book 2, chapter 33). The romantic irony that floods the novel before Book 2, chapter 35, and *stops* there alerts the reader that our immature hero is going to mature. This also happens, on a lesser scale, in *La Chartreuse* and *Lucien Leuwen,* in which the relatively small amount of irony directed at the hero is found only in the first part of the novel and simply depicts, in Fabrice's case, an eager adolescent yearning to have been in a real battle and, in Lucien's case, a charmingly normal young man flustered by his first love. The mild irony directed at the latter is further tempered by the future tense, which predicts the hero's progress: "In the opinion of the hero, who is mad and who will correct his faults. . ." (p. 768). A similar future is found in *Armance:* "There reigns moreover in his depiction of that element of society that he has never seen a tone of ridiculous animosity of which he will break himself" (p. 101). Likewise, in *Le Rouge* Stendhal frequently uses the verbs *annoncer* and *augurer* to indicate that Julien's strengths will eventually overcome his weaknesses.

> He saw and exaggerated his absurdity; but what one did not see was the expression of his eyes; they were so beautiful and *announced* such an ardent soul that, like good actors, they sometimes gave a charming meaning to what did not have any. (P. 257; emphasis added)

> I *augur* well of your mind. (L'abbé Chélan speaking to Julien, p. 259; emphasis added)

> One must not *augur* too ill of Julien. (P. 260; emphasis added)

> In my opinion it is one of the finest traits of his character; a person capable of such effort on himself *can go far.* (P. 463; emphasis added)

As Julien matures, the irony decreases. The movement of this novel, a bildungsroman, is not from youthful idealism to the disenchantment of experience, but the reverse: Julien in the end begins to rid himself of distrust and total self-preoccupation and learns to love.

> He was still quite young; but in my opinion this was a fine plant. Instead of moving from the tender to the sly, like most men, age would have given him a goodness easily aroused, he would have cured himself of insane distrust. (P. 560)

Note that now the conditionals are used in Julien's *favor.*

Stendhal also uses romantic irony as an exercise in sadomasochism. To compensate for his own disappointments, the author can revel in the discomfiture of his scapegoat hero. The following passage, for instance, clearly suggests, if not downright sadism, at least an unsubtle form of schadenfreude: "Oh how they were punished, at that moment, the outbursts of pride which had led Julien to consider himself superior to people like Caylus and Croisenois! With what deep-felt unhappiness he exaggerated their slightest advantages! With what burning good faith did he scorn himself!" (p. 550). But since Julien is an autobiographical figure, the author is identifying with his victim.

Stendhal's romantic irony is also a defensive ploy against those famous readers who inspire such fear in him; for example, the hard-to-please ladies of Paris: "The ladies of Paris . . . are devilishly severe when it comes to *extraordinary* events. As soon as an event seems to be brought on at just the right moment to make the hero shine, they throw the book away and the author is ridiculous in their eyes."[10] Here the unstable point of view can be looked upon as a compromise between the portrait Stendhal would have preferred to paint and the one his prejudiced public would have commissioned him to do. Romantic irony confers authorial immunity not only from the immoral but also from the sublime.

It can also be used as an antidote to counteract certain noxious features of romantic and preromantic style, such as hyperbole, sentimentality, melodrama, excessive lyricism, and bathos. Stendhal's hostility toward what he called "le style d'*Atala*" is well known. The best remedy against it, he thought, is a strong dose of the *code civil*. Among the epigraphs to each chapter in *Le Rouge* are several from Byron's *Don Juan*, a poem whose tonality recalls that of Stendhal's novel. Probably more than any other poem (since Stendhal professed not to like poetry), it gave the author some training in this particular use of romantic irony. In many passages of *Don Juan*, for example, Byron mocks his hero's sentimental hyperboles and, in other passages, his own. In *Namouna*, as we have seen, Musset pokes fun at *his* Don Juan figure, Hassan, as well as at his own rambling poem. Romantic irony can protect an author from his own enthusiasms, which can be extreme in a romantic age.

One of the romantic things about romantic irony is its kinship with the baroque, the irregular shape and paradoxical texture it gives to the work as a whole. It is born of the same impulse that urged Hugo to seek a mixture of the comic and the tragic in the romantic drama. There are many analogies between romantic irony and baroque poetry, for example, the love of paradox, contrast, and surprise. Julien, as Leo Spitzer has said of another protagonist, is a walking oxymoron. He surprises us at every turn. We are never sure what this irrepressible and unpredictable youngster will do or feel next—often it is the exact opposite of what he is doing and feeling now. *Le Rouge* reflects the baroque emphasis on movement, energy, and realism, the wild, the unexpected, the picaresque, the avoidance of repose, tranquillity, and complacency. There is even a significant analogy between the unusual rhythmic and syntactical effects of baroque poetry and Stendhal's prose. The Stendhalian sentence is founded on classical syntax, but as Martin Turnell points out, the movement of his paragraphs is quite different: "Stendhal's prose is continually twisting and turning, changing direction, and producing startling juxtapositions between the 'perpendicular' sentences."[11] The adjective alludes to an adverb Gide once used to describe the Stendhalian paragraph: "With Stendhal, one sentence never calls the next into being, nor is it born of the one that went before. Each of them stands perpendicularly to the fact or idea."[12] Another adverb, very much in fashion these days, would also be appropriate: dialectically. Romantic irony, like the baroque, is concerned with complex themes such as the dialectics of carnal and cerebral love, of artifice and sincerity.

The *mélange des genres,* of which romantic irony can be considered a species (or, more accurately, the genus), was an attempt, on the technical side, to avoid classical "monotony" and, on the psychological side, to present modern man as a complex creature of dualism, ambivalence, and paradox. Julien's particular ambivalence is not so much a question of dichotomies between reason and emotion or innocence and experience; it is rather a constant tension between what Henri Beyle called *l'espagnolisme* and *la logique,* that is, between the courage and energy required to create one's own identity, to carve out one's career, and the instinctive (and intelligent) prudence that knows and observes the ground rules of the stadium in which society and history, whether we like it or not, force us to play. Julien's *logique* is frequently illogical, and his prudence often borders on paranoia—which does not at all spoil the reader's pleasure. On the comic level he can enjoy a sense of superiority over the likable hero, a compensation for and a catharsis of his own weaknesses; on the tragic level he can look forward to the hero's moral progress. What is remarkable about romantic irony is that it allows the reader to feel all this *simultaneously.*

Despite his many comic moments and antics, Julien is not properly a comic hero. And despite his many sublime or near-sublime moments, his tragic dignity, and his tragic flaw, he is not properly a tragic hero either. Romantic irony creates a hybrid genre delicately poised between comedy, in which the protagonist is a victim-fool, and tragedy, in which the protagonist is a hero-victim; it produces *pathedy,* in which the protagonist is a hero-fool.[13] As John Nist has said, both tragedy and comedy squint; they look at man with one eye closed. Pathedy looks at man with both eyes wide open. It sees his sublimity and his grotesqueness but does not nail him to either pole. Nist says of Chaucer—the supreme pathedist of English literature—that he sees man as something of immense yet limited value. Pathedy, of which romantic irony is an important new species (an older species is the picaresque), involves, as I see it, an awareness of man's potential for greatness and of his inevitable limitations. Julien's sublimity has its limits, but so, too, does his silliness—he is a much more noble and certainly more interesting specimen than the traditional pi-

caro. Through romantic irony Stendhal has created a unique form of
pathedy. He has given us a protagonist who is eight or nine parts hero to
one or two parts fool. At times we want to put Julien on a pedestal; at
other times we want to wring his neck. Those who see in Julien a higher
percentage of fool (the term includes "schemer," "rogue," and "roué" as
well as *ingénu*) than I have suggested would do well to take the beam out
of their own eye before casting the first stone; for one thing, it will
improve their aim. Stendhal has simply chosen to *show* rather than conceal his hero's faults and limitations. Julien, then, is neither comic nor
tragic; he is *pathedic*. He is a unique kind of romantic hero. Scoured with
irony and ambivalence, he is cleansed of both bathos and self-pity. He
inspires admiration, sympathy, and empathy—but also Hobbesian
laughter.

Romantic irony involves not only the hero's ambivalence but also the
author's; there is never an uninterrupted flow of sympathy or antipathy
but a constant rotation, often a commingling, of the two. In *Le Rouge* it is
not so much a question of authorial alienation as of a pre-Brechtian
Verfremdungseffekt (alienation-effect). The reader is invited to examine
the hero's deeds critically rather than to be lulled into an unthinking
identification with an idealized hero. Julien's comic flaws, indeed, become a tragic flaw in the end. As Alvin Eustis has wisely observed: "In
each of Julien's love affairs, his motives are not so much social ambition
as the need to increase his importance in his own eyes. His downfall is
not to be attributed, in the cant phrase of the critics, to society's narrow
victory over a threat to its existence, but to a tragic flaw in his character:
an acute sensitivity that takes the form of sudden, unreasoning rages."[14]

Stendhal knew he would pay a price for refusing to present a flawless hero. He knew that his book would be appreciated only by "the
happy few" and that his hero was destined to be maligned. In the first
chapter I mentioned Robert Penn Warren's explanation of the coarse
humor of Mercutio in *Romeo and Juliet*. His remarks are also apposite
here: "The poet wishes to indicate that his vision has been earned, that it
can survive reference to the complexities and contradictions of experience." In giving us a sympathetic portrayal of a hero so complex that his
flaws outnumber, although they do not outweigh, his good qualities,
Stendhal has achieved this earned vision. And he has achieved it in large
measure through romantic irony.

5

The Earnest but Skeptical Questor: Gautier's *Albertus* and *Mademoiselle de Maupin*

I laugh in my own face.
(Mademoiselle de Maupin)

No French author has better epitomized the romantic dilemma than Théophile Gautier. His lifelong yearning for the ideal was accompanied by a career-long pessimism that told him his frantic search was futile. He suffered the agonizing dual awareness that, on the one hand, the human condition was intolerable and, on the other, transcendence was impossible. One tries to spread one's wings, says the heroine of *Mademoiselle de Maupin*, but they are weighed down by slime, the corrupt body anchors the soul to earth. Critics have spoken of Gautier's Gnostic and Manichaean dualism, of his view of the universe as a battleground upon which the forces of good and evil fight for dominance. But for this unbeliever, orthodox Christianity—especially its analysis of man's dualism—provided the central text, and Gautier found it eloquently expressed in Hugo's preface to *Cromwell*, which "shone in our eyes," says Gautier of himself and his fellow romantics of 1827, "like the Tables of the Law on Sinai."[1]

Gautier's aesthetic was likewise dualistic. He never fully abandoned his romantic belief in the relativity of taste and the importance of the artist's private vision, his individual genius, imagination, and inspiration, but even during the days of the Petit Cénacle he also thought of art in terms of craftsmanship, hard work, and the universality of the classical ideal. Even as late as *Emaux et camées* (first published in 1852) Gautier combines impassive and impersonal texts inspired by the doctrine of art for art's sake with other texts expressing an intense personal lyricism.

Johanna Richardson *(Théophile Gautier,* pp. 132–33) and James Smith ("Gautier," pp. 37–38) have shown that Gautier's belief that everything useful is ugly, that only those things having no purpose can be beautiful, had to cohabit with a conflicting doctrine: that art and artists must be *practical.* "Nowadays," says Gautier, "Benvenuto Cellini would not refuse to make tops for . . . canes and paperweights."[2] Gautier was capable both of railing against the railroads and against the ugliness of industrial progress in general and of praising with genuine enthusiasm the inauguration of new railway lines.

Gautier's aesthetic was indeed elastic enough to include objectivity and subjectivity, discipline and caprice. Caprice could even take the extreme form of preciosity: "The most exquisite preciosity pushes right and left its capricious tendrils and its bizarre flowers with their intoxicating perfumes—preciosity, that beautiful French flower."[3] And his conception of the well-wrought artifact does not preclude what Friedrich von Schlegel had boldly touted: buffoonery and the baroque arabesque.

> Beyond the compositions that can be called classical . . . there exists a genre for which the name "arabesque" would be appropriate, in which, without great concern for linear purity, the pencil engages in a thousand baroque fantasies.[4]

> We believe that one can admit these comic caprices into poetry just as one admits arabesques into painting.[5]

Two of Gautier's major themes are the impermanence of life and of love and the uncertainty of "reality." Short stories like *Une Nuit de Cléopâtre* (1838) and *Le roman de la momie* (1857) treat of impossible love while Gautier's report on his extensive travels in Spain speaks of the inevitable decay and destruction even of great civilizations and religions. Georges Poulet has noted *(Etudes,* p. 291) that Gautier's visual power made him more painfully aware than other writers of the perishable nature of things:

> The object appears simultaneously as beautiful—and beauty seems invested with eternity or atemporality—and as already corroded by time. Nothing must have seemed more intolerable to Gautier than this *simultaneous* apperception of "eternal beauty" and of the eternal work of

dissolution that accompanies its presence. The sensible object was seen, *simultaneously, at the very same time,* as eternal and ephemeral, as unalterable *and* deteriorating. (Emphasis added)

To take a single example:

> Marble, pearl, rose, dove,
> Everything is dissolved, everything is destroyed;
> The pearl melts, the marble falls,
> The flower fades and the bird flies away.
>
> ("Affinités secrètes" in *Poésies Complètes* 3)

The futility of everything is the major theme of Gautier's ironic romance, *Le Capitaine Fracasse* (1861), and the uncertainty of everything underlies the plot of *La Morte amoureuse* (1836). In the latter work ontological uncertainty is joined with moral ambiguity. As Richard Grant *(Gautier,* p. 124) sums up: "It is not only hard to know who one is but also who one ought to be."

Gautier was an admirer of E. T. A. Hoffmann, and Hoffmann's direct influence can be seen in works like *Onuphrius Wphly* (1832) and *Deux acteurs pour un rôle* (1841). The *fantastique,* of which Gautier was not only a great admirer but a prolific producer, has been related by critics such as Hubert Juin, Roger Caillois, and Tzvetan Todorov to what can be called an uncertainty principle. Caillois, for instance, defines the fantastic as "a break in the recognizable order of things, the eruption of the unacceptable in the midst of the unchanging daily legality."[6] The main source of terror in the fantastic, says Richard Grant *(Gautier,* p. 118), is the sudden discovery that what was thought to be an orderly, rational world breaks down, "one can no longer be certain of the rules of the game." Gautier, the visual poet for whom the external world exists, is also a poet possessed by a "feeling for the invisible world" *(Italia).* Michael Riffaterre ("Rêve et réalité," pp. 18–25) has shown that even in Gautier's most objective and realistic descriptions, as in the *récit de voyage,* there are sudden eruptions of the supernatural or the fantastic.

> Mobility is conferred on that which in real life is immobile, animation on that which is inert: movement surrealizes, so to speak, the real. (P. 24)

> Solids dissolve, lines are displaced, landmarks change, in short, every certainty of the real is called into question once again. (P. 23)

Gautier only half-believed many of his most cherished convictions. Even his belief in the divinity of art was tempered at times by the gnawing thought that art is an illusory good. Beginning his career as one of the most excessively ardent romantics, as his history of romanticism vividly tells us, he soon became an ardent critic of romantic excesses, including his own. He and Musset were among the first romantics to criticize romanticism in general as well as *their own romanticism,* that is, to indulge in self-irony and self-parody. The key texts for Gautier in this regard are *Albertus* (1832), *Les Jeunes-France* (1833), and the vaudeville, *Un voyage en Espagne* (1843), first published under the title of *Tra los montes.* Even as late as *Spirite* (1865) we witness an author who warns his readers to beware of unreliable authors and their narrators and who deliberately deflates a theme—the problem of reality versus ideality— that he obviously takes seriously. It is not surprising, then, to find Gautier indulging in parabasis and the destruction of artistic illusion in a play like *Une Larme du diable* (1839) in which the author appears as one of the characters and speaks directly to the audience about the inadequacy of the play's structure. In a somewhat similar vein the hero of *Le Capitaine Fracasse,* who has joined a wandering theatrical troupe, varies the tone of his voice within the same scene and wears only a half-mask so that the audience can see both the actor and the real man.

*

Albertus and d'Albert, both of whom are autobiographical figures, tell us much of the author's most intimate feelings during his early, romantic period. The entire first section (chapters 1–5) of *Mademoiselle de Maupin* is devoted not to the heroine but to the hero, who gives us a lyrical confession in the *enfant du siècle* mode, although the *siècle* is displaced for the sake of historical accuracy to the turn of the eighteenth century. The main components of d'Albert's psyche are ones we would expect to find in a romantic hero: boredom, melancholy, misanthropy, cynicism, solitude, and the vague *élans sans but,* yearnings prompted by no precise object. Such yearnings are also felt by the heroine, who is an alter ego of d'Albert and the author as well as the incarnation of their ideal (i.e., perfection symbolized by the heroine's bisexuality and by her obsession with hermaphroditism, which represents completeness and perfection through the [impossible] harmony of opposites).

Mademoiselle de Maupin begins exactly like Senancour's *Obermann,* with the hero writing to a friend not of the events of his life, since there aren't any, but of his ideas and feelings. The language is identical: "But, since you insist that I write to you, then I must tell you what I think and what I feel, and I must tell you the story of my ideas, for lack of events and actions."[7] A passive hero, he spends his life, like Obermann, "waiting." For what? He does not know. He is tormented by the same vague desires and passions as René; like René's, one of the objects of these desires is an ideal woman; but another component is latent homosexuality.

Like Benjamin Constant's Adolphe, d'Albert is supremely indifferent to everything around him and, like him, enjoys a lukewarm affection for a mistress he soon wants to be rid of. The hero's indecisiveness in this regard is finely analyzed and is worthy of the pen of Constant: "I am almost angry at her for the very sincerity of her passion, which is one more shackle, and which makes a breaking of our relations more difficult or less excusable" (p. 127). Like Adolphe, d'Albert speaks to his mistress of love for fear of speaking of its disappearance.

When he describes for us his heroic otherness, d'Albert gives us an almost direct translation from *Manfred:* "My heart beats for none of the things that make most men's heart beat.—My sorrows and my joys are not those of my fellow beings" (p. 242). Manfred had proclaimed,

> From my youth upwards
> My spirit walked not with the souls of men,
> Nor looked upon the earth with human eyes;
> The thirst of their ambitions was not mine,
> The aim of their existence was not mine;
> My joys, my griefs, my passions, and my powers
> Made me a stranger. Although I wore the form,
> I had no sympathy with breathing flesh.

At times d'Albert is a stranger even to himself: "The meaning of my existence escapes me completely. The sound of my own voice surprises me to an unimaginable degree, and I would be tempted at times to take it for the voice of another" (p. 243)—a disconcerting sensation that will be retold by Malraux in *La Condition humaine.*

The hero describes himself as a romantic *puer senex.*

> Is it not strange that I, who am still in the blondest months of adolescence, I have reached that degree of satiety as to be no longer tickled by anything except by the bizarre or the difficult. . . ?

> I am stricken by that malady that attacks whole populations and powerful men in their old age:—the impossible. (Pp. 140–41)

He is explicitly called by Rosette a *beau ténébreux,* a hero wrapped in Byronic gloom, and he calls himself a marked man, a fated and fatal hero: "Everyone is born with a black or white seal. Apparently mine is black" (p. 250).

However, we are not allowed to take d'Albert's problems, which are real and grave, with tragic seriousness. The novel is frequently interrupted by allusions to the fact that this *is* a novel, a "glorious novel," an "illustrious novel," a "truly French novel," and so on. The author tells us that it is boring to write a novel and even more boring to read one (p. 231). In one place the author will apologize for an awkward simile; in another the narrator will bemoan the inordinate length of a really fine and sincere burst of lyricism: "Ouf! there's a tirade of interminable length, almost straight out of the epistolary style. —What a long-winded passage!" (p. 67). And at another point the author tells us that he cannot go on with his story; his idea of perfection makes him feel nothing but disgust for this inferior novel he is writing.

The story proper is framed with ironic detachment. Here is the beginning:

> At this point in the story, if the debonair reader is willing to allow us, we are going for a time to leave to his reveries the worthy character who up to now has occupied stage center all by himself and speaks for himself, and return to the ordinary form of the novel, without however forbidding ourselves to assume later on the dramatic form, if the need arises, and reserving for ourselves the right to dip again into that kind of epistolary confession that the aforesaid young man was addressing to his friend, persuaded as we are that, however penetrating and sagacious we may be, we surely ought to know less about these things than he himself. (P. 146)

And here is the ending, the moment when d'Albert finally receives Madeleine's nocturnal visit, which is both the climax of the "plot" and the beginning of the dénouement: "Who was surprised?" says the narrator to the reader. "It's neither you nor I, for you and I have been prepared for this visit for quite a while now" (p. 360). Thus, d'Albert's great moment is deflated more cruelly than Stendhal would ever have done to Julien. The reader is not allowed to share the hero's excitement vicariously: "He uttered a little cry of surprise midway between oh! and ah! However I have every reason to believe that it was closer to ah! than oh!" (p. 361). The novel's sad ending is punctured by a final ironic intervention:

> At the end of the week, the unhappy, disappointed lover received a letter from Théodore [Madeleine], which we are going to transcribe. I do fear that it may not satisfy either my male or my female readers; but, in all truth, the letter was such and not otherwise, and this glorious novel will have no other conclusion. (P. 369)

*

Not only is Gautier's Albertus still another incarnation of the romantic hero, but the author seems to go to some pains to ensure that he is a stereotypical one. A number of critics have condemned the lack of originality in the poem, but I don't believe that the presentation of a unique hero is really one of the author's or, better, the work's intentions. At any rate Albertus is indeed a stereotype of the romantic hero. He has, for instance, the *regard de lion* of the Hugoesque hero—

> His lion's stare and the wild spark
> That leaped at times from his eyes
> Made you shiver and pale despite yourself.[8]

—a reminiscence, too, of the Byronic hero whose cold stare dazzles but also "chills" the vulgar heart. Albertus's lip is "severe" and forms the mocking smile of the Giaour. But his principal expression, the narrator tells us, is a "great disdain" for everything and everyone. He is a sad, bored, solitary misanthrope; "his door is closed to all." He is, inevitably, a *puer senex:*

> —Having always inquired, ever since his birth,
> About the why and wherefore, he was pessimistic
> As is a man grown old.
>
> (69)
>
> —A great knowledge is a great scourge;
> It turns a child into an old man. . . .
> . . . .
>
> As soon as the cause is seen, one already knows the effect.
> Existence weighs down upon you and everything seems insipid.
> . . . .

Love is now but a spasm, and glory an empty word,
Like a squeezed lemon the heart becomes arid.
—Don Juan arrives after Werther.

(70)

Driven by a Faustian urge to obtain divine omniscience and omnipotence, he learns all of human knowledge that one can learn and, possessing that, promptly wants to die. Only fear deters his suicidal hand. But at twenty he is already ripe for death.

Like Musset's Hassan, Albertus does not believe in true love and settles for a quantitative ethic in which repeated superficial pleasures serve as opiate to his anguish.

... What does it matter, after all, if the cause
Be sad, provided the effect produced be sweet?
—Let's enjoy ourselves, let's make for ourselves a superficial bliss;
A beautiful mask is better than an ugly face.

(72)

Although good-hearted at bottom, he believes in neither worldly nor otherworldly values and proposes for his life no lofty goals: "He let his life go at random" (123).

In a second Faustian impulse, he sells his soul to the Devil in exchange for a brief moment of love with the beautiful witch, Véronique. Although he knows perfectly well that the love won't last, he is still greatly shocked when the beautiful maiden at midnight (the conventional hour should warn us not to take with excessive gravity the conventionality of the hero) turns into the old hag once again, and the Devil, after an orgy in which all the inhabitants of hell participate, comes to claim him for his own.

A sad career indeed, but the tale is not told, of course, in the lugubrious tone that my résumé suggests. We are advised in the Preface that the tale is only "semi-diabolique"; it is also "semi-fashionable"; the latter, significantly, is the most prominent adjective in the poem and tells us at once that the clichés and plagiarisms are meant to be ironically transparent and the hero something less than heroic. The poem is half-serious and half-ironic, the mixture producing romantic irony since the ironic does not simply cohabit with the serious, it invades it. We need not linger over the devices used to produce this irony; we have seen them before: authorial intrusions, some of which disparage the very poem in progress, digressions (i.e., structural irony), asides to the reader, and especially a constant short-circuiting of the narrative in favor of allusions to the *composition* of the narrative. In stanza 59, to take a single example, the poet tells us that it is "now time to get back to the subject" of this rambling and disconnected tale; then, instead of simply introducing us to the hero, he tells us that "before going further, it might be a good idea to sketch his physical portrait." The portrait itself is done with a certain playfulness and *désinvolture*.

> —His hair, thrown into disorder by his fingers,
> Fell around a brow that Gall, in ecstasy,
> Would have examined for six months and used as source
>   For a dozen treatises.

Gautier, then, uses most of the basic strategies of the romantic ironist. Rather than give a detailed rehearsal of them, it would seem more profitable at this point to explore the serious implications of the irony in both works, especially since this is still largely unexplored territory. As late as 1975 a critic can wonder whether *Albertus* can be interpreted at all,[9] and another critic considers the poem unsuccessful because "the style continually distracts from the subject."[10] Similarly, *Maupin* has been condemned by a good number of critics for its incoherent structure.[11] In my view the style of the poem and the novel, especially their romantic irony, is both the foundation of their subject matter and the key to their interpretation. I also believe that Gautier, as much as any other French or German writer, gives us many insights into the mainsprings of romantic irony.

Consider first the concluding stanza of *Albertus*.

> —This heroic and unequaled poem
> Offers an admirable and profound allegory;
> But, in order to suck the marrow, one must break the bone,
> . . . .
> —I could have clearly explained every detail,
> Nailed a learned commentary to every word.—
> I believe, dear reader, that you are intelligent enough
> To understand me. —So, goodnight. —Close the door,
> Give me a kiss goodnight, and tell them to bring me
>   A volume of Pantagruel.

(122)

Despite the cavalier, tongue-in-cheek tonality, there is a half-serious Rabelaisian invitation to find the "substantific marrow" within the bone, to find serious subject matter despite the playful treatment. The invitation is convincingly reinforced by the fact that roughly 50 percent of *Albertus* and 95 percent of *Maupin* are dead serious.

A serious theme running throughout the poem that can be considered its chief one is the instability of human sentiments. In one of his digressions the narrator tells us about his own love life, which was an ecstatic but evanescent affair.

> All that happiness is no more. Who would have thought it?
> We are as strangers to one another; all men
> Are thus; —their "forever" does not last six months.

Their "forever" does not last six months—this antithesis catches one of the moods behind romantic irony. A philosopher-critic who has captured the mood well is Vladimir Jankélévitch.

> Our feelings are ephemeral and our beliefs unstable. . . . the passion will end, despite all our pledges; we swear to heaven that the loved person is irreplaceable and, when we have replaced her, we envisage, not without a smile, that disappointing absolute which is always eternal during the occurrence and provisional afterwards. Attrition or conversion—a feeling is eternal only until further notice! A definitive vow is definitive only until Easter! What creature here below can say Forever?[12]

Even the witch Véronique recognizes this sad truth:

> Man loves as he lives: one day.
>
> (146)

The romantic ironist presents us with sudden shifts of tone or mood that are playful on the surface, but if one looks beneath this surface, one sees the dangerous undertow. In *Mademoiselle de Maupin,* for instance, the author shows us how the romantic *vague des passions* can lead to cynicism, then to emotional aridity, and finally to self-irony. For lack of the right nourishment the passions *feed on each other* and become internecine:

> All my unoccupied passions are quietly snarling in my heart, and devour each other for lack of any other nourishment. (P. 45)

> Tossing and turning within me are vague desires that fuse together and give birth to others which then devour them. (P. 160)
>
> Nothing is so tiring as those motiveless whirlwinds of desire and those yearnings without an object. . . . I laugh in my own face. (Pp. 43–44)

Even when a man's heart is not filled with vague passions, it is filled with "absurdities," irreconcilable "contradictions" that prevent him from ever being more than "half-happy" or half-sad, half-moral or half-immoral, half-serious or half-ironic. Romantic irony is the science of the half rather than the whole. Not only do human sentiments keep changing, they change with such alarming rapidity that one's actions cannot keep up with them.

> Whenever I write a sentence, the thought that it renders is already as far from me as if a century had passed instead of a second, and *I often mix with it, in spite of myself, something of the thought that has replaced it in my mind.*
>
> That is why I would never be able to discover how to live, —either as a poet or as a lover. —I cannot render the ideas that I no longer have; —I possess women only when I have forgotten them and when I am in love with others; . . . how could I express my will, since, no matter how much I hasten, I no longer have the feeling that corresponds to what I am doing. (P. 248; emphasis added)

How, then, can one measure the moral worth of others or even of oneself at any particular moment? "There are moments when I recognize only God above me, and other moments when I judge myself to be the equal of the bug under the rock or the mollusc on its sandbank" (p. 92). Romantic irony expresses a moral agnosticism ("I have completely lost the knowledge of good and evil" [p. 177]) based partly on the fact that human sentiments are contradictory and fleeting and also on the conviction that there are no absolute standards. The heroic mode, under these conditions, seems "silly" (p. 178); the mock-heroic is the best defense against disillusion; self-mockery is a protection against self-deception. All this can be read on Albertus's face:

> The imperial brow of the artist and poet
> Occupying all by itself *half* of his head,
> Broad and full, bending under the inspiration,

Which hides in each premature wrinkle
A superhuman hope, a great thought,
And bears written these words: —Strength and conviction.—
The rest of the face corresponded to this grandiose
Brow. —However it had something
Unpleasant about it and, although faultless,
One would have wished it different. —Irony
And sarcasm shone there more than genius.
        The lower part seemed to mock the upper.

                                                        (60)

The peculiar tension produced by romantic irony also reflects the unbridgeable gap between reality and ideality. In *Albertus* we catch a fleeting view of the gap in the following lines:

Benevolent reader, this is my entire story
Faithfully told, as well as my memory,
A disorganized register, has been able to remind me
Of those nothings that were everything, of which
Love is composed and of which later one makes fun.
—Excuse this pause: The bubble I enjoyed
Blowing and which floated in the air, multicolored,
Has suddenly collapsed into a drop of water;
It broke on the corner of a pointed roof.
—Because it knocked against the Real, my pleasant
Chimera broke. . . .

                                                        (57)

And in *Maupin* we have a vivid image of this romantic dilemma:

I can neither walk nor fly; the sky attracts me when I am on the ground, the earth when I am in the sky; above, the North wind pulls off my feathers; below, the pebbles offend my feet. The soles of my feet are too tender to walk on the broken glass of reality; my wingspread too narrow to soar above things. (P. 240)

Romantic heroes, even those not treated with romantic irony, all share this predicament. In each one the idealist is restrained by the cynical realist, and the latter is restrained by the *idéaliste malgré lui*. Since he has a home in neither world, he yearns for the one while immersed in the other, or when presented from the viewpoint of romantic irony, he shuttles—playfully *and* painfully—between the two.

In *Maupin* the hero describes his life in terms of this shuttle but also as "an absurd treadmill." And when the narrator of *Albertus* speaks of "this silly story," both the general and the immediate context make the epithet polyvalent: it applies simultaneously to the poem in progress, to the hero's entire career, and to life in general. It is an intimation of the Absurd.

Before the romantic period, with the notable exceptions of Sterne and Diderot, the narrator's attitude toward his hero or his story, or the hero's attitude toward himself in first-person narratives, was usually unequivocal: it was either positive or negative. Or if it was ambivalent, the ambivalence was clearly stated and explained; or if it was ironic, the irony was transparent, since it was almost always a form of antiphrasis, the narrator obviously blaming the person or thing he was pretending to praise, or vice versa. With the romantic period the narrative point of view begins to become more and more problematic; we cannot measure the exact dosage of antipathy or sympathy, of authorial identification or alienation in works informed by romantic irony. We can only feel the tensions, observe the shuttlings and oscillations, admire the complexities and, finally, puzzle at the paradoxes.

6

The Coexistence of Contraries:
Baudelaire's *La Fanfarlo*
and *Les Fleurs du mal*

I am the wound and the knife,
....
Both the victim and the torturer.
("L'Héautontimorouménos")

LL roads of modern French literature seem to lead to and from
Baudelaire. In his article on romantic irony Maurice Boucher
("L'ironie romantique," p. 29) defined it as "consciousness of the
coexistence of contraries." And Dominique Rincé *(Baudelaire,* p. 180) has
spoken of Baudelaire's modernity precisely as "consciousness quartered
between its contradictory postulates." Baudelaire's entire opus is cen-
tered on his vision of the irreducible duality of *homo duplex* and his two
contradictory and *simultaneous* postulations: "There is in every man, at
every hour, two simultaneous postulations, one toward God, the other
toward Satan. The invitation to God, or spirituality, is a desire to rise in
stature; that of Satan, or animality, is a joy in descending."[1] The poet has
said that even as a child he had felt in his heart two contradictory feelings: the horror of life and the ecstasy of life.[2] Man's painful consciousness of these and other contradictory feelings and impulses has been
exacerbated by modern civilization, of which Baudelaire is perhaps the
chief poet. Verlaine *(OEuvres posthumes* 2:9–10) correctly saw Baudelaire's originality as that of depicting "modern physical man with
his sharpened and vibrant senses, his painfully subtle mind." Paul Valéry
has said that to be modern is to unite in oneself the most contradictory

96

features and to live with that monstrous juxtaposition. And Carl Jung considered disagreement with oneself the distinctive sign of modern civilized man. What Baudelaire saw as modern man's unique illness— spiritual apathy or ennui—is countered by a desperate longing for spiritual health, but this dialectical opposition does not produce, either in the poet's life or in his work, a wholesome synthesis or resolution, just physical and metaphysical tension, grating contradictions.

René Bourgeois *(L'Ironie romantique,* p. 34) has said that romantic irony "has this which is peculiar to it that it unites in the same movement 'the victim and the torturer' and that the writer feels himself both in the object and outside the object." This sadomasochistic side of romantic irony is an essential aspect of Baudelaire's work: the torturer identifies with the victim; in fact he *is* the victim. The mocker is looking in a mirror.

> I am the wound and the knife,
> . . . .
> Both the victim and the torturer.
>
> ("L'Héautontimorouménos")

> It would perhaps be pleasant to be alternately victim and torturer. *(Mon coeur mis à nu)*

Baudelaire's imaginative world includes a vision of a cruelly ironic Heaven or Ideal mocking the inadequate poet (Mallarmé will develop this theme even more insistently), the incorrigible sinner, and all those conscious of being mired in material reality, exiled, like the poet's Albatross and his Swan, from the realm of Beauty, Truth, and Goodness.

> . . . the ironical and cruelly blue sky
>
> ("Le Cygne")

> And now the depth of the sky fills me with dismay; its limpidity exasperates me. . . . The study of the beautiful is a duel in which the artist shouts with fright before being vanquished. ("Le *Confiteor* de l'artiste")

> I am like a painter whom a mocking God
> Condemns to paint, alas, on shadows.
>
> ("Un Fantôme")

> Sometimes in a beautiful garden
> Where I was dragging along my atony
> I felt, like an irony,
> The sun tearing apart my heart.
>
> ("Confession")

The poet is conscious of another irony, that of Death mocking the laughably short-lived contortions of humanity.

> In every clime, under every sun, Death admires you
> In your contortions, laughable Humanity,
> And often, like you, perfuming herself in myrrh,
> Mingles her irony with your insanity!
>
> ("Danse macabre")

The clock is a constant reminder that man's inadequacies are compounded by the inexorable flight of time.

> The clock, sounding midnight,
> Ironically forces us
> To remember what use
> We made of the fleeting day.
>
> ("L'Examen de minuit")

The poet's self-conscious lucidity, his painful awareness of the ironies engulfing him, turns to self-irony.

> Am I not a false chord
> In the divine symphony
> Thanks to the voracious Irony
> That shakes and bites me?
>
> ("L'Héautontimorouménos")

Baudelaire speaks of irony as a "beacon" (*phare ironique*), as a "consciousness within evil" (cf. the end of "L'Irrémédiable" and of "Les Phares"); it does not excuse the sinner but does raise him above the beasts of the field: "One is never excusable in being wicked, but there is some merit in knowing that one is; and the most irreparable of vices is to do evil through sheer stupidity" ("La fausse monnaie"). It also provides a punishment coterminous with and exquisitely appropriate to the particular evil committed. Claude Pichois (OC, p. 987) is correct in claiming that it is with Baudelaire that irony enters French poetry, by which he means not that Baudelaire is the first ironist in French poetry, but that for the first time, in *Les Fleurs du mal*, irony is not just a strategy but a subject, an important poetic theme in its own right. Baudelaire was conscious of his role as the chief ironist of French poetry: "I am the real representative of irony, and my sickness is of an absolutely incurable kind."[3]

Baudelaire's romantic irony contains several interrelated components:

(1) the always painful and occasionally playful consciousness of the coexistence of contraries;

(2) the yearning and anguished search for the Ideal combined with the *simultaneous* awareness of the search's futility, which we have also seen in Musset and Gautier (Baudelaire will turn this metaphysical perspective into an aesthetic principle: "Two fundamental literary qualities: supernaturalism and irony" [*Fusées*]);

(3) the perpetual oscillating movement between the two poles, a movement caused also by moments of exhilaration inevitably followed by premonitions of entropy—

> Everything cracks, love and beauty.
>
> ("Confession")

by the realization that Time not only leads to Death in an imminent future but is at every moment turning the present into a dead past—

> Now says: I am Formerly.
>
> ("L'Horloge")

(4) the sadomasochistic impulse to insult what one loves and to praise what one abhors—

> We have, to please the brute,
> Worthy vassal of the Demons,
> Insulted what we love,
> And flattered what repulses us.
>
> ("L'Examen de minuit")

(5) in his aesthetics, the Schlegel-like admiration of the convoluted arabesque—

> The arabesque design is the most spiritualistic of designs. . . . The arabesque design is the most ideal of all. *(Fusées)*

the taste for the irregular, the surprising, the bizarre, the *mélange des genres,* and the "aristocratic" pleasure of displeasing the reader through

the display of bad taste, which is not unrelated to the dandy's delight in
displeasing the vulgar through the display of excessive refinement—

> What is not slightly deformed appears insensible; —whence it fol-
> lows that irregularity, that is, the unexpected, surprise, astonishment
> are an essential part and the basic characteristic of beauty. *(Fusées)*

> The mixture of the grotesque and the tragic is pleasing to the mind
> just as dissonance is to blasé ears.
> What is intoxicating about bad taste is the aristocratic pleasure of
> displeasing. *(Fusées)*

(6) the poet's irreducible ambivalence toward everything: toward
politics and humanitarian social schemes, toward sin and death—

> To plunge to the depths of the abyss, Hell or Heaven,
>   what does it matter?
>
>   ("Le Voyage")

toward beauty—

> Do you come from the deep heaven or from the deep abyss,
> O Beauty?. . . .
> From Satan or from God, what does it matter?
>
>   ("Hymne à la Beauté")

toward love—

> I hate you as much as I love you
> . . . .
> Infamous one to whom I am tightly bound.
>
>   ("A celle qui est trop gaie")

toward God—

> Even if God did not exist, Religion would still be Holy and Di-
> vine. . . . God is the only being who, to reign, does not even need to
> exist. *(Fusées)*

(7) and finally, the curious, ambivalent blend of romanticism and
antiromanticism.

T. S. Eliot has said of Baudelaire that he was inevitably the son of
romanticism and at the same time, by his nature, the first antiromantic in
poetry.[4] This fact alone is enough for Baudelaire to qualify as a romantic
ironist according to Morton Gurewitch, who declares ("European
Romantic Irony," p. 3): "The full-fledged romantic ironists are those

who, in one movement of mind, both impressively absorb and mockingly disject the romantic heritage. The romantic ironist blends a romantic ardor with an anti-romantic animus." Baudelaire's romanticism (e.g., sensibility, passion, lyricism, modernity, revolt, the concrete, the addition of strangeness to beauty, the renascence of wonder) is countered, corrected, and chastised by an instinctive classicism (e.g., lucidity, analysis, order, the general and abstract, art as craft and constraint rather than inspiration); this fruitful clash produced a poetry of controlled violence, but also an irony of calculated contradictions that remained excruciating despite the formal control exerted upon them.

*

Baudelaire's work is of especial interest in that it contains both early and late forms of romantic irony. The early, even by then (the mid-1840s) traditional or neo-Byronic form, is displayed in his novella, *La Fanfarlo,* which was written between 1843 and 1847 and is therefore contemporaneous with some of the earliest poems of *Les Fleurs du mal.* While informed by many of the same philosophical problems as the poetry, it is written in the casual, playful, and ironic style of Gautier's tales, borrowing especially from *Mademoiselle de Maupin.* It is an autobiographical work, but the self-portrait is an ambivalent rather than a flattering one.[5]

The protagonist, Samuel Cramer, is "the contradictory product of a pale German, a Chilean brunette . . . a French education and a literary civilization" *(La Fanfarlo,* OC, p. 553), which accounts for the bizarre complications of his character. The psychological complications are suggested by his physical portrait, in which concrete substantives are modified by moral epithets: "Samuel has a pure and noble brow, shining eyes . . . a teasing and mocking nose, impudent and sensual lips, a square and despotic chin, pretentiously Raphaelesque hair" (p. 553).

I said in the preceding chapter that romantic irony is the science of the half rather than the whole. The hero-antihero of *La Fanfarlo,* we learn, is "a great idler," never having had in his life anything but "half-ideas." The sun of laziness has vaporized his "half-genius." Ranking among the "half-great men," Samuel is the creator of "beautiful failures."

A paradoxical creature, made of shadows and brilliant flashes of light, of laziness and ambition, of erudition and ignorance, of "naive

and respectful impudence," of "equally violent" habits of monklike re-
clusion and rakelike dissipation, an avid reader of both philosophy and
pornography, a materialistic idealist, a credulous cynic, his language
combines mystical terms and enormous crudities. "He possessed the
logic of every good sentiment and the knowledge of every deceitful trick,
and nevertheless never succeeded at anything, because he believed too
much in the impossible" *(La Fanfarlo,* p. 555). His relationship with Mme
de Cosmelly, his attempt to console and seduce her simultaneously, has
been called "jesuitical tartufferie."

Samuel will expatiate passionately on metaphysical anguish and
spiritual ennui, but the narrator warns us that his speech is that of a
"brutal and hypocritical actor" proud of the fine tears he inspires in
himself and in others, which he considers his "literary property." In his
conversations with Mme de Cosmelly he will interrupt himself with
dramatic moments of silence—"the classical silence of emotion"; the
narrator tells us the problem with our hero—"our young roué"—is that
one can never be sure when he is not acting.

The narrator pokes fun at his hero's derivative romanticism: "His
volume on the *Sea-hawks,* a collection of sonnets, such as we have all
composed and all read, at that time when we had such short judgment
and such long hair" (p. 558). At one point Samuel resembles a comically
distraught and desperate Julien Sorel: "Ashamed of having been so
stupid, he tried to be sly; he spoke to her for some time in the patois of
the seminarian" (p. 569). His conversations with Mme de Cosmelly are
mocked in the same terms that Stendhal used to characterize Julien's
initial conversations with Mme de Rênal: "laughable silliness," "bombastic clumsiness," and so forth.

The dénouement is ironically anticlimactic. The elegant dandy, who
had prided himself on astonishing others while never allowing anything
or anyone to astonish him, ends up unpoetically, as a hack writer. A good
example of the self-conscious narrator's playful tone is the following
passage reminiscent of Sterne, whom Baudelaire admired greatly and
who is specifically mentioned in *La Fanfarlo.*

> One of the most natural faults of Samuel was to consider himself
> the equal of those he had learned to admire. . . . *"there* is something
> beautiful enough to be *my* creation!"—and from there to the thought: it
> is, then, my creation—there is only the space of a double hyphen. (P.
> 554)

In *Les Fleurs du mal* romantic irony becomes more shrill and sardonic, more macabre, in short, more modern. The Byronic breeziness, flippancy, and casualness disappear; the humor becomes grating. This was inevitable since Baudelaire came to view laughter as the indisputable sign of man's fall from grace and into sin. Like Hobbes's, Baudelaire's theory of laughter is based on the feelings of pride and superiority experienced by the laugher (mocker) at the expense of his victim—"A satanic notion if ever there was one" *(L'Essence du rire)*. Baudelaire's laughter is closely related, then, to the melancholy, "destructive laughter" of Jean-Paul, for whom the greatest humorist of all would be the Devil. This theory explains in part why Baudelaire's humor is so often mordant ("Man bites with laughter") and self-deprecating. The mirthless humor of *Les Fleurs* expresses the poet's feelings of inferiority, not in relation to human norms—he knows that his fellowmen ("mes semblables, mes frères") are hardly better moral specimens than he—but in relation to Christian ideals he had always revered but never succeeded in actualizing. As everywhere, Baudelaire finds in laughter still another manifestation of man's eternal duality.

> Laughter is satanic, it is therefore profoundly human . . . and . . . as laughter is essentially human, it is essentially contradictory, that is, it is simultaneously the sign of an infinite greatness and of an infinite destitution, an infinite destitution relative to the absolute Being of which he possesses an idea, an infinite greatness relative to the animals. It is from the perpetual shock of these two infinites that laughter arises. *(L'Essence du rire)*

Baudelaire's "laughter" is not far removed from the metaphysical anguish created by the shock of Pascal's two infinites. It is a nervous laughter.

In the self-mockery of *Les Fleurs du mal* there is sarcastic, sneering, and sardonic humor but only latent playfulness. The self-derision is kept within the confines of the solemn confession, which precludes the complacency of other types of self-deprecating humor. In the hands of a lighter-hearted poet the self-deflating similes and metaphors could have produced uproarious laughter.

> I am an old boudoir filled with faded roses
> Where lies a thicket of old-fashioned styles.
>
> ("Spleen," 76)

I am a cemetery abhorred by the moon.

("Spleen," 76)

I am like the king of a rainy country,
Rich, but powerless, young and yet very old.

("Spleen," 77)

My heart is a palace dilapidated by the throng.

("Causerie")

My mind is like the tower that succumbs
Beneath the blows of the heavy and indefatigable
                          battering ram.

("Chant d'automne")

My soul is a tomb that, bad monk,
I have been dwelling in and roaming through forever.
Nothing embellishes the walls of this odious cloister.

("Le mauvais moine")

As for me, my soul is cracked.

("La Cloche fêlée")

In other passages he compares himself to a shadow of Hamlet, to a ham actor on vacation ("La Béatrice"), to an old horse stumbling at every obstacle ("Le Goût du néant"), to a drum veiled in crepe ("Le Guignon"), to a theater in which the long-awaited savior, fairy princess, or *deus ex machina* ("L'Etre aux ailes de gaze") fails to appear ("L'Irréparable").

Baudelaire's is a grim, bitter, and unsmiling laughter:

            That bitter laughter
Of the vanquished man.

("Obsession")

[I am] one of those great abandoned souls,
Condemned to eternal laughter
And who can no longer smile.

("L'Héautontimorouménos")

At times it is a hysterical laughter; at other times it is the hollow mechanical and funereal laughter affected by harlots past their prime:

The funeral gaiety of those old whores.

("Le Jeu")

In many passages of *Les Fleurs* Baudelaire strives to achieve a highly provocative moral irony, as when he indulges in, or rather experiments imaginatively with, sadism and satanism.

> Thus would I like, one night,
> When the hour of sensual pleasure sounds,
> To crawl noiselessly, like a coward,
> Toward the treasures of your person,
>
> To punish your joyful flesh,
> To bruise your forgiven breast,
> And to make in your astonished side,
> A wide and deep wound,
>
> And, dizzying pleasure!
> Between those new lips,
> More dazzling and more beautiful,
> To infuse my poison, my sister!

("A celle qui est trop gaie")

> Glory and praise be unto thee, Satan.

("Litanies de Satan")

> Race of Cain, mount to heaven,
> And cast God down to earth.

("Abel et Caïn")

> Saint Peter renounced Jesus . . . he did well!

("Le Reniement de Saint Pierre")

I speak of imaginative experimentation rather than actual experience since much of the autobiographical aspect of *Les Fleurs* deals with latent sins, sins of which the poet is capable, not culpable.

> Faithful to his painful program, the author of the *Fleurs du mal*, like a perfect actor has had to mold his mind to every sophism and to every corruption. (OC, p. 1076)

> . . . having boasted (why?) of several villainous actions that I never committed, and having like a coward denied some other misdeeds that I accomplished with joy. (OC, p. 288)

Similarly, it is latent, not actual evil that informs the black humor of prose poems like "Le mauvais vitrier" and "Assommons les pauvres" in which the reader is encouraged to despise the implied author.

A work significantly informed by romantic irony must betray ambivalence at every turn. In *Les Fleurs du mal* a generalized ambivalence is
felt not only in the opening section, explicitly scored "Spleen et Idéal,"
not only in the cycles of love and perversion, the latter paradoxically
scored "Fleurs du mal," but in every section of the volume. Part of the
distinctive quality of the "Tableaux parisiens," in pieces like "Les sept
vieillards," "Les petites vieilles," and "Les Aveugles," is the ironic mixture of genuine pity and instinctive revulsion inspired by the downtrod-
den and the mixture of excitement and horror inspired by the great city.
The very change in the placement of the Wine Cycle from the 1857 to
the 1861 edition suggests ambivalence. In the first edition the section was
placed after the blasphemies of "La Révolte," thus emphasizing the
search for an artificial paradise; in 1861 the section follows the "Tableaux
parisiens" and precedes "Fleurs du mal," "La Révolte," and "La Mort,"
suggesting as Claude Pichois has noted (OC, p. 1045) no longer paradise
but "a gradation in damnation." The blasphemy of "La Révolte" is by
definition ambivalent and paradoxical. The genuine blasphemer is
deeply hurt by a God in whom he deeply believes; an avowed atheist who
would curse God would be a hypocrite. In the Death Cycle there is a
double ambivalence, the first dealing with the poet's mixed emotions,

> Desire mixed with horror,
> Anguish and keen hope,
> Bitter and delicious torture. . .

("Le Rêve d'un curieux")

the second dealing with his dualistic evaluation of the afterlife ("Hell or
Heaven, what does it matter?"). He will even wonder whether the afterlife will show him anything new and interesting or whether it will be still
another disappointing anticlimax.

> The curtain was raised and I was still waiting.

("Le Rêve d'un curieux")

Ambivalence is so intrinsic to *Les Fleurs du mal* that examining it
closely and exhaustively would require a thick volume of commentary
and analysis. In the interests of concreteness I shall examine ambivalence briefly in just one thematic area: love.

The three main cycles of Baudelaire's love poetry are often said to
represent three different types of love: *l'amour-passion* (Jeanne Duval),
l'amour spirituel (Mme Sabatier), and *l'amour-tendresse* (Marie Daubrun).

But not only do the three cycles contrast with each other, they exhibit within themselves conflicting moods and themes that belie the simple labels.

In the 1857 edition the Jeanne Duval cycle opened with "Les Bijoux," which, while corresponding to the "coup de foudre" (love at first sight) phase, contains sly and subtle ambivalences and latent hostility. The lover, in ecstasy before his beautiful mistress clothed only in her "sonorous jewels," describes her in images drawn from stone and metal, thus tempering the adoration of beauty with the simultaneous awareness of a coldness and hardness that can turn to cruel mockery.

> When it sends forth, while dancing, this sharp and mocking noise,
> This world radiant with metal and stone
> Puts me in ecstasy and I love to distraction
> Things in which sound is mingled with light.

This mixture of brilliant light and metallic sounds is found again in "Avec ses vêtements ondoyants et nacrés" where Jeanne's eyes are made of "charming minerals," hard minerals

> In which everything is gold, steel, light and diamonds

The poet admires the "cold majesty" of the sterile woman, the "useless star." In "Le Chat" her eyes are metallic, and in "Le Serpent qui danse" they are again "cold jewels" in which brilliant gold is mingled with hard iron.

"Parfum exotique" and "La Chevelure" belong to "the honeymoon period," but are immediately followed by "Je t'adore à l'égal de la voûte nocturne" in which masochistic adoration is mingled with poorly concealed hatred.

> And I cherish, o cruel and implacable beast,
> Even the coldness by which you are all the more beautiful to me.

The poet's ambivalence is at its most explicit in "Sed non satiata" in which Jeanne is portrayed as both a "bizarre deity" and "a pitiless demon" whose bed is "hell."

In "Une Charogne" and "Remords posthume" the lover imagines with sadistic glee the future decomposition of his mistress's now-beautiful body. He curses his beloved in "Le Vampire." But in "Le Balcon" and "Un Fantôme" he returns to tender reminiscences of erotic ecstasy.

In contrast to Jeanne, who is addressed as a "cruel beast," and to
Sara "La Louchette," who is called a "vile animal," Mme Sabatier is
lauded as an angel full of gaiety, goodness, health, beauty, bliss. But even
in this cycle, which stresses—or attempts to stress—spiritual and platonic
love, there are intriguing tensions and ambivalences. In "Le Flambeau
vivant" her eyes, shining with a mystical brightness, lead the poet toward
the realm of spiritual Beauty, "dans la route du Beau." But this piece is
followed in the first edition by "A celle qui est trop gaie" in which the
poet plots sadistic revenge for her annoyingly constant good cheer. "Ré-
versibilité," in which the adoring invocation to the Angel is accompanied
by a suggestion of reproach for the Angel's indifference, is followed by
"Confession," in which Mme Sabatier appears as a callous, superficial
coquette, even a courtesan tired of amorous betrayals and of the
mechanical smiles required by her "difficult trade." "Harmonie du soir"
presents unadulterated ecstasy but is followed by "Le Flacon," which
ends the cycle and in which the poet's love has been downgraded to an
ambivalent "aimable pestilence."

The poet's ambivalence toward Marie Daubrun is expressed directly: "Amante ou soeur," "Madone, ma maïtresse." There is much
tenderness in this cycle but also much contempt. Marie is compared, for
instance, to a sinister sky; poison as well as beauty stream from her green
eyes. She is seen as "alternately tender, gentle and cruel." "A une
madone," perhaps the most interesting poem in the cycle, employs the
language of mysticism to express a love twisted by jealousy and a thirst
for sadistic revenge.

> Finally, to complete your role as Marie,
> And to mingle love with barbarity,
> Black poison! of the seven capital Sins
> I shall make, torturer filled with remorse, seven sharp
> Knives, and like an insensitive mountebank,
> Taking the deepest part of your Heart as target,
> I shall plant them all in your panting Heart,
> In your bleeding Heart, in your dripping Heart!

The "Fleurs du mal" section of the volume deals with the problem of
unnatural love and sexual perversion: homosexuality, sadism, prostitu-
tion, necrophilia. As we have come to expect, the poet's point of view
varies from poem to poem. The ambivalence—guilt versus unremorse-
ful self-indulgence, attraction versus repulsion—is the result of what

might be called ethical experimentation, the goal of which is to explore
(imaginatively) the insidious attractiveness of evil—the flowers of evil—
and, on the other side, the frightening destructiveness of the sins of the
flesh.

In "Lesbos" the poet acts as an apologist for female homosexuality.

Let old Plato's austere eye frown.
You obtain your forgiveness from the excess of kisses.
. . . .

You obtain your forgiveness from the eternal martyrdom
Inflicted without relaxation upon ambitious hearts.

Which of the Gods will dare to be your judge, Lesbos,
And condemn your pallid brow to forced labor?

What have the laws of the just and the unjust to do with us?
Virgins of sublime heart, honor of the archipelago . . .
Your religion, like another, is august.
And love will laugh at Hell or Heaven!

Similarly in "Allégorie" the beautiful prostitute "knows"

That the beauty of the body is a sublime gift
That steals forgiveness for any infamy.

and she will face death without fear or regret and without remorse. But
at the end of "Delphine et Hippolyte" the poet castigates lesbianism in
the manner of a fiery, furious preacher.

The bitter sterility of your sensual pleasure
Makes your thirst worse and stiffens your skin,
And the furious wind of concupiscence
Makes your flesh flap like an old flag.

Far from the land of the living, across the deserts,
Run like wolves, wandering and condemned;
Create your destiny, disordered souls,
And flee the infinite that you carry within you!

*

Stylistically, Baudelaire's romantic irony is expressed by a radical
mixture of styles and tonalities and by a marked tendency toward catachresis, antithesis, and oxymoron.

Baudelaire successfully combined the grand manner ("Be a poet

always, even in prose. Grand style . . ." [OC, p. 670]) and classical diction
("Nothing is more beautiful than the commonplace" [OC, p. 670]) with
brutal realism and with the casual, colloquial, and conversational style.
His lyricism is basically oratorical; *Les Fleurs* abounds in apostrophes,
invocations, rhetorical questions, exclamations, enumerations, person-
ifications, allegories, archaisms, sententious sentences, proper nouns,
and abstract nouns. He also tends to use nouns in a generic sense, the
generic plural, for instance: *les chats, les aveugles, les femmes damnées —*

> Les amoureux fervents et les savants austères

and the generic singular—

> And the man is tired of writing and the woman of loving.

He also uses vague, generic adjectives, even in the erotic poetry: *profond,
long, vaste, divin, plein, beau, grand.*[6] This is due in part to the fact that
Baudelaire's is a lyrical "poetry of ideas." He once claimed that poetry is
always, although involuntarily, philosophical, and has explicitly expressed his enthusiasm for abstractions: "Enthusiasm applied to anything other than abstractions is a sign of weakness or sickness" *(Fusées).*
But as Laforgue noted, Baudelaire was also one of the first modern poets
to use a crude simile or prosaic word to introduce a note of flatness in the
middle of a harmonious period, and he will often switch suddenly from
the solemn to the ludicrous or from excitement to anticlimax, creating a
type of irony that Corbière and Laforgue were to develop successfully.[7]

> Our soul is a three-master searching for its Icaria;
> A voice resounds on the deck: "Keep a sharp eye!"
> A voice from the crow's nest, ardent and wild, shouts:
> "Love . . . glory . . . bliss!" Hell, it's a reef!
>
> ("Le Voyage")

Erich Auerbach has studied sympathetically a stylistic trait for which
Baudelaire was roundly criticized by his contemporaries: strange and
violent contrasts between the lofty and solemn tone established by traditional rhetorical devices and, on the other hand, the indignity of the
subject treated and the abjectness of many details.[8] A Baudelairean love
sonnet can begin with what appears to be a ritual compliment to the lady
and to the poet's own "haughty rhymes" that will confer immortality
upon her—

> I offer you these verses so that if my name
> Happily reaches far-distant ages. . . .
>
> ("Je te donne. . . ," 39)

But the apostrophe developed in the tercets combines, on the one hand, an apotheosis of adoration ("angel") and admiration ("statue") and, on the other, a bitter curse, producing a bizarre coupling of laudation and imprecation.

> Cursèd creature, to whom from the deep abyss
> To the height of heaven, none replies but me!

Even in those love poems where the beloved is treated as a Muse, a Madonna, or an Angel there is always a slight hint of irony; the hyperboles are not sarcastic, but they smack of ambivalence, especially when the poems are read in the context of the entire cycle.

In "Au Lecteur" Baudelaire uses the conventional devices of moral declamation and religious oratory: personification, enumeration, periodic syntax, the abuse of synonyms and reiteration ("yelping," "howling," "grumbling," "crawling"), traditional metonymies of instrument (the dagger, poison) and of effect-for-cause ("vile tears" for hypocritical remorse), the archaism (*appas* for "charms"), noble clichés of the elevated style ("the muddy path," "wash away our stains")—but the poet will also deflate the lofty tonality with grotesque similes.

> And we feed our pleasant remorse
> As beggars feed their lice.
> . . . .
> Just like an indigent débauché, who kisses and eats
> The martyrized breast of an old whore,
> We steal in passing a clandestine pleasure
> That we squeeze very hard like an old orange.

Similarly, the rhetorical phrase "a host of Demons" is deflated by a grotesque image ("like a million intestinal worms") and a colloquial verb (*ribote*, "goes on a binge").[9]

What Auerbach has called "breaches of style" and what Brunetière called Baudelaire's "genius for stylistic impropriety" has been analyzed by Jean Royère as catachresis. For Royère, catachresis is any trope—but especially simile, metaphor, hyperbole, and metonymy—that offends logic but expresses an emotional truth or renders a visual image compelling, suggestive, or impressionistic (e.g., "blue hair"). Most often it involves the concretization ("physication") and elaboration of an abstraction, producing "concrete thoughts" or "sonorous and pictural ideas." The tropes range from the unexpected but immediately comprehensible (e.g., eyes shining like boutiques, swelling breasts equated with a beautiful *armoire*, the rhythmic movements of a beautiful young woman bringing to mind a sleek ship going out to sea)—that is, images in which the ground of the simile or metaphor, the relation between tenor and vehicle, is obvious—to the logically bizarre (e.g., a sun that doesn't "stagger" in horror, a bottle of perfume that "remembers").

A striking example of catachresis concretizing the abstract is found in "Hymne à la Beauté." Like wine, Beauty's look "pours out" good and evil *(le bienfait et le crime);* Destiny, bewitched, follows her skirts like a faithful dog; Honor is one of her charming jewels; one of her dearest trinkets, Murder, dances lovingly on her proud belly. Beauty then becomes a candle toward which the dazzled butterfly flies willingly to its death. Beauty's lover looks like a dying man caressing his tomb.

Other catachreses juxtapose incongruous or discordant images in which, for example, passionate love is mingled, as above, with thoughts of death, a compliment is tempered by an insult, or a description is composed of elements drawn from vastly different semantic fields or connotative values.

In one of the draft prefaces for *Les Fleurs* Baudelaire indicated one of his literary strategies as that of joining "contrary words." Often it is the joining of the concrete to the abstract.

mystic attic	the claws of love
mystic food	the foam of pleasure
mystic eyes	the whip of Pleasure
magic grottoes	the pillow of evil
magic curves	the naked and crimson breasts
celestial harvests	of temptation[10]

Often it is the coupling of positive and negative terms. The main effect achieved by the latter is a moral irony designed to shake or shock the reader out of his complacency and force him to see the world with the poet's ambivalent and dualistic vision. The two terms of his antitheses are brought so close together that they form ironic *alliances de mots.*

decrepit and charming	black and yet luminous
charming and sepulchral	monsters, o martyrs
sublime and ridiculous	pious women, lechers
bitter and delicious	Madonna, my mistress
infernal and divine	o sweetness, o poison

We *gaily* return to the *muddy* paths.

In *repugnant* objects we find *sweet charms.*

That *wingèd* voyager, how *awkward* and *feeble!*

As moral ironist, the poet speaks of "the pleasing designs" of crime, of the soft "pillow of evil," of the harsh "whip of Pleasure, that mercilous torturer," of débauchés returning home "broken by their work," of the brow of thieves and lesbians grown pale by their "work," and of the "martyrized breast of an old whore." The brutal pictures of big city life in "Tableaux parisiens" are prefaced by a poet wishing to lie under the open sky in order "to compose chastely" his "eclogues."

The ironic juxtaposition of opposites reaches its climax in the frequently recurring oxymoron, which the poet uses to put into stark relief the ironic *simultaneity* of two conflicting impulses, feelings, or moral judgments clashing in the consciousness of a single being. It underscores the inescapable dualism of man's nature, his "connivance in corruption" (Nathaniel Wing), and expresses the poet's "alchemy of pain," his negative capability of changing no longer mud into gold, but gold into base metal, paradise into hell.

smiling Regret	hideous delights
pleasant remorse	spiritual flesh
pleasant pestilence	magnificent carcass
pleasant horror	filthy grandeur
dear poison	sublime ignominy
dear Beelzebub	savory pain
funereal gaiety	prosperous litter
fearsome pleasures	icy sun
frightful pleasures	

It was Marcel Ruff, I believe, who noted that Baudelaire's oxymorons are distinctive in that they are not used simply as arresting or imaginatively compelling stylistic devices; the poet *believes* in them.

7

Ambivalent and Uncertain Irony in Flaubert's *Madame Bovary*

> The comic reaching the extreme, the comic
> that does not make one laugh . . . is for me
> what is most appealing as a writer.
> (Letter to Louise Colet)

WHEN teaching Flaubert in the classroom, I often have occasion to speak of his "realistic irony." The task of this chapter is to demonstrate how Flaubert can be a producer of both "realistic" and "romantic" irony, often simultaneously.

By "realistic irony" I mean irony that belittles, disparages, or deflates a character while managing to maintain the realistic author's apparent objectivity, self-effacement, impassivity, impartiality, and impersonality, his (impossible) goal of being, like God, everywhere present but nowhere visible. The depersonalized and unidentified narrator will not wink at the reader, cast knowing glances at him, or nudge him with the overt signals of rhetorical irony. He makes the reader feel the ironic perspective strictly from the choice of detail: biographical "facts" that speak for themselves or "objective" descriptions and scenes that interpret themselves. The author's commentary is, one might say, a *sous-commentaire;* it is not directly expressed by the narrator but only inferred by the reader from the "almost cinematographical manipulation of detail" (Harry Levin). Erich Auerbach speaks of "pure pictures."

Clear examples of realistic irony are provided in Flaubert's celebrated short story, *Un Coeur simple.* In one passage the naive and simple-minded heroine is impressed with Monsieur Bourais.

114

> She opened [the door] with pleasure for Monsieur Bourais, a former attorney. His white tie and his baldness, the ruffle on his shirt, his ample brown coat, his way of taking snuff by rounding his arm, his entire person produced in her that agitation inspired in us by the sight of extraordinary men.[1]

The irony here turns on the deflation of the honorific term that ends the passage. This is not rhetorical irony since the antiphrasis that develops is not the result of direct insinuation; it results strictly from the selection of detail. The "extraordinary" Monsieur Bourais is not a handsome young man; he is a "former attorney," that is, retired and presumably old. He is bald, and his coat is "ample" because he is fat. There are intimations, but *not* direct insinuations, that he is pretentious: the frilly ruffle and the affected manner in which he takes snuff. The reader is not told of pretentiousness or affectation but infers this simply from the narrator's insistence on the gesture. The "us" of the last clause, meaning, first, the common run of humanity and, second, a shared perspective between narrator and reader, is ironic without being an actual insinuation. It indicates a norm that is violated by Felicity since the object of her admiration seems unworthy of "us."

Another example is found on the same page. After deflating, with traditional irony, Felicity's "literary" education, which consisted entirely of listening to a child's explanation of the pictures in a geography book—the only book she had ever looked at in her life—the narrator of *Un Coeur simple* tells us that the children's formal education was furnished by a certain Guyot, "a poor devil employed at the Town Hall, famous for his fine handwriting and who enjoyed rubbing his pocket knife against his boot." The suggestion of Guyot's pedagogical incompetence is accomplished without offering the slightest commentary (except for the vague "poor devil") but by simply showing (through the use of the iterative past tense) a tic, the habitual gesture of a petty bourgeois of peasant stock rubbing his pocket knife against his heavy boot.

Examples of this type of irony abound in *Madame Bovary*. The narrator condemns most of the characters simply by letting them perform typical actions or letting them speak for themselves in direct discourse or in "free indirect discourse." Homais, the bumptious pedant who tries to pass for the village intellectual, is not directly ridiculed by the narrator; there is no need for him to do so since Homais is condemned in the reader's eyes by the words the author puts in the character's mouth, as

when Homais calls his mere looking at a thermometer scientific "observations," when he gratuitously converts twenty-four degrees Réaumur
to fifty-four degrees Fahrenheit, or when he tells his interlocutors
that his God is the God of Voltaire, Rousseau, Franklin, and . . .
Béranger.

Emma's lovers, Léon and Rodolphe, are most often ridiculed without the narrator having to pass explicit subjective judgment on them; for
example, those scenes in which Emma and Léon engage in a ritualistic
exchange of clichés. In one such scene Emma, hypocritically and self-
pityingly, laments her useless existence: "If only our sorrows could be of
use to someone, one could console oneself in the thought of sacrifice."[2]
Léon immediately concurs of course: "Léon started praising virtue, duty
and silent immolations, having himself an incredible need for self-
sacrifice that he could not assuage" (p. 309). The narrator makes no
comment at all (the thought expressed in the last clause being in the *style
indirect libre* and thus attributable only to the character), but the force of
the *passé simple*—"Léon started praising . . ."—signals to the reader a
too-automatic and hypocritical reply suggesting that the narrator pro-
nounces the "incredible need for self-sacrifice" with a subtle smirk. And
when Emma goes on to say that it is a pity she did not die from her
illness, for she would no longer be suffering now, "Léon immediately
envied *the calm of the grave*" (p. 309). While the end of the sentence
offers an overt signal of irony, the underlining, which is the equivalent
here of sarcastic quotation marks indicating an empty cliché to be attributed to the character rather than the narrator, the irony at the beginning of the sentence is conveyed simply by the adverb "immediately,"
which reinforces the *passé simple* and signals—without commentary
again—an automatic and hypocritical response.

But the case of Charles Bovary is more complex. Charles is the
victim of this same realistic irony that deflates him without explicit
commentary, but the irony is no longer one-dimensional and one-
directional. Flaubert ridicules Charles, but not totally and not mer-
cilessly; there is in the irony an admixture not of great admiration
certainly, but of muted and perhaps grudging respect, of mild sympathy
and, at times, mild pathos.

The novel's first word, "we," presents us with a first-person narrator
who, after introducing Charles to us, disappears suddenly and completely from the story. This "we," which has intrigued, baffled, and

annoyed critics for over a century, has been explained by Sartre as a device by which the author puts himself on the side of the mockers by presenting Charles's character in all its opacity, but objectively, *"from the outside" (L'Idiot de la famille* 2:1202; Sartre's italics). The "we" of Madame Bovary is not unrelated, I think, to the "us" of *Un Coeur simple;* in both cases it represents a norm (of intelligence merely, not of ethical values) from which the deflated character departs. And in both cases it is used in the service of realistic irony since the generalized "we" creates a depersonalized narrator who does not speak for himself alone.

We immediately learn an objective fact: Charles, who is entering "the fifth form," should be in a higher grade because of his age. We learn this not from the narrator but from the headmaster, who is introducing Charles to his proctor. Then there is a visual form of objective irony: the new boy, who is so much taller than his younger classmates, will be allowed, if his work and conduct are deserving, to join "les grands," the older boys. Thus, this "country's boy's" very physical appearance will be a constant reminder to his mocking classmates from the city—the "we"—that he is an awkward creature of below-average intelligence.

Later, when Charles is a student at the Collège de Rouen, his below-average intelligence is indicated by another objective fact: it is only by dint of applying himself diligently that he manages to keep "near" the average of his class.

Still later, when pursuing his medical studies, Charles takes an impressive array of courses—anatomy, pathology, physiology, pharmacy, chemistry, botany, clinical practice, therapeutics, hygiene—but he doesn't understand a word. The irony is produced not only by the objective fact of Charles's incomprehension but by the structure and sequence of the sentences. A resounding enumeration is followed by an abrupt anticlimax.

The seeming plethora of minutiae in *Madame Bovary* has a dual function: it is used in the service of traditional realism—or, if you prefer, the referential illusion (a convincing accumulation of the *effet de réel*)— and it is used in the service of realistic irony, that is, the replacement of direct commentary by circumstantial detail that the reader, *on his own initiative,* interprets as insinuations.

But the irony of which Charles is the victim is more complex than that aimed at Homais, Léon, Rodolphe, or Father Bournisien. The author does not hide from us the positive side of his character. While it is

true that Charles does not understand the theoretical or even the practical side of the medical profession, he does possess an admirable earnestness of purpose: "He worked hard, however, he had purchased bound
notebooks, he took every course, he did not miss a single hospital round"
(p. 29). In context the sentence is a development of the same theme—
Charles's lack of intelligence—and prepares for the image of the stupid
workhorse that immediately follows. But it does more; it indicates
Charles's positive qualities: perseverance, assiduousness, conscientious-
ness. This positive side of his character is suggested even in the famous
description of his cap at the beginning of the novel. The cap—a
monstrosity that Charles has concocted by combining elements of the fur
bonnet, the military cap, the round hat, the otter-skin cap, and the
cotton bonnet—is "one of those pathetic things . . . the mute ugliness of
which has depths of expression like the face of an imbecile." The cap—
shapeless from having too many shapes—symbolizes the lack of intelligence and taste of its owner-creator but also his good qualities, the same
ones as noted above. Flaubert suggests these qualities at several different
points in the novel along with another quality that the heroine lacks: a
warm heart.

The case of Emma is still more complex. The author ridicules
her—often with objective, realistic irony—but not only does he suggest
certain good qualities in her, he partially identifies with her and forces
his readers to do the same, although, again, only partially.

The episode of Emma's wedding is an exercise in objective, "realistic" description. Flaubert insists on the external details. There is, for
example, a leisurely description of the variety of carriages that arrive at
the wedding and later a lengthy description of the wedding cake, which
becomes symbolic and ironic through the mere selection of detail, and
even more ironic when the reader makes a retroactive connection between the cake and the cap worn by Charles as a schoolboy. The cake
and the cap (and the architecture of the pharmacy in Yonville that
echoes them ironically later on) are complicated, several-tiered structures exhibiting a grotesque mixture of styles; both are supreme examples of bad taste. The omniscient narrator does not even bother to use
his omniscience to report the inner feelings of the wedding couple—a
narrative decision subtly signaling to the reader that their feelings are
not worth reporting.

When, in the novel's sixth chapter, the narrator does report on
Emma's inner life, it is done mainly with realistic irony; we are given

facts, not commentary, value judgments, or Balzacian opinions and generalizations. For example, whenever she went to confession as an adolescent schoolgirl, she invented little sins in order to stay there longer in the mysterious and romantic atmosphere of the confessional. When, in the Sunday sermons, Christ was referred to as the heavenly fiancé, the celestial husband and lover—the priest no doubt playing to the celibate and sexually frustrated nuns of the convent school by exploiting the clichés of the convent—Emma's sensual religiosity is stirred again. Unbeknownst to the nuns she manages to get her hands on some popular romantic novels whose stereotyped heroes are clichés on legs; they are "brave as lions, gentle as lambs," and "cry like urns." The historical novels of Walter Scott initiate her into romantic escapism; she imagines herself sitting by the casement window of a medieval manor, spending her days watching a white-plumed knight galloping toward her on a black steed. Such biographical and psychological facts are piled up in paragraph after paragraph in support of one of those rare sentences in which Flaubert drops the mask of impartiality and explicitly condemns the egocentrism and sentimentalism of his heroine (and, implicitly, of romantic art):

> It was necessary that she be able to draw from things a sort of personal profit; she rejected as useless anything that did not contribute to the immediate gratification of her heart,—being by nature more sentimental than artistic, seeking emotions and not landscapes. (Pp. 63–64)

Flaubert uses many other forms of irony that avoid direct commentary or insinuation. For example, the ironic reversal of Emma's expectations produces dramatic and situational irony. Her marriage turns out to be not the expected escape from, but an imprisonment within, tedium and boredom. Later, adultery turns out to be not an escape from, but a continuation of "all the platitudes of marriage."

Flaubert also manages to make his ironic points without direct commentary by the subtle manner in which he controls narrative point of view. After the beginning chapters, the omniscient narrator often slyly withdraws and allows us to see the unfolding events mainly in the eyes of one or another of the characters, especially, but not exclusively, Emma's. There is, in fact, an ironic rotation of points of view that prevents us from seeing things from a single vantage point.

The shifting viewpoints in *Madame Bovary* create a generalized ambivalence reinforced by the subtle changes in aesthetic distance. As Benjamin Bart explains: "When the distance remains considerable, irony is usually present and bitter. The distance sometimes narrows, however, and the irony becomes gentler or even disappears."[3] Flaubert creates his ironic distance not through the transparent devices of rhetorical irony but through the subtle handling of point of view just mentioned, through a network of ironic cross-references, implicit analogies, and unobtrusive symbols (e.g., butterflies suggesting the frivolousness and fragile morality of *une femme qui papillonne*—a woman who flits about like a butterfly, from one man to another), and through ironic counterpoint, as in the famous scene at the Agricultural Fair.

A subtle technique that contributes to this generalized ambivalence and lends itself simultaneously to both realistic and romantic irony is the insistent use of the *style indirect libre*. We are given—without commentary and without "authorial grammatical intervention" (John P. Houston)— Emma's thoughts and words, which tend to make us sympathize and identify with her. But these words and thoughts are uttered not by her directly but by the narrator, who does not interrupt his narration or his basic narrative tense, the *imparfait*. The precise borderline between dialogue and narration (i.e., between two distinct points of view) is blurred. Emma's thoughts are thus *filtered by another consciousness*. An ironic distance or screen is placed between the heroine and the reader despite the psychological close-up. To take a single example:

> She kept repeating to herself: "I have a lover! a lover!" reveling in this idea as in that of another puberty that she would have reached suddenly. . . .
>
> Moreover, Emma was experiencing the satisfaction of revenge. Hadn't she suffered enough? (P. 219)

In the last sentence we are given the privileged observer's direct view into Emma's mind: the thoughts, the very words, the very *intonation*. But at the same time we are aware of the ambiguity created by both the presence and the *voice* of the narrator (the voice that quotes Emma directly in the first sentence and that is *still speaking here*). One senses that the narrator is not in total agreement with the sentiment expressed in the last sentence, that Emma is exaggerating her suffering and is deceiving herself once again. She is not a superior woman worthy of an extraordinary husband; she has simply married a man even more mediocre than herself.

We are dealing here with romantic irony or, better, with a new development of it, because we have the double-edged or two-directional point of view, an ambiguous and ambivalent amalgam of identification and alienation.[4]

The mobility and instability of point of view in *Madame Bovary* create a great uncertainty in the mind of the reader as to how to pass any kind of final judgment on the heroine. Emma emerges from the novel neither as a tragic heroine—she does not possess enough dignity for that—nor as a comic heroine; there is, despite the mirthless humor and comedy of which she is the butt, too much sympathy and identification established for that. We can both blame her and pity her; we cannot measure her. We sense that Flaubert, while castigating Emma's specific and concrete aspirations, sympathizes with her yearning for self-realization. "What she desires—furnishing her house, Léon, Rodolphe—may be petty, but her desire itself—to transcend Yonville—is neither tawdry nor wrong" (B. F. Bart, *Flaubert,* p. 318).

The narrator's attitude toward his heroine remains ambiguous and ambivalent from beginning to end. The negative edge of the irony—the negative pole of the ambivalence—is clearly felt, but as in the case of Charles and even more so, we also feel the presence of a modicum of muted sympathy and empathy, so that we are not surprised when the author tells us, after the fact, that he has identified with the victim of his cruel irony, that "Bovary, c'est moi." We are clearly shown the many weaknesses of the heroine, but the author goes to some pains to make us aware also of the extenuating circumstances: Emma's unfortunate (i.e., romantic) education, a matter more of chance than choice, the mediocrity and callousness, in fact the downright *bêtise,* of all the men in her life.

*

Lilian Furst, who brilliantly summarizes most of Flaubert's major ironic devices, feels that they do not add up to romantic irony. She sees Emma as an enigma, not a paradox, in "a world that can be evaluated with certainty" *(Fictions of Romantic Irony,* p. 42), and she sees Flaubert as a traditional ironist, one whose irony is amenable to "reasonably confident reconstruction" (p. 84). But in the light of this assessment she makes some startling admissions and self-contradictions. She admits on the same page, for instance, that the novel's focalization "is so variable and the shifts of viewpoint so rapid and elusive that it is difficult to determine who speaks or from where" and that in the portrayal of Emma and Charles the fluctuations in ironic stance are most disconcerting; on page 75 that "the mobility of viewpoint and the withdrawal of the omniscient narrator behind his protagonists' view deprives [sic] us of ultimate assurance"; on page 78 that "the very technique that allows the reader to see the alternative view also puts onto him a burden of choice such as never faces him in *Pride and Prejudice*"; and on page 79 that "the shifting viewpoint undercuts every position, leaving the reader in an uncertainty tantalizing in its resistance to resolution." What happened to that "reasonably confident reconstruction"?

In a curious statement Furst claims: "The fragility of the viewpoint is counteracted by a firmness of perspective" (p. 91). And in an even more curious statement she says that Flaubert's position "is one of certainty except in regard to Emma and Charles" (p. 91). This, of course, is a very large exception!

Furst's problem is that she is emphasizing the unambiguous irony focused on the minor characters who serve as the furniture of Emma's world and is de-emphasizing what the author stresses when dealing with the heroine: an uncertain irony that cannot be easily resolved or reconstructed.

In attacking Emma's romantic mentality Flaubert is desperately trying to disgorge the persistent vestiges of his own. The resultant ambivalence is one of the chief sources of his romantic irony. Morton Gurewitch ("European Romantic Irony") puts the matter this way:

> The romantic ironist blends romantic ardor with an anti-romantic animus. (P. 3)

> Flaubert walked the tightrope of romantic irony with much preliminary tigerish ardor and anguish. . . . And he let it be known, not only in *Madame Bovary* but also in *The Sentimental Education* that romanticism is both inspiration and sick nerves, both elixir and destructiveness. (P. 131)

Romantic irony could be defined in terms of such ambivalence alone, although the definition is unnecessarily reductive. We do find this ambivalence toward "the romantic" in Schlegel, Byron, Musset, Stendhal, Gautier, and Baudelaire as well as Flaubert; in Sterne and Diderot the relevant term is *sensibility*. A broader view, however, would include the radical indeterminacy of meaning such ambivalent irony deliberately produces. In his correspondence Flaubert often claims that the greatest works of art, those that unleash the power to dream, are "incomprehensible"—a claim akin to Schlegel's notion of incomprehensibility as an artistic virtue. Flaubert also admitted on several occasions his desire to baffle the reader. And early in his career he had dreams of a text so written that the reader would not know whether he is being made fun of or not. Another Flaubertian attribute directly related to Schlegel is a self-consciousness that "turns into an ironic and parodistic strategy that blurs genres and becomes . . . creatively deconstructive" (Victor Brombert, "Status of the Subject," p. 104). Roland Barthes (S/Z, p. 140) tells us that Flaubert's is "an irony impregnated with uncertainty . . . one never knows if he is responsible for what he writes." Who is speaking and from where? Postmodernist critics have stressed the ways in which Flaubert's text eludes meaning: its subversion of traditional narrative, its thematic elusiveness, its devaluation of content, its antimimetic and self-referential nature, its semiotic excess that foregrounds the *signifiant* at the expense of the *signifié*, "the excess of the sign which, more than and other than its own referent, imperiously insists on its own primacy."[5]

Jonathan Culler has investigated the strategies by which Flaubert attempts to make the novel an aesthetic object rather than a communicative act, an autonomous system of functional relations that are to be aesthetically admired rather than decoded as parts of a message. Like Barthes, he stresses Flaubert's "uncertain irony" produced, for example, by the disconcerting rotation of narrative point of view in *Madame Bovary* and by the fact that not a single character of importance in the novel suggests alternative ways of living or provides ethical norms in terms of which Emma's deviance can be characterized. Flaubert's style, then, becomes the instrument of what Hegel and Kierkegaard, in connection with Schlegelian irony, called "infinite absolute negativity," an irony that suggests no alternatives to its negatives. One simply does not know where the author stands. Culler concludes,

> We seem to be faced, then, with a version of what is often called Romantic irony: the posture of a work which contains within itself an awareness of the fact that while pretending to give a true account of reality it is in fact fiction and that one must view with an ironic smile the act of writing a novel in the first place. *(Flaubert: The Uses of Uncertainty,* pp. 210–12)

Even Lilian Furst has admitted (*Fictions of Romantic Irony*, p. 91) that Flaubert's wavering stance in *Madame Bovary* may reflect an irony executed at his own expense; the author mocks and censures his own inclination to empathize with his victim. Such self-irony is, of course, another sure sign of romantic irony.[6]

*

The vastness of Flaubert's ambivalence and of the uncertainty that results can be seen in those passages in which the aesthetic distance narrows considerably and the irony almost disappears. The narrowing of the distance in such passages is so considerable that even a perceptive critic like B. F. Bart can claim, erroneously, that the irony has completely disappeared.

Here is one such passage:

> Then she remembered the heroines of the books she had read and the lyrical legion of those adulterous women began to sing in her memory with voices as of sisters which captivated her. (P. 219)

Bart says ("Art, Energy and Aesthetic Distance," p. 90) that we are invited not to analyze Emma's emotions here, but to live them vicariously with her and to feel with her. But there are three signals of irony in the "lyrical legion of those adulterous women": the pejorative "legion," the alliteration, and the demonstrative which, like the pluperfect tense later on, points back to the ironic perspective of the chapter that first told us of Emma's dangerous readings and her dangerous (and ludicrous) identifications with such heroines. Even without the signals, the pressure of the entire context, the macrocontext, forces the reader to read this as a *continuation* of the ironic perspective so painstakingly established up to this point. That is, our perception of irony is governed by a formal expectation derived from our sense of the function of earlier descriptions.[7]

The passage continues:

> She was becoming herself a veritable part of these fictions and, realizing the long reverie of her youth, she saw herself as that type of lover she had so much envied. (P. 219)

The "long reverie of her youth" takes the reader back to the devastating ironies of the beginning, as do the specific pointers: the demonstratives ("these fictions"; "that type of lover") and the pluperfect that concludes the sentence. Bart claims (p. 92) that the reader now "accepts Emma's feelings as valid and joins with her. Irony has disappeared." But the irony has not disappeared, and if Emma's feelings were felt as perfectly valid, *Madame Bovary* would be little better than those second-rate romantic novels so violently condemned by Flaubert at the beginning of his own novel.

Here is another such passage:

> But if there existed somewhere a strong and handsome being, a valorous nature, full of both exaltation and refinement, a poet's heart in the form of an angel, a lyre with brazen strings, sounding, heavenward, elegiac epithalamia, why, perchance, would she not find him? Oh! what an impossibility! Nothing moreover was worth the trouble of a search; everything was deceitful! Every smile hid a yawn of boredom, every joy a curse, every pleasure its unpleasant aftertaste, and the best of kisses left on your lip an unachievable desire for a higher passion. (P. 368)

Bart says (p. 96) that we are drawn closer to Emma here and the irony is entirely suspended, "and we join with her in her disabused view of life." But surely we cannot accept her sudden switch from one extreme— romantic illusion—to the other extreme of total and facile cynicism. Flaubert's main signals of irony are the enumeration of idealized creatures in the first sentence and the accumulation of cynical hyperboles: "*Nothing* . . . was worth the trouble"; "*everything* was deceitful"; "*every* smile"; "*every* joy"; "*curse*"; "*every* pleasure"; "the *best* of kisses." Other ironic signals are the alliterated "elegiac epithalamia" and the mock-heroic exclamation, "Oh! what an impossibility!" The *style indirect libre* and the immediacy of the imperfect tense narrow the aesthetic distance, but we still feel the ironic presence and voice of the narrator whom we can well imagine smiling condescendingly at this petulant self-pity and exaggerated disillusionment. It may be true that Flaubert was often guilty of such "immature cynicism" (Martin Turnell) and of a neurotic view of life (Sartre), as evidenced in his correspondence, in his autobiographical juvenilia and even, arguably, in *Madame Bovary* itself. But in the passage under discussion Flaubert is parodying, not parading, his own weakness.

Bart goes on to say of this passage: "No writer will use irony when a character is phrasing the author's own intimate beliefs: it would destroy the point he is trying to make, his 'thesis' " (p. 97). But an apotheosis of cynicism is not the point Flaubert is trying to make. The author does feel that his heroine merits some measure of pity and that her cynicism is in some measure justified, but *not* to the degree she does. Irony lurks behind every hyperbole and behind every exclamation mark in the novel, and there is a striking convergence of them here. The irony of this passage is not contemptuous but is condescending enough to maintain the author's invincible ambivalence.

Bart's greatest error is in his evaluation of the novel's conclusion and then of the novel as a whole.

> If the book is to achieve towering stature, it must in the end forthrightly elect either irony or pity as its foundation and erect thereon a structure which will be conditioned by that basis. Within the shorter compass of a play it had long been clear that the choice had to be made at the outset: if tragedy were sought, aesthetic distance had to be maintained and a sympathetic pity evoking pathos had to be eschewed. The longer forms, the epic for instance, gave ample proof that a greater compass permitted wider ranges in aesthetic distance during the course of the work; for the conclusion, however, the requirements were as rigid as for drama. The novel, for which Flaubert was trying to establish new molds, seems to be equally rigid. The complementary polarities, irony-pity and tragedy-pathos, must be resolved in Emma's last moments.
>
> Flaubert must finally hammer out in unmistakable terms the meaning he finds in her life: inconsistency will mean a book that falters in the end, when it should rather be rising to a clear conclusion. (Pp. 98–99)

There are already several problematic areas here, even before we look at Bart's detailed analysis of the passage that presents the end of Emma's life. First, the a priori dogma that Flaubert must resolve the irony-pity polarity, that is, the ambivalence, and that all novels must have a clear conclusion. Ever since Flaubert (i.e., largely thanks to him), ambivalence, unclear conclusions, and the eschewal of closure are found in some of the finest works of modern fiction. The uncertainty is part of what makes them modern, not only from a technical point of view but from the point of view of the modern sensibility. Second, the a priori notion that the novel, like the epic, has "rigid" constraints with regard to its conclusion. On the contrary, the novel is distinguished from other genres precisely by its aesthetic freedom in both form and content. Third, the a priori notion that Flaubert was trying to mold his novel into a tragedy. On the contrary, Flaubert, commenting specifically on *Madame Bovary*, explicitly affirmed that tragedy and bourgeois vulgarity are incompatible: "The *hideousness* of bourgeois subjects must replace the *tragic*, which is incompatible with them" (Letter to Louise Colet, November 29, 1853). A term such as *tragédie bourgeoise* would be for Flaubert an oxymoron.

Then there is the a priori notion that tragedy and pathos are incompatible. This flies in the face of a large critical consensus established ever since Aristotle that pity, like fear, is one of the defining ingredients of tragedy. Erich Auerbach is much closer to the truth when stating that, despite the fact that *Madame Bovary* is not a tragedy, there are times when the reader is moved to something like "tragic pity." There is an ideal aesthetic distance for tragedy; the reader cannot be so close to the protagonist that he cannot see the tragic flaw, nor can he be so far removed that he cannot identify with the hero or at least feel the pathos of his tragic situation. If the fluctuations in aesthetic distance in *Madame Bovary* mean that Flaubert has not observed the "rigid" and "severe" focus of classical tragedy, he nevertheless has remained faithful to the norms of the modern novel, which for many practitioners and theoreticians is a fundamentally ironic genre. Both Flaubert and his ungrateful descendant, Sartre, agree that the novel is an action presented from various and thus relativized points of view.

In demanding that Flaubert choose between irony or pity, Bart puts the author in a no-win situation. If he chooses irony, he has "demeaned" his potentially tragic heroine. If he chooses pity and pathos, according to Bart's rigid view of the tragic, Flaubert has eschewed "tragedy" altogether.

My thesis is that Flaubert is consistent, that he maintains the novel's principal perspective from beginning to end. The perspective does not involve an either/or choice between pity or irony; it is an ambivalent amalgam of pity *and* irony, with the emphasis on the latter. The ambivalence is maintained even in those passages of reduced aesthetic distance, and the novel, without ever achieving the status of tragedy, does possess tragic overtones, the tragic pity, however, *always* being tempered by irony.

Let us now examine the crucial passage itself.

> Emma, her chin against her chest, opened her eyes inordinately; and her poor hand dragged along the sheets with that hideous and

> gentle gesture of the dying who seem to want already to cover them-
> selves with the shroud. (P. 415)

Bart claims (p. 99) that the adjectives "poor" and "gentle" set a new tone:
"On the one hand, we do stand apart from Emma, observing her actions,
but not sharing them. . . . On the other hand, the appeal of her actions
('pauvres,' 'doux') breaks down the distance by calling directly upon our
emotions and seeking to make us personally involved in the scene." We
now have, says Bart, "unconcealed tenderness," and tenderness "invites
pathos," and pathos "is not consonant with the severity of tragedy" (pp.
99–100). While allowing that tenderness, when accompanied by nobility,
is permissible and may even heighten the tragedy, Bart concludes (p.
100) that "art," in Emma's death scene, "is giving place to sentiment."

But we must object. Art is the enemy not of sentiment but of sentimentality. Furthermore, Flaubert does not tell us that Emma's gesture is
"gentle"; it is described as "hideous and gentle," an oxymoron that preserves the ambivalence. In this context, and in the light of all that has
preceded this passage, even "poor" must be construed as the ambivalent
"pathetic," not simply as "much to be pitied."

Bart requires that Emma attain "nobility" (p. 102) if she is to become
a symbol of mankind. But the dying heroine hears the song of the ugly,
scrofulous Blindman outside her window.

> And Emma started to laugh, with an atrocious, frenetic, desperate
> laughter, thinking she was seeing the hideous face of the poor wretch
> who was standing in the eternal shadows like a figure of horror. (P. 418)

It is not just the blindness and the sickness that unite Emma to her
symbol; it is the epithet "hideous." Flaubert, true to the aesthetic an-
nounced in his letter to Louise Colet, emphasizes *la hideur* at the expense
of *le tragique*. Emma's demonic laughter, the last act of her life, symbolizes a bitter realization: her romantic illusion (her blindness) was
ludicrous; her inner nature is rotten. Like some horrified existentialist
on his deathbed, she has summed up her existence and made it into an
eternal essence (cf. "eternal shadows")—what non-Christians call failure
and what Christians call sin.

Another author could have given Emma an antidote to the arsenic,
saved her physically and later spiritually. Her sudden awareness could
have turned into a truly tragic awareness or epiphany and served as the

beginning of "a new life." But Flaubert scrupulously avoided this temptation. Emma has reached the logical end of her destiny: failure.

Bart sums up: Flaubert's long association with his heroine, even his battles with her, had drawn him close to her, and when writing the end of his novel, "he was no longer trying to treat it merely as a *sujet bourgeois,*" he was now "striving for tragedy" (p. 105). But he did not achieve his goal, says Bart. Emma does not emerge from the novel with enough dignity, despite the narrowed aesthetic distance at the end (which Bart had demanded and has been given!), to become a symbol of mankind. Bart notes, "We have stood off to condemn her too often for it to be satisfactory to accept her now as one of us, and a book which might have pointed the way toward a form of tragedy in the modern novel closes without achieving this stature" (p. 105).

But Emma does achieve a certain degree of symbolic value. Both her praiseworthy desire for self-actualization and her disgustingly self-indulgent *bovarysme* are endemic to human nature (the latter defined not within an essentialistic ontology but simply in terms of a vague and unmeasurable norm that allows human beings to generalize about themselves). What was said earlier of Julien Sorel could be said of her: let the reader who has never been guilty of self-deception cast the first stone. She is representative not only of Flaubert's but of a widespread view of mankind in that she is neither angel nor beast but a vivid example of Baudelaire's "double postulation," *homo duplex.* A true stoic (Flaubert, says one critic, is only a stoic comedian) would condemn her beyond all possibility of redemption or forgiveness; a true Christian (Flaubert, as Sartre says in *L'Idiot de la famille,* is a *chrétien malgré lui)* would sympathize and empathize with her irreducible dualism.

I agree that Flaubert did not manage to write a tragedy. Rather, he created an ironic and profoundly ambivalent work; *the irony itself is ambivalent.* If he failed to achieve something he never attempted, he succeeded in creating something he never heard of: romantic irony. The lack of nobility in the subject matter and the author's disconcerting ambivalence toward his material deprive *Madame Bovary* of the austere dignity of ancient tragedy, but at the same time they make of it, from this perspective and from several others, the first modern novel.

8

The Multiple Ironies of Black Humor: Michaux's *Plume*, "Clown"

I was born full of holes.

My heart, emptied periodically of its wickedness, is opened to goodness, and one could almost trust a little girl with me for a few hours.
(L'Espace du dedans)

THREE main roads lead from Baudelairean irony to that of the twentieth century: a masochistic self-irony—the *bourreau-victime* complex; a ferocious moral irony aimed not only at the poet himself but also at mankind in general and modern man in particular; and black humor, as found in certain moments of Baudelaire's satanism, sadism, and schadenfreude and those moments when he indulges in what Flaubert calls mirthless laughter and what Beckett calls dianoetic laughter, the laughter that laughs at itself and at what is unhappy. Whatever road one takes, one encounters Lautréamont, whose destructive, sadomasochistic humor is related to romantic irony in that it expresses not only revolt against traditional values but even attacks the author's ideas, his literary style, and his very being. Other forms of ironic ambivalence are found in the sardonic humor of Charles Cros, aimed principally at the straight people, "the people who are always right," in the wry, sickly smile of Corbière's "yellow laughter," his "bilious verve," aimed at himself as well as others, and especially in the bittersweet ironies of Laforgue.

In *Les Chants de Maldoror* Lautréamont presents us with a sadistically cruel hero, a frighteningly satanic creature whose self-proclaimed thirst for the infinite is in reality a form of inordinate pride, the desire "to equal God" in power and glory but as the incarnation of evil rather than good. He corrupts, seduces, rapes, and murders his victims with obvious relish. Like Genet, he speaks of the "sanctity" of crime and, like Genet again, uses the epithet "sublime" to describe scenes of crime and horror. The narrator himself identifies with this point of view and declares on two different occasions that the goal of his poem is nothing less than to attack man and The One who created him.

But this macabre tale, told by an obviously tortured consciousness, makes us laugh as much as it makes us shudder. Starting with the fourth canto, there is a radical change of dominant tone, from seriousness (or mock-seriousness—we are never quite sure) to black humor. From beginning to end, the work is filled with self-conscious devices that destroy the fictional illusion: the declamatory lyricism; the weird imagery and bizarre associations; the constant banter with the reader; the convoluted circumlocutions; the tongue-in-cheek pedantry displayed not only by the narrator and his hero but by every character in the work, including the young and the uneducated; the self-contradictions (e.g., when the narrator boasts about his concise style precisely after a particularly laborious and labyrinthine sentence); and the comic similes—

> beautiful as a scholarly paper on the curve described by a dog running after its master. (5.3)[1]

> beautiful as the law of arrested development in the chest of adults, whose propensity toward growth is not in direct correlation with the quantity of molecules assimilated by their organism. (5.3)

> beautiful . . . as the fortuitous encounter on a dissection table of a sewing machine and an umbrella. (6.3)

C. A. Hackett (*Modern French Poetry*, p. 124) speaks of Lautréamont's constant "use of irony to destroy the very means by which he achieves his effects." Imitating Byron and Gautier and anticipating Beckett, the narrator criticizes a figure of speech he has just composed: "All those tombs that are scattered in a cemetery like flowers in a prairie, a simile that lacks truth" (1.12).

The reader finds it difficult to take seriously a fiction riddled with metafictional comments such as these:

> I propose, without being moved, to declaim in a loud voice the serious and cold strophe that you are about to hear. (1.9)

I want this to be the last strophe of my invocation. (1.9)

If it is sometimes logical to rely on appearances, the first canto ends here. (1.14)

Alas! I should like to unfold my reasonings and my similes slowly and with much magnificence (but who disposes of his time?). (4.7)

We are no longer in the narration. (5.7)[2]

. . . divesting myself of the frivolous and skeptical style of ordinary conversation, and prudent enough not to . . . I forget what I intended to say, for I don't remember the beginning of this sentence. (6.2)

. . . every dramatic trick [truc à effet] will appear in due time and place, when the plot of this fiction sees no objection to it. (6.8)

A unique scene, this, which no novelist will ever equal! (6.9)

The author makes it impossible for the reader to measure the degree of seriousness and sincerity in this enigmatic work. Is the empirical author poking fun at the implied author, the narrator, and at himself? Is the whole thing a comic hoax? The narrator declares that he is not certain that what he asserts is true (4.1) and warns the reader that the latter's most unshakable convictions are shaky and that there exists a universal uncertainty principle, a law of indeterminacy:

It is not useful for you to encrust yourself in the cartilaginous carapace of an axiom that you believe to be unshakable. There are other axioms too that are unshakable and that walk parallel to your own. (5.1)

Charles Cros's humour noir, so greatly admired by André Breton and the surrealists, is directed generally at the self-satisfied bourgeois, as in "Red Herring":

I have composed this story—simple, simple, simple,
To infuriate people who are grave, grave, grave,
And to amuse children—little, little, little.[3]

But his attack against the vain and "grave" bourgeois is done with a self-conscious playfulness that points to the poem's own artifices. The poem is an attack but also a joke. Even in his most serious poems, expressing deep-felt and often painful feelings, the seriousness is often tempered by the playfulness of the rhyme schemes and of the rhymes themselves. Many poems create an all-pervasive irony that ricochets back onto the serious passages. At one point the poet dismisses all his poems as "bibelots d'emplois incertains"—trinkets of uncertain uses.

Tristan Corbière fulfills Morton Gurewitch's requirements for a romantic ironist: the mixture of romanticism and antiromanticism. While Corbière's major themes are romantic, especially the expression of a tormented existence, his work is a violent reaction against romantic tonality and style, against lyricism, self-pitying sentimentality, and grandiloquence. His antidotes are humor, often self-deprecating humor, and a poetics of instability, of "bad" taste, of intentional cacophony and unbalanced rhythms, a grating abruptness of style, and in general the eschewal of any device that smacks of conventional writing or conventional feeling. Pierre-Olivier Walzer, in the introduction to the Pléiade edition of *Les Amours jaunes*, says that the poet polishes his verses to give them the appearance of something spontaneous and *un*finished. This is accomplished by violent contrasts in tone and imagery, rough-hewn versification, "chaotic" enumerations in Spitzer's sense, and a plethora of gratuitous punctuation—dashes, colons, suspension points, italics, capitalization—that create staccato effects, indeed harsh static.

Self-irony, self-mockery, and self-contradiction are other components of Corbière's romantic irony. Verlaine called him "the Disdainful One and the Mocker of everything and everyone, including himself." In his important autobiographical poem, "Epitaphe," for example, he describes himself thus:

> He killed himself with ardor, or died from laziness.
> If he still lives, it's an oversight. . . .
> [He was] an adulterous mixture of everything.
> . . . .
> Nerves—without nerve. Vigor without strength.
> . . . .
> A poet, despite his verse;
> An artist without art. . . .
> . . . .
> An actor, he didn't learn his lines.
> Misunderstood—especially by himself.
> . . . .
> Too naive, being too cynical.
> . . . .
> Believing in nothing, believing everything.
> . . . .

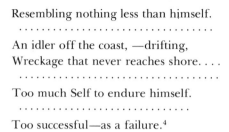

Resembling nothing less than himself.
....
An idler off the coast, —drifting,
Wreckage that never reaches shore. . . .
....
Too much Self to endure himself.
....
Too successful—as a failure.[4]

In "Le Poète contumace" ("The In-absentia Poet") he says of himself,

The thing is certain,
It's really me, I'm really here—but like an erasure.[5]

C. A. Hackett *(Modern French Poetry,* p. 226) has said that Laforgue's use of irony makes his work a complete contrast to that of the romantics. This is not true since Laforguean irony is directly descended from romantic irony; in fact, it *is* romantic irony. As Henri Peyre points out in his essay "Laforgue among the Symbolists" (p. 45), "Ever since the romantics . . . irony has served to convey the contrast between the author's assertion of his own freedom and his realization that he cannot reach the infinite of his dreams; his creation remains finite and paltry, and the creator can only look at it with mockery." "Paltry" is precisely Laforgue's estimate of himself and his work.

He will take a serious romantic theme, for example, disgust with everyday reality, and invest it with an irony that deflates both the theme and the poet.

Ah! how daily is life . . .
And as true as one can remember
How paltry and ungifted one was.[6]

Laforgue's irony is informed by a feeling of the transience and futility of everything, including love and art. Once again, Vladimir Jankélévitch *(L'ironie ou la bonne conscience,* pp. 21–22) renders the feeling with precision:

Attrition or conversion—a feeling is eternal only until further notice! A definitive vow is definitive only until Easter! What creature here below can say Forever? Thus the fickle consciousness already sees the end of its own pleasure; it gauges it in length and breadth, it knows it, in other words, as an object.

An excellent example of this detached, "mathematical" view of love can be seen in the *Pierrot amoureux* of "Autre Complainte de Lord Pierrot" (*Poésies complètes* 1). The would-be lover does not allow himself to get overly excited about the prospect of meeting his First True Love; he already suspects that it is likely to be an ephemeral and trivial affair.

> She who is to inform me about Woman!
> We will tell her first of all, with my least cold air:
> "The sum of the angles of a triangle, dear soul,
>   Is equal to two right ones."

The beloved is deflated by the periphrastic formula, the poet is deflated by the "we" that clashes grammatically with the "my," the passion is deflated by the negative superlative, and the protestation of love is deflated by the *reductio ad theorem*. As Warren Ramsey (*Jules Laforgue*, p. 137) has observed, the geometrical theorem has deeper implications than mere deflation; it is one of the symbols of Laforgue's sense of fatality: "The speaker of the poem is, among other things, telling the lady that what will be is bound to be." But this sense of fatality is rendered in terms of self-parody. As with Corbière, the tone established is one of self-pity tempered by self-mockery. Pierrot's fear of overrating and overstating his love is clownishly squeamish; when addressing his Beloved, he will replace hyperbole by its more ridiculous opposite: the fear of expressing his emotion at all.

Pierrot's irony, his bitter smile, is not simply the result of a fear of overstatement or disillusionment. His emotions are constantly upended because they must compete with conflicting ones. In other words, the poet's contradictory impulses neutralize each other. This dissociation of sensibility, which so greatly impressed the younger Eliot, is expressed in a unique style. In a typical poem by Laforgue there will be a conflicting counterpoint between theme and mood; or there will be a sudden reversal of sentiments; or the direct expression of a feeling will suddenly yield to a deflationary objective correlative of the feeling; or a deeply felt emotion will be controlled, chastened, or canceled by an anticlimactic detail, or as two contemporary critics have nicely put it, since the poet's difficulty seems insoluble, the issue will suddenly be suspended, the problem shelved.[7]

More typical of the humor of this century are the multiple ironies of black humor. The twentieth century did not invent black humor. André

Breton traces it back to Swift; and a case could be made for several earlier antecedents. But black humor has been used more consistently by writers of this century than of any other to express the many frustrations of the modern sensibility suffering in an Age of Anxiety, Anguish, and Angst—its polymorphous revolts and, on the other side, its passivity and resignation. Black humor is directly related to romantic irony in that it is so often imbued with philosophical irony and in that it is so often an uncertain irony lending itself to varied, even contradictory, interpretations and providing more questions than answers. For convenience of classification black humor could be divided into its sadistic and masochistic modalities. Jarry's *ubuesque* farces can be taken as one of the most seminal influences on the sadistic type of black humor in the twentieth century. The masochistic type is vividly expressed in the work of Franz Kafka whose influence on contemporary French literature has been enormous. Breton *(Anthologie de l'humour noir,* p. 322) has summarized the philosophical import of Kafka's black humor: "The human individual struggles at the center of a play of forces whose meaning he has generally despaired of discovering, and his total lack of curiosity in this regard may well be the very precondition for his adaptation to social life." This description also applies perfectly to a hauntingly disturbing antihero, Henri Michaux's Plume.

Plume: the very name suggests a Kafkaesque, Thurberesque, and Chaplinesque vulnerability and the lightness of body and mind of the classic comic Stan Laurel. (Michaux has created similar feather-light creatures in his paintings, sketches, and water colors.) The lightweight protagonist expresses in part the author's obsession with his own ontological fragility ("I was born *troué,*" he says, full of holes). Plume, like the heroes of Raymond Queneau, suffers from *ontalgie:* pain of being, caused partly by external circumstances but also by the self-conscious self's perceived lack of fullness of being. He travels in the familiar world of trains, boats, restaurants, and hotels, but the people he encounters treat him with a cruelty comic in its gratuitousness and frightening in its implications: "Some people walk right over him without warning, others calmly wipe their hands on his jacket. He's finally gotten used to it. He tries to travel modestly."[8]

The underlying theme of *Un certain Plume* is "powerlessness, power of others" *(Plume,* p. 57). The most frequently recurring leitmotif is the hero's persistent troubles with people in authority. In "Un homme paisible" it is the judge who condemns him to death on purely circumstantial evidence. In "Les Appartements de la reine" it is the Queen who seduces a willing but apathetic Plume, and later the King who catches him with the Queen and who perhaps (we are given only suspension points) has him castrated. In "La Nuit des Bulgares" it is the train conductor who demands that Plume and his accomplices stay in the same compartment with the foreigners they have murdered. Without registering any emotion, Plume acquiesces as usual, complaining inwardly but with comic mildness ("It is always preferable not to travel with a dead man, especially when he has been the victim of a revolver bullet, for the blood that has flowed gives him a nasty look" [p. 154]). In "Plume avait mal au doigt" it is the surgeon who insists on amputation as the best remedy for a sore finger; his two main arguments are that Plume, being well off, doesn't need ten fingers and that he will be able to pick from a wide selection of "extremely graceful" artificial fingers. In Casablanca Plume is so preoccupied with the customs officials and the ship's doctor he must see the next day that he forgets the purpose of his sight-seeing trip.

In "Plume au restaurant" he asks a waiter for something that is not on the menu and is immediately accosted and accused by authorities of greater and greater rank: the maître d'hôtel, the manager, a policeman, the police commissioner, the head of the *Sûreté*, and finally the chief of the forbidding *Secrète*. Each encounter ends with the comic refrain: "Plume apologized immediately." In restaurants he is refused the meal he has ordered; in hotels he is refused a room; on ships he is relegated to the baggage hold. When he gets on a train, the tractable, self-effacing hero is immediately thrown off ("Fine, fine, I understand perfectly. I had gotten on, oh, just to take a look around"). In Rome he is not allowed even to *look* at the Coliseum ("Fine, fine. It was just . . . I just wanted to ask you for a post card, a photo maybe"). In Berlin five pimply prostitutes rob him, force him to accept their wares, and then throw him down the stairs of a sleazy hotel ("Well," thought Plume, "that will make a great memory of this trip later on").

When Plume is a guest at a banquet of the Bren Club (a Joycean pun formed on Pen Club and *bren,* an archaic synonym of *merde*), he is forced to eat an unappetizing meal.

> The turkey was stuffed with maggots, the salad had been rinsed in dirty engine oil, the potatoes had been spit out. The grapefruit tree

must have grown in a field of mothballs, the mushrooms smelled of steel, the pâté smelled of armpits. (P. 171)

Somehow a snake falls from a bunch of bananas and out of politeness (that is, to spare his hostess any embarrassment) he swallows it. At the end of the episode the polite and considerate guest of honor is simultaneously kissed and beaten by the hostess.

The main source of irony in *Un certain Plume* is the matter-of-fact tone of both the hero and the narrator during the most horrendous misadventures. But at two points the narrative voice becomes lyrically plaintive and expresses directly the anguish of both the protagonist and the implied author.

Frightening adventures, whatever your developments and your beginnings, painful adventures, guided by an implacable enemy. (P. 149)

Fatigue! Fatigue! Will we never be let go, then? (P. 176)

The last cry can be related to the autobiographical musings of *Idées de traverse:* "The extreme and exhausting fatigue to which any activity and any exercise lead me rather quickly, makes me withdraw rather considerably from the familiar world" *(Passages,* p. 14).

The first section of *Un certain Plume,* entitled "A Peaceful Man"—an ironic understatement worthy of Swift's "modest proposal"—would have been better placed at the end. It summarizes Plume's placidity and passiveness and suggests deeper implications. (In its original version this chapter was entitled "La philosophie de Plume.") Plume has become so accustomed to hostility that he has also become dehumanized into an unfeeling vegetable or, as Michaux has expressed it, a *mutilé psychique*—a psychically mutilated being.[9] Plume awakens to discover that all the walls of his house are missing ("Ants must have eaten them . . . anyway, the thing is over and done with"). And he goes back to sleep. Shortly he is reawakened by a train rushing at him and his wife at full speed, but after expressing mild annoyance he goes back to sleep. Finally, awakened by the cold, he finds himself dripping in blood and his wife lying in pieces next to him: "I sure wish that train hadn't passed through here like that, but since it has. . . ." And he goes back to sleep.

"Come now," said the judge, "how do you explain the fact that your wife was hurt to such a degree that she was found divided into eight

pieces without you, who were right next to her, having made one gesture, to keep her from it, without you even noticing it? That's the
mystery. The whole case rests on that point."
    "On that score, I can't help him," thought Plume, and he went back
to sleep.
    "The execution will take place tomorrow. Defendant, have you
anything to add?"
    "I'm sorry," he said, "I haven't been following the proceedings."
And he went back to sleep. (P. 138)

Critics have seen a positive side to Plume, his courage and stoicism,
his inextinguishable hopefulness. Even his indifference is seen as an
effective shield, making him, like Chaplin, emotionally invulnerable to
the misfortunes and persecutions that constantly befall him. Evidence
for such a view is provided by the following text.

> Don't weigh more than a flame and everything will be fine,
> A flame from a zephyr, a flame coming from a hot and
>   bloody lung,
> In a word: a flame.
> Ruin in the face, pleasant and well rested,
> Ruin can say all, ruin.
> Don't weigh more than a crow's nest and everything
>   will be fine. (ED, p. 73)

But I read Plume as one who has no choice in the matter, who *must* yield
to the inevitable, the inevitability of suffering and of the active cruelty or
cruel indifference of others, and finally the inevitability of his own impotence. His only recourse in each horrible situation is to absent himself
mentally, to be absent-minded. In "Ecce Homo" Michaux summarizes
quite explicitly the implicit view that subtends *Un certain Plume.*

> I have seen man. . . .
>   I have seen man, with his weak torch, bent over and searching. He
> had the seriousness of a flea leaping, but his leap was rare and regi-
> mented.
>   His cathedral had a soft spire. He was preoccupied.
>   I have seen him agitated and worried. . . . His worries were his real
> children.
>   For a long time the sun had no longer turned around the Earth.
> Quite the contrary.

Then it had been necessary that he be descended from the mon-
keys. . . .

I have not seen man counting for man. I have seen: "Here, men are
broken." Here they are broken, there a hat is put on them and he is still
of some use. Stamped on like a road, he is of use. . . .

He was, when I knew him, about a hundred thousand years old and
was traveling around the Earth with ease. He hadn't yet learned how to
be a good neighbor. (ED, pp. 277–79)

The irony of *Plume* is related to romantic irony partly by its autobiographical dimension, its self-irony, and especially by virtue of its
being an uncertain irony. The author's attitude toward his hero and
toward the world at large remains forever ambiguous. Elizabeth A.
Howe ("Irony in Michaux's *Plume*," p. 896), specifically connecting
Plume to romantic irony, writes, "*Plume* clearly cannot be characterized
as an example of stable irony; there is no invitation here to correct a
surface meaning by a covert one, since the possible 'meanings' of *Plume*
are vague and problematical and could not be substituted for some
other, literal meaning. Nor does *Plume* aim at correcting the world."

Despite any positive dimension that can be read into his "character,"
Plume's comic passivity has inescapably disturbing overtones. He partakes of the twentieth-century myths of the Little Man as Tragic Hero,
the Passive Hero, and the Hero as Clown—comically awkward and frail
creatures overwhelmed by unknown forces beyond their control, bewil-
dered by a hostile, decadent, and polluted environment, the victims of
cosmic indifference and malevolence. We certainly have moved a great
distance from the Cornelian Hero, master of himself and of the universe, and from the confident anthropocentrism of pre-Copernican
days.

*

Rarely in the history of French literature has self-irony been expressed with such extreme anguish as in the work of Henri Michaux. He
tells us that he was born *trouvé* and *troué*, a spiritual foundling and an
ontological lightweight. He felt that his own mother's prediction that
his life would be one of "poverty" and "nullity" was a self-fulfilling
prophecy. At the age of eight he was already wishing "to be accepted as a
member of the plant family" (ED, p. 334). Throughout his life he remained "ashamed," like Lautréamont, "of being only what he is." Speak-

ing of his "prodigious lack of ability," he claims to have made "only blunders" in his life (ED, p. 50). He would have preferred a pseudonym, he tells us, but continues to sign his works with his ordinary name like a label that says "qualité inférieure." He would also prefer that readers refer to him thus: "Well! There's another book by number 367!"[10] His "autobiography," "Quelques renseignements sur cinquante-neuf années d'existence," is written in the third person and in the impersonal index-card style of the Bureau of Public Records. What has been called his "militant masochism" is frequently expressed by reflexive verbs: *I make fun of myself; I scalp myself; I skin myself alive; I strike myself; I seduce myself; I irritate myself; I put myself out of joint.*

> I kill myself in my rage
> I scatter myself with each step
> I throw myself at my feet
> I swallow myself in my saliva
> I mourn myself
> . . . .
> I refuse myself absolution
> . . . .
> I refuse myself any review of my case
>
> (*Qui je fus*, pp. 63–64)

In "Repos dans le malheur" the poet's persona will have a solemn colloquy with his Unhappiness. But the unhappiness is objectified through apostrophe and personification as in Baudelaire's "Recueillement," and the self-pity is further tempered by the playful tonality that erupts unexpectedly.

> Unhappiness, my great plowman,
> Unhappiness, sit down,
> Rest yourself
> Let's both rest ourselves a bit you and I
> Rest,
> You find me, you test me, you prove it to me.
>
> (ED, p. 100)

The translation does not capture the playful paronomasia of the last line:

> Tu me trouves, tu m'éprouves, tu me le prouves.

Michaux's most important self-portrait is appropriately entitled "Clown." It is a remarkable piece of self-condemnation.

Someday.
Someday, soon maybe.
Someday I am going to pull up the anchor that's
        holding my ship far from the seas.
With the sort of courage it takes to be nothing and
        nothing but nothing.

I will let go of what seemed indissolubly close to me.
I'll chop it off, I'll knock it over, I'll break it,
        I'll make it tumble down.
Disgorging all at once my miserable modesty, my
        miserable schemes and piecemeal thoughts and acts,
Emptied of the abscess of being somebody, I shall drink
        anew of nourishing space.

By means of ridicule and downfalls (what are downfalls?)
by explosion, by emptiness, by a total dissipation-
derision-purgation, I shall expel from myself the form
that people thought so well attached, composed,
coordinated, matching my surroundings and my peers,
so worthy, so worthy, my peers.

Reduced to a humility of catastrophe, to a perfect
leveling as after an intense scare.
Brought back down, beyond measurement, to my real rank,
        to the lowly rank that I don't know what ambition-
        idea had made me desert.
Annihilated with regard to eminence and esteem.
Lost in a faraway place (or not even that,
        without a name, without an identity).

CLOWN, demolishing in derision, in roars of
        laughter, in the grotesque, the sense of
        my importance that I had made for myself
        despite all evidence to the contrary,
I shall plunge.
Without a purse in the subjacent infinite-spirit
        open to all,

open myself to a new and incredible dew
by dint of being null
and shorn. . .
and ridiculous. . .

(ED, pp. 249–50)

The clown has become one of the chief heroes of modern art. He
has figured in modern French poetry from Banville's *Odes funambulesques*
(1857) through Laforgue to Jacob, Apollinaire, and Cocteau; he has
been even more prominent in modern painting, particularly in the
works of Picasso, Rouault, Chagall, and Buffet. The title, "Clown," refers
not only to the subject of the poem but to an extraliterary genre.
Michaux was a painter, and this poem is part of a volume entitled *Pein-
tures* and is accompanied by reproductions of his paintings, sketches, and
drawings, including one of a sad clown. Michaux's reference, then, is not
just to the world of the circus but to the discourse of painting.

Most of the paintings of clowns and harlequins created in this century have revealed or suggested the tragedy behind the comic mask, but
Michaux, while exploiting this association, has given the subject a different interpretation. Michaux's clown is not the tragic man behind the
mask. The grotesque mask of the clown is the real man, "shorn" of all
pretentions, rationalizations, and false identities (the dignified masks
that he and his "dignified peers"—*mes semblables si dignes*—wear in society), the man as he really is "shorn . . . and ridiculous." Beneath the
social mask is that of the clown; beneath that of the clown is nothing.

Michaux, then, takes a step farther than the painters in the direction
of ontological anguish. His clown does not possess a shred of tragic
dignity. The absurd figure he cuts is the true picture. One of the several
ironies in "Clown" is the conflict it establishes with the now traditional
connotations of tragic dignity or dignified humanity in the sad clown
topos of twentieth-century painting. All the sentences, both complete
and elliptical, in "Clown" are variations on a matrix that could be called
"my utter absurdity" and that negate the stereotypes of dignified sorrow
in the canvas clowns.

Just as important as the poet's realization of his utter insignificance
is his inability to assume his true role as clown before the world. "Someday I am going to pull up the anchor that's holding my ship far from the
seas": but unlike Rimbaud's *bateau ivre,* the poet has *not* pulled up his

anchor; he is still bogged down in those "impassive [not impassible] Rivers" that Rimbaud's boat successfully (at first) left behind—his conventional self or false identity. Like Prufrock, he cannot ride "seaward on the waves"; like Prufrock, he cannot "plunge" into the refreshing sea except in dream and imagination. He still clings to his main source of gratification, the fact that a number of people (his public) consider him a person of some importance. The real confession in this autobiographical poem is the poet's inability to admit he is a clown. The indefiniteness of "someday" and the future tense give him away. Like Prufrock, he needs a disguise to face the world; like Prufrock, he cannot admit to others that on life's stage he is not the hero but the Fool.

> No! I am not Prince Hamlet, nor was meant to be;
> Am an attendant lord, one that will do
> To swell a progress, start a scene or two,
> Advise the prince; no doubt an easy tool,
> Deferential, glad to be of use,
> Politic, cautious, and meticulous;
> Full of high sentence, but a bit obtuse;
> At times, indeed, almost ridiculous—
> Almost, at times, the Fool.[11]

"Clown" is the poet's commentary on himself to himself. But the uncomfortable feeling that the poem creates in the reader suggests that the self-irony has been subtly generalized. The ironic antimetabole, "mes semblables, si dignes, si dignes, mes semblables," leaves no doubt as to Michaux's opinion of the rest of humanity. The most relevant intertext here is Baudelaire's "hypocrite lecteur, mon semblable, mon frère" (hypocritical reader, my peer, my brother). In *Passages* the poet explicitly universalizes the Fool topos by employing the syntax of proverbs:

> Qui cache son fou meurt sans voix.

> Whoever hides his fool dies without a voice.

The poem can easily be read at another level. The death wish is implicit in nearly every line. The insistent repetition of being "nothing and nothing but nothing" and the violent "Emptied of the abscess of being somebody" speak of death at least as much as of loss of a spurious identity. It is only as nonbeing that the poet will partake of "nourishing space" and the "incredible dew" of the grave. In fact death is the most logical link between these disparate images. It is only by death that he will shake off all claims to a personal identity and all ties with his fellow-men. The "total dissipation-derision-purgation" suggests not only death but decomposition.

The courage required by the poet on this level, then, is the courage to kill himself.

The second line attenuates the first despite the repetition. If the double "Someday" is fairly aggressive, the phrase "soon maybe" suggests procrastination and indecision, as if the poet were trying to convince himself. Throughout the rest of the poem there is an ambivalent interplay of aggressiveness and reluctance that I have analyzed in detail in an earlier essay.[12] This tonal fluctuation is consonant with all three themes: the poet as clown, the inability to admit it to others, the death wish.

Like *Le Bateau ivre,* the first section of "Clown" is organized around a boat metaphor and ends with a longing for a new energy in the form of "drinking anew of nourishing space," which would be a release from the stifling atmosphere surrounding the poet hemmed in by his own defense mechanisms. But the double aposiopesis concluding the poem suggests that the "tropism" is over. As at the end of *Le Bateau ivre,* there is a hint of fatigue and discouragement. The quietness of the finale suggests that the poet is not going to act on his courageous impulse.

Michaux's selection of the clown to embody and translate his pessimism is an attempt at mythopoesis, an attempt to transcend self-irony. The canvas clown, the Charlie Chaplin–Samuel Beckett tramp, Kafka's K, and Eliot's Fool are all part of the most enduring myth we have had in the twentieth century. The poem on first reading seems only a self-confession; upon further investigation it yields a commentary on the human condition and, finally, a reformulation of what Camus considered today's most important philosophical question, Prufrock's "overwhelming question"—and Hamlet's: suicide.

*

The hero of the early Chaplin films was often mean. Similarly, Plume is *not* always a passive creature. He, too, exhibits the *agressé-agresseur* duality. On two occasions his frustrations and repressed anger lead to violence. In "La Nuit des Bulgares" his misanthropy, taking here the form of xenophobia, pushes him to sadistic murder. In "L'Arrachage des têtes" Plume, while not named, participates in an orgy of gratuitous beheadings. The sadomasochistic dualism of *Un certain Plume* is also reflected in Michaux's opus at large, the major themes of which range between fatigue and combativeness, between passiveness and violent resistance. Michaux most often uses his prose and poetry as imaginative "interventions" and "exorcisms," the former designed to strike back— for compensation, revenge, and catharsis—at a hostile world, the latter to keep it at bay ("to hold in check the surrounding powers of the hostile world").[13]

Michaux's magical interventions attempt to overthrow the world's physical and metaphysical status quo. One method is to throw disorder into the natural order.

> In the past I had too much respect for nature. I stood before things and landscapes and let them do as they pleased.
> Finished, now *I shall intervene.*
> So, I was in Honfleur and was bored. And so I very resolutely put in some camel there.
> . . . .
> I had likewise launched a passenger train. It left from the Grand Plaza and advanced resolutely toward the sea with no concern for the heaviness of the matériel; it sped forward, saved by faith.
>
> ("Intervention," ED, p. 60)

The resultant disorder is described in precise and concrete detail and with the matter-of-fact tone of a newspaper account, creating latent humor and irony that must be actualized by the reader.

In other situations the combative poet intervenes directly.

> I can rarely see someone without beating him. Others prefer interior monologue. Not me. I prefer to beat people up.
> There are people sitting opposite me in the restaurant and saying nothing, they stay for a while, for they have decided to eat.
> Here's one of them.
> I grab him, toc.
> I grab him again, toc.
> I hang him up on the coatrack.
> I unhook him.
> I hang him up again.
> I unhook him again.
> I put him on the table, I pound him and choke him.
>
> ("Mes Occupations," ED, p. 33)

Our mean magician has many tricks. One is the "bag session."

> It started when I was a child. There was a big bothersome adult.
> How to avenge myself on him? I put him in a bag. There I could
> beat him easily. He would cry out, but I didn't listen to him. He wasn't
> interesting.
> I have wisely kept this habit of my childhood. The possibilities of
> intervention that one acquires in becoming an adult, in addition to the
> fact that they don't go very far, I didn't trust them.
> ("La Séance de sac," ED, pp. 287–88)

Other interventions take the form of ubuesque inventions like the *fronde à hommes* (a slingshot to be used against people), the *appareil à éventrer* (an eviscerating machine), and the *mitrailleuse à gifles* (a machine gun that distributes slaps in the face). His imaginary murders and rapes have a particularly effective cathartic value: "My heart, emptied periodically of its wickedness, is opened to goodness, and one could almost entrust a little girl to me for a few hours" (ED, p. 290). The vast self-irony produced here by the little adverb "almost" is typical of Michaux's sadistic humor: "It must not be thought that massacres (except for *little* judicial executions) are done in cold blood. Often we are seized with frenzy" (ED, p. 206). In another passage he tells us that the possession of the *mitrailleuse à gifles* disposes one toward patience; that is why he "occasionally" advises tolerance toward members of one's family!

Michaux's exorcisms are related to traditional forms in that they, too, are verbal exercises designed to cast out the world's evil spirits. Ordinary language alone does not suffice to express Michaux's anger and (imaginery) aggressiveness. He will often compose rasping, grating cacophonies and pugilistic neologisms to express his savage revenge on the hostile world with which he struggles. A good case in point is the untranslatable beginning of "Le grand combat."

> Il l'emparouille et l'endosque contre terre;
> Il le rague et le roupète jusqu'à son drâle;
> Il le pratèle et le libucque et lui baruffle les ouillais;
> Il le tocarde et le marmine,
> Le manage rape à ri et ripe à ra.
> Enfin il l'écorcobalisse.
>
> (ED, p. 14)

We know immediately that most of these neologisms are verbs, not because they denote any specific action or state, but because they fill the

verb "slots" in their sentences. We know that they are active and transi-
tive verbs because they are given a direct object: the victim in this "great
combat" called Life (Michaux, among other stylistic traits, is a synecdoch-
ist). We know that these verbs denote violent actions of some sort because of their adverbial complements, "contre terre" (against the
ground), "jusqu'à son" (right up to his), and the like. The first verb does
bear a resemblance to *s'emparer de* (to seize); "endosque" suggests that the
victim's back is involved; "lui baruffle les ouillais" suggests "lui bat les
oreilles" (boxes his ears) for several reasons, phonetic, syntactic, and
morphological (e.g., *ouïe*, hearing). "Tocarde" is formed on the violent
onomatopoeia used in "Mes Occupations": "I grab him, *toc.*" The very
volume of the five-syllable verb *écorcobalisse,* whatever it means, expresses
an apotheosis of violence. A similar use of enumeration to lead a series of
neologisms and onomatopoeias to a violent polysyllabic climax is found
in "Gli et glu":

> et glo
> et glu
> et déglutit sa bru
> gli et glo
> et déglutit son pied
> glu et gli
> et s'englugluglolera.
>
> (ED, p. 12)

Michaux's poetry frequently takes the form of invective, imprecation, anathema—

> Ah! que je hais Boileau   [Ah! how I hate Boileau]
> Boileux, Boignetière, Boiloux, Boigermain,
> Boirops, Boitel, Boivery,
> Boicamille,
> Boit de travers
> Bois ça.   [Drink that]
>
> (ED, p. 13)

or the Faustian curse—

> Glas! Glas! Glas sur vous tous, néant sur les vivants!
>
> (ED, p. 147)

> Knell! Knell! Knell on you all, nothingness on the living!

The prose often takes the form of cynical maxims, sayings, aphorisms, proverbs, "truisms," and uncommon commonplaces worthy of the Ionesco of *La Cantatrice chauve.*

> He who has a pin in his eye, the future of the English navy doesn't interest him. (ED, p. 115)

> The microbe doesn't have the time to examine the biologist. (ED, p. 82)

> How one would detest men less if they all didn't wear a face. (ED, p. 42)

*

Michaux's misanthropic irony—his black humor—is part of a larger, cosmic irony. His work expresses a metaphysical revolt against the limitations and inadequacies of the human condition. One critic has said of him that he suffers from claustrophobia on a cosmic scale. Michaux himself has said the same: "Never, no NEVER, do what you will, you will never know what a wretched suburb the Earth was. How wretched we were and famished for something Greater!" *(Plume,* p. 103). His motto is EVEN IF IT'S TRUE, IT'S FALSE (ED, p. 339)—which is precisely the motto implicitly adopted by most romantic ironists. His experimentation with drugs, what he calls his "experimental schizophrenia," was not only an escape from reality but, much more important for him, an attempt at multiplying the possibilities of his being. Seeing the real as "absurd" (ED, p. 41), Michaux has tried to live principally in his "inner space," on the still swampy terrain of his inner "property." His imaginary countries, such as Grande Garabagne, are buffer states set up between himself and the real world. Even his many real-life travels to exotic lands were voyages "against": "He travels against. In order to expel from himself his native land, his attachments of all sorts, and what has attached itself to him, despite himself, of Greek or Roman or Germanic culture or of Belgian habits."[14]

Contre, both the preposition (against) and the verb (to counter), is a key word in his work.

> I have lived against my father and against my mother and against my grandfather, my grandmother, my great-grandparents. *(Plume,* p. 211)

O world, strangled world, cold belly!
Not even a symbol, but sheer nothingness, I counter,
    I counter,
I counter and stuff you with dead dogs.

("Contre," ED, pp. 147–48)

I row
I row
I row against your life. . . .
I multiply myself into innumerable rowers
To row more strongly against you.

(*Face aux verroux*, p. 27)

Against Versailles
Against Chopin
Against the alexandrine
Against Rome
. . . .
Against Bossuet
Against analysis

(ED, p. 314)

Among his many rhetorical combats there is his daily struggle with his King, which seems to be an oblique reference to the poet wrestling with his guilty conscience and also with the god he has renounced and blasphemed. Here we see once again the romantic ironist as ambivalent iconoclast. (In his youth Michaux had wanted to take religious orders.)

In my night, I attack my King, I arise progressively and I twist his neck.

He regains strength, I come back at him, and twist his neck again.

I shake him and shake him, like an old plum tree, and his crown trembles on his head.

And yet, he is my King, I know it and he knows it, and it is quite clear that I am in his service.
. . . .
Wherever he goes, he installs himself.

And no one is surprised, it seems that his place has been there forever.

(ED, p. 131)

The principal god of Grande Garabagne reminds one of the remote or dead God of the contemporary Western world: "The god *Mna* is the deafest of all and the greatest. They well know that if he heard them, their troubles would be over. . . . Ah! if he could see at least, that hard-of-hearing god!" (ED, pp. 180–81).

Like Kafka's K, even when Michaux's narrator arrives at the gates of the City-That-Counts, he can never enter *(Face aux verroux)*. And even though the road leading to the Federal Capital has been shown him "I don't know how many times," it remains forever inaccessible *(Ailleurs)*. The countryside is indifferent, and "the sky is without intentions" (ED, p. 58).

But Michaux, mired in the Absurd, still awaits his Godot.

> One waits, one doesn't say a word, one waits until He decides. (ED, p. 134)

> Man, impatient for a brief while, keeps waiting and would like a bit of light. (ED, p. 281)

> But You, when will You come?
> Someday, stretching out Your hand
> Over the neighborhood I live in,
> at the moment when I am really giving up hope;
> . . . .
> You will come, if You exist.
> . . . .

Then, in the very same passage expressing the very same theological anguish, the tone suddenly turns to comic sarcasm and cynicism. The "blackness" of the humor gives a distinctively modern ring to the romantic irony.

> Or else, what?
> Never? No?
> Say, Big Prize, where do You want to land?
>
> *(Plume, pp. 97–98)*

Lilian Furst has suggested *(Fictions of Romantic Irony,* p. 27) that Kafka and Beckett belong within the tradition of romantic irony because for them, as for Schlegel, irony is "the consciousness of eternal mobility, of the infinite fullness of chaos," and because of the malaise engendered in the reader by this irony. Michaux, too, is obviously part of the tradition. His world is one in which "everything trembles, always, always" *(Plume,* p. 75). His "nomadic consciousness" (Max Bense) is seldom at rest. Indeed, human consciousness is characterized by its perpetual movement: "The inner being has all the movements, it bursts forth with the speed of an arrow, then it returns like a mole. . . . What a creature of movement" *(Plume,* p. 132). Michaux can say, with Montaigne, "Je ne peints pas l'estre, je peints le passage" (I don't depict being, I depict passage). *Passages* (1950) is one of many significant titles pointing to the mobile, transitory nature of human existence and of the individual self. Another significant title is *Qui je fus* (Who I Was). Still others are *La nuit remue* (The Night Moves), *Ailleurs* (Elsewhere), *Mouvements, vents et poussières* (Movements, Winds and Dusts), *Par la voie des rythmes* (By the Path of Rhythms), and *Déplacements, Dégagements* (Displacements, Disengagements). A recent monograph (Laurie Edson, *Henri Michaux and the Poetics of Movement*) has focused on Michaux's "poetics of movement."[15]

> Movements of quartering and inner exasperation more than movements of walking,
>   movements of explosions, of refusals, of stretching in all directions. . . .
> Movements of withdrawals and of coilings upon oneself.
>
> *(Face aux verroux,* p. 13)

> I am one of those who like movement, the movement that breaks inertia, that confuses lines, that undoes alignments, frees me of constructions. Movement as of disobedience, as of reshuffling.
>
> *(Emergences-Résurgences,* p. 65)

Like Schlegel's, Michaux's work privileges striving rather than completion, becoming rather than being.[16] Consciousness is "an oscillatory state" *(Connaissance par les gouffres,* p. 29). The self is always transitory, in transition.

> The SELF is always provisional.
>
> *(Plume,* p. 216)

> Transformation is our infinite, and one cannot depend on anything that does not transform itself, and if one is, one is only successively.
>
> *(Qui je fus,* p. 15)

> Signs of the ten thousand ways of being in a state of equilibrium in this moving world that laughs at adaptation. . . .

> Signs, not in order to be complete, not in order to conjugate, but in order to be faithful to one's transitory nature.
>
> *(Face aux verroux,* p. 18)

Such "signs" are found not only in Michaux's prose and poetry but in his drawings in which a single wandering line that never arrives at a fixed destination imitates Michaux's eternal wanderings through foreign and imaginary countries, through drug experiences, through his favorite enigmatic paintings, like those of Magritte and Klee, and finally through himself: "J'écris pour me parcourir" (I write in order to travel through myself).

One of Michaux's favorite movements, as Georges Poulet has noted ("Michaux et le supplice des faibles," pp. 166–71), is the fall, including the clownish, farcical pratfall: "One is in a good position only when one falls" *(Passages,* p. 15). This yearning for a fall from spurious stability, self-identity, and dignity is compellingly expressed in "Clown."

Schlegel's "infinite fullness of chaos" is suggested by another significant title: *L'Infini turbulent* (1957). The universe, like the self, is in a never-ending state of flux, of "oscillation." In the last years of his life Michaux attempted, through Eastern mysticism, to find some harmony between the restless self and the restless universe, but the burden of his work bears witness not to the oneness of the cosmos but to its disquieting diversity. His black humor, in both its masochistic and its sadistic modalities, is a brilliant expression of dismal truths. Like that of Kafka and Beckett, his "transcendental buffoonery," which defies literary genres ("des ennemis") and which refuses to take itself too seriously, bears both playful and excruciatingly painful witness to the metaphysical anguish of modern man.

9

Intellectual Gamesmanship: Queneau's *Le Chiendent*

—I am observing a man.
—Gee. [Are you] a novelist?
—No. A character.
(Le Chiendent)

R AYMOND QUENEAU is a self-deprecating humorist and an ironist who often points his weapon at himself. Conscious of the two possible etymologies of his name, for example, he identifies at times with the noble oak tree, more frequently with the humble dog—not the faithful friend, but the filthy beast and "cynical" cur.

> The animal devours and defiles,
> such are his two qualities;
> he is ferocious and impulsive,
> one knows where he likes to put his nose.
> ....
> The dog is a dog to the bone,
> he is brazen, indelicate.[1]
>
> *(Chêne et chien* [Oak and Dog])

The title of one of his collections of poems, *Le Chien à la mandoline* (1965), is a periphrasis for "Queneau le poète." And the title of the long autobiographical "novel" in verse, *Chêne et chien* (1937), refers to his dual nature.

> A dog would feed on acorns
> if he didn't frequent garbage cans.
> The branch of the oak tree stretches
> toward the sky.

The novel describes his eventual restoration to mental equilibrium, even joy, after several years of psychoanalysis, but the burden of the work deals with his unhappy childhood and the many complexes of his young adulthood.

> I am incapable of working
> in our society in short
> I am a maladjusted disadjusted fellow
> neu-
> rotic
> impotent
> so on a divan
> here I am telling how I use my time

In other texts Queneau presents himself as an absurd caricaturist of the Absurd.

> Infirm is all of nature
> Infirm are beasts and rocks
> Infirm is caricature
> Infirm is the idiot who says stupid things.
>
> ("Sourde est la nuit" in *Si tu t'imagines*)

> Here I am getting gray
> Here I am getting fat
> I cough and say stupid things.
>
> ("Vieillir" in *Si tu t'imagines*)

> Come back among us o indulgent Muses
> And please forgive this little joker
> His poems are hollow his prose indigent
> But in none of his witticisms is there any evil intent.
>
> ("Muses et lézards" in *Si tu t'imagines*)

> I ain't ever gonna know happiness on this earth
>   I'm really too stupid
> Everything makes me suffer, and everything is a misery
>   for me poor stupid jerk.
> . . . .
> Anguish grabs me strangles me and I get worse
>   more and more stupid.
>
> ("Complainte" in *Si tu t'imagines*)

A constant feature of Queneau's writing, in both his poetry and his fiction, is the text's self-referentiality. As poet, Queneau has produced

poems that self-consciously examine themselves and question their own
rhetoric and prosody.

> Far from time, from space, a man is lost,
> Thin as a hair, wide as the dawn.
> His nostrils foaming, his eyes turned upwards in fright,
> And his hands out in front of him to feel the décor
>
> which is, moreover, nonexistent. But what, people will say,
> Is the meaning of that simile:
> "Thin as a hair, wide as the dawn"?
> And why those nostrils beyond the three dimensions?
>   ("L'Explication des métaphores" in *Si tu t'imagines*)

In *Petite Cosmogonie portative* (Small Portable Cosmogony, 1950) the poet
offers an explanation of the poem's meaning, *within the poem itself* (Canto
3). Similarly the reader of Queneau's poetry is made constantly aware of
the poet's presence and of the poem as artifact by the use of words that
often call more attention to themselves than to their referents outside
the poem and by ludic licenses that are striking because of their frequency as well as their comic extravagance. The poet will offer false
rhymes, facetious rhymes, syncopated rhymes

> s'éloigne/témoign/-age
> gazomètres/géométr/-ie
> infâme/hame/-çon
> n'ose/l'adipos/-ité

and verses facetiously forced into "regular" versification (here octosylla-
bles) by pseudodieresis:

> Hélas! quel paüvre jeune homme
> plus tard je süis devenu
>
> Alas! what a poooor young man
> later I beeeecame

There are Rabelaisian enumerations, amphigoric alliterations, mis-
spellings reflecting popular mispronunciations (or, rather, faithful tran-
scriptions of what Queneau calls Neo-French), archaic spellings
("avecque"), anacoluthons ("j'avec soin déchirai"), and parenthetical
asides to the reader ("it's the genre that requires that").

At the beginning of the last canto of *Petite Cosmogonie portative* the
poet offers an entire "history of humanity"—in two lines.

Le singe (ou son cousin) le singe devint homme
lequel un peu plus tard désagrégea l'atome.

The monkey (or his cousin) the monkey became man
Who a bit later split the atom.

Queneau's novels are steeped in everyday reality, indeed in all its
realistic banality and sordidness, but in few of his fictional works does the
author strive for pure mimetic realism or consistent realistic illusion. In
Les Enfants du limon (1938) and *Loin de Rueil* (1944) Queneau steps into
the novel as a character himself. (In the latter novel his name is his-
panized and anglicized to "Ramon Curnough.") In *Le Dimanche de la vie*
(1952) he reminds the reader of the author's presence by changing the
spelling of a character's name every time the character reappears, much
like Kurt Vonnegut, who in *Galápagos* places an asterisk beside the
names of all the characters who die during the course of the self-
consciously ironic story. Near the end of *Pierrot mon ami* (1942) the hero
muses about the various episodes of his recent life: "He could see the
novel that that might make . . . and he could see the novel that it did
make." In *Zazie dans le métro* (1959) the author, in a Schlegelian parabasis,
steps forward to offer the following metacommentary:

> Gabriel is only a dream (a charming one), Zazie only the dream
> about a dream (or about a nightmare) and this entire story is but the
> reverie about a reverie, the dream about a dream, hardly more than a
> delirium typewritten by an idiotic novelist (oh! sorry).

Throughout his fictional work there are many intrusive *mots d'auteur,*
bravura passages, and, more significantly, abrupt changes in tone,
theme, stylistic register, or narrative mode. *Le Chiendent* (1933) is a veritable encyclopedia of moods and modes. We shall examine them in detail
after a few other preliminary remarks.

*

For Friedrich von Schlegel, literature was a serious game. For
Queneau, it is an intellectual game that plays down the partially hidden
seriousness. His early, but ephemeral, infatuation with surrealism may
have been the most important impetus for Queneau's ludic impulse since
it occurred at the very beginning of his literary career. In any event
Queneau is a poet for whom form is prior to content and who sees

poetry primarily as technique, as a craft that follows self-imposed constraints, rules, formulas, even recipes.

> Take a word take two of them
> cook 'em like eggs
> take a little bit of meaning
> then a large dose of innocence
> heat on a low flame
> the low flame of technique
> pour in the enigmatic sauce
> sprinkle with a few stars
> pepper and then get the hell out of there.
>
> ("Pour un art poétique" in *Si tu t'imagines*)

The poet often plays "semiotic games" (Renée Baligand) in which the signs are separated from their *signifiés* and are led around by the sounds of neighboring words. There is no need to translate the following passages since the sounds swallow up the sense.

> on retouve tout à coup des pieux sculptés
> des dieux peut-être
> des dieux pieux des pieux dieux
>
> ("Souviens-toi du vase de Vix" in *Courir les rues*)

> . . . la lave
> pierre ponce ponceu pilote pilâtreu
>
> *(Petite Cosmogonie)*

In 1960 Queneau became the cofounder of Oulipo, the Ouvroir de Littérature Potentielle (Workshop for Potential Literature), a subgroup of the Collège of 'Pataphysics, devoted to the invention of new literary forms or the renewal of old ones. Among their recognized ancestors were the Grands Rhétoriqueurs of the late Middle Ages. Texts were generated by following, with mathematical rigor, the preestablished rules of a literary game (i.e., genre). Queneau admits *(Bâtons,* p. 323) that the work of the Oulipo group resembles games of wit, parlor games, and intellectual *amusettes.*

One method favored by the members of Oulipo was *lipogrammatie,* the art of writing prose or poetry by strictly avoiding one letter of the alphabet. In particular favor were the *poèmes à forme fixe: pantoum, virelai, rondel, vilanelle, sextine.* One experiment was to compose sonnets in monosyllabic verse. The *sextine*—six stanzas of six-syllable verse—was structured upon rhyme schemes following rigid mathematical permutations of numbers 1–6. If, for example, the rhyme words of the first stanza were as follows—

feuillages	1
soleil	2
volages	3
rivages	4
vermeil	5
sommeil	6

those of the second stanza had to be—

sommeil	6
feuillages	1
vermeil	5
soleil	2
rivages	4
volages	3

The total scheme is immensely complex:

I	1 2 3 4 5 6
II	6 1 5 2 4 3
III	3 6 4 1 2 5
IV	5 3 2 6 1 4
V	4 5 1 3 6 2
VI	2 4 6 5 3 1

The S+7 method consisted of taking an already written literary text and replacing each substantive by the seventh noun that follows it in a given dictionary. Different (i.e., more or less pleasing) results were obtained by using different dictionaries. The "isomorphic" method involved taking an already existing text, say Mallarmé's "Le vierge, le vivace et le bel aujourd'hui," and changing the words while preserving the phonetic and syntactic patterns and rhymes. The result is an amusing, if meaningless, exercise in intertextuality.

> Le liège, le titane et le sel aujourd'hui
> Vont-ils nous repiquer avec un bout d'aine ivre
> Ce mac pur oublié que tente sous le givre
> Le cancanant gravier des coques qui n'ont pas fui

Un singe d'ocre lui me soutient que c'est lui
Satirique qui sans versoir se délivre
Pour n'avoir pas planté la lésion où vivre
Quand du puéril pivert a rententi l'ennui

Tout ce porc tatouera cette grande agonie
Par l'escale intimée au poireau qui le nie
Mais non l'odeur du corps où le curare est pris

Grand pâle qu'à ce pieu son dur ébat assigne
Il cintre, ô cytise, un bonze droit de mépris
Que met parmi le style obnubilé le Cygne.

The generation of literary texts through gamesmanship is brilliantly
demonstrated in Queneau's *Exercices de style* (1947) in which the same
trivial episode is related ninety-nine times, each in a different style,
system of spelling, or narrative point of view. This passion for writing
within rigid constraints was more than a parlor game for Queneau. He
used similar constraints to structure some of his most important novels,
including *La Gueule de pierre* (later incorporated into *Saint Glinglin*, 1948),
Les derniers jours (1936), *Pierrot mon ami*, and *Le Chiendent.*

*

In addition to exhibiting the many tricks of the trade, Queneau's
work is informed by most of the basic philosophical underpinnings of
romantic irony. His nonstop irony is based in great measure upon his
recognition of the limits of science, mathematics, philosophy, and
literature—and his sense of his own limitations as a creative artist and
thinker. As editor of the ambitious *Encyclopédie de la Pléiade*, Queneau
warns the reader in his "Présentation" (1956) that he will learn *not* to
know and to doubt and that he will become aware of the immensity of
man's "non-Savoir," his nonknowledge. Here is the author speaking (in a
radio interview) of the limits of his own literary style and of his
metaphysical knowledge.

> Do you find the form of expression which is yours sufficient, or do
> you have the feeling that it limits you?
> —It limits me.
> Do you believe in life after death?
> —It's not a question of believing, but of knowing. Well, I don't
> know anything. I behave as if I didn't know anything.[2]

The second statement, borrowed from Eluard, was incorporated into Queneau's novel, *Le Dimanche de la vie* (1952). As a metaphysician, then, Queneau withdraws into a *que sais-je?* agnosticism. As a 'pataphysician, he views mathematics and the exact sciences as intellectual games that reveal relationships *between* things but that cannot lessen our ignorance of things as they are in themselves, as noumena. Language, too, pins labels on things but cannot describe them in their very essence: "We learn words, but real things, we don't know them. We know names, but we are completely ignorant of what it is about" *(Les derniers jours).*

Reality for Queneau, as it was for most of the romantic ironists who preceded him, is eternal mobility, entropy, and chaos.

Mobility:

> One never washes one's feet twice in the same water. . . . Nothing holds, everything moves. *(Pierrot mon ami)*

> In Queneau's novels one always sees people moving. The dialogues are always accompanied by gestures. Even the interior discourse, the monologues, are carried on in an animated setting. . . .

> Things move. Raymond Queneau manifests a singular delight in movement, that of the body and of the mind. (Jacques Bens, *Queneau,* pp. 62, 67)

> The being of things is only a flickering, a metamorphosis, a transition. . . .

> His fundamental experience seems to be the *panta rhei* (everything is in flux) of Heraclitus, who refuses to admit the immutable nature of things. (Jan Prokop, "Raymond Queneau," pp. 18–19)

Entropy:

> Everything seems to disappear without a trace
> > even the agile mountains.
> > > > > ("Nuit" in *Si tu t'imagines)*

> At the very bottom of their viscera
> at the very bottom of their dust
> are fermenting the stains and wear and tear of
> > people
> > > > > ("L'Usure" in *Battre la campagne)*

> crevassed by little rains
> by timid erosions

by ploughshares of vanished plants
the rock continues on its path
. . . .
it too sails toward its fi-
nal transformation into dust
which will be gone with the wind

("Solide comme un roc" in *Battre la campagne)*

Chaos: In a 'pataphysical universe there are no laws, only exceptions, no generalities, only particulars. And no hierarchy of values: in a universe without absolutes all things are equal—equally valid and equally vain—even contraries. This equivalence of contraries is, of course, a basic assumption not only of 'pataphysics but of romantic irony. 'Pataphysics is the science of imaginary solutions, the most imaginary of which is the idea of "truth." Since life is absurd, only the comic is serious.

Queneau was always fascinated by the heretical doctrines of Gnosticism and Manichaeism, especially their emphasis on the Creation as the work of an evil Creator who deliberately keeps man in eternal darkness, hiding from him the true god of light.[3] He sees existence as polarized between conflicting—and coequal—forces of good and evil, of light and darkness.

For these gods are demons; they crawl in space
. . . .
Yes, they are demons. One descends, the other mounts.
For every night its day, for every hill its vale.
For every day its night, for every tree its shadow.
For every being its No, for every good its evil.

("L'Explication des métaphores" in *Si tu t'imagines)*

Queneau's philosophical irony is nowhere better illustrated than in *Le Chiendent,* his first novel and perhaps his most brilliant. His best-seller, *Zazie,* certainly pales in comparison. We shall examine this important novel now.

*

Everything in Queneau's fiction—plot, characterization, structure, style, even setting—has philosophical implications. The setting of *Le Chiendent* is a typical one: Paris and its suburbs. Not the well-groomed suburbs of country manors but the dreary suburbs of dirty little towns filled with ramshackle shanties and hovels, whose filthy rivers are polluted by chemical factories, whose streets are filled with potholes, whose vacant lots are littered with debris, soiled papers, and garbage, whose inhabitants are run down at the heels, and whose greasy, foul-smelling restaurants serve gamy and rancid food. In one such restaurant, for example, a character is served "the most frightening shoe sole that ever haunted the nightmares of a hypochondriacal shoemaker; several nails of charcoal were joined to it. It took him a few moments to understand that the whole thing is called steak and fries."[4]

As Gaëton Picon has pointed out, the setting of Queneau's most typical novels is that of a vulgar and sordid twentieth century, places "in parentheses": vacant lots, amusement parks, flea markets, dingy cafés and movie theaters, brothels, the criminal underground, buses, trains, and subways hurtling people around in a Heraclitean flux—places where meaningful work is not accomplished. Queneau's characters are for the most part insignificant people living marginal lives in marginal milieus and seldom engaged in meaningful activity for one reason or another: the retired, the unemployed, unread authors, idle moviegoers, people at amusement parks, soldiers on latrine duty, transvestite dancers, fortune-tellers, junk dealers, pimps, and crooks. Germaine Brée and Margaret Guîton have noticed (An Age of Fiction, p. 171) that almost all human activity in Queneau's novels is ceremonial in nature: "assiduous movie attendance, shopkeeping (devoid of profit), walks (devoid of destination), conversations (devoid of meaning), quests (devoid of objects), courting rites (devoid of consummation)." One could add to the list, in connection with Le Chiendent, apartment buildings devoid of tenants and houses missing a floor.

The atmosphere, then, resembles that of Eliot's Wasteland. Well before Sartre and Camus (as well as after them) Queneau described the essential meaninglessness of life. His inconsequential characters move through arbitrary plots mirroring the arbitrariness and contingency of human existence. Many of the more self-conscious of them suffer from an "existential disease": ontalgia. But Queneau's world is even more cruel than that of a Sartre or a Camus because no noble revolt against the Absurd, no commitment to noble causes, illuminates the lives of his seedy characters. But if the picture is crueler, it is also more entertaining because Queneau's world is saturated with laughter, joyful, lighthearted laughter as well as the sardonic laughter of black humor, which Queneau both publicly repudiated and diligently practiced with great verve.

Here are three brief descriptive passages, typical of Queneau's "squalid picturesqueness," the last containing what might be called explicit implications.

> The air, perfectly purified by the night, started stinking slightly again. (P. 25)

> Garbage and soiled papers complete the landscape of vacant lots and boards. The Warsaw express passes by, making the old yellowed newspapers fly about. (P. 36)

> He noticed, casually, that his shoes were run down at the heels; those of his neighbor too and those over there as well; suddenly, he saw a whole civilization of worn-down shoes, a culture of chipped heels. (P. 9)

At the beginning of *Le Chiendent* the main character, Etienne Marcel, a bank clerk who has been leading a completely routine existence, realizes that he suffers from acute "ontalgia"; he suffers in his very being mainly because of a perceived lack of being. He has no personality or character to speak of, almost no being—the narrator refers to him as "the being of lesser reality" and "the being of minimal reality"—because he does not think: *non cogitat ergo non est*. My allusion to Descartes is not gratuitous. In the first place there are many references to the Cartesian *cogito* in the novel itself; the most explicit is this one: "Before I didn't think I didn't exist . . . when I looked at the world I started existing maybe they talk about that in philosophy books" (pp. 79–80). In fact, one impetus behind the writing of the novel was to translate the *Discourse on Method* into the vernacular French of this century just as Descartes had translated it from his original Latin into the literary French of the seventeenth century. Descartes himself is alluded to in the novel: Saturnin Belhotel, a philosophical concierge (most of Queneau's characters are walking oxymorons), wonders why it is that card players in cafés always call the waiter Descartes, shouting to him, "Descartes, des cartes!" (some cards [p. 65]). Misinterpretation of things and people, by the way, is one of the novel's major themes.

Etienne's philosophical awakening—his sudden consciousness of things around him and then of himself—begins with a ludicrously banal event; he notices for the first time a display in a shop window he had passed by for two years: a demonstration of a waterproof hat filled with water and two rubber ducks. This makes him late for his train, which he has always taken at the same hour, always sitting in the same compartment and in the same seat. "Something had changed" in his routine.

Etienne's philosophical development begins with his sudden awareness, his "astonishment," that things *exist*. ("Why is there something instead of nothing?" is the first sentence of Heidegger's *Was ist Metaphysik?*) Then he wonders what they essentially *are*. He immediately develops Cartesian systematic doubt. In fact it is only later (p. 222) that he considers methodical doubt as a necessary preliminary to any philosophical inquiry. His initial stance is one of genuine, not procedural, doubt.

> Then Etienne doubted everything he thought he knew, everything he thought he understood, everything he thought he saw and heard. *Naturally*, Etienne doubted the world. The world was playing a trick on him [cf. Descartes's God as possible deceiver]. . . .
> —I was saying that even a cigarette butt, no one knows what it is. I don't know what it is. I don't know. I DON'T KNOW! . . .
> And myself, eh? who am I? . . . That question in itself, does it have a meaning? Does the word *being* have any meaning? (Pp. 148–49)

Etienne's thoughts develop in the direction of modern existentialism. First, the notion of the subjectivity of meaning and truth.

> —Do you think that birds and pebbles and stars and crustaceans and clouds have a meaning? That they were made for some purpose?
> —I don't think so, replied Etienne. . . . In any case, what is natural can acquire a meaning; when men give it one. (P. 127)

His friend Pierre rejects the possibility of even subjective meaning, preferring to see the universe in nihilist terms.

> —For me too, said Pierre, things, the world doesn't have the meaning it gives itself, it is not what it claims to be; but I don't believe there is any other meaning. It doesn't have any. (P. 127)

From the subjectivity of meaning Etienne moves on to the total absence of meaning and value in the universe, to the Absurd, a word he uses on page 33.

> Existence was losing all value, things all meaning—and it wasn't just this existence right here that was losing all value; it wasn't just these things right here that were being stripped of all their significance, but also that existence that was behind and above and over there, and everything that was located elsewhere and everywhere. The universe

squeezed like a lemon seemed to him only a contemptible peeling. (P. 140)

Looking at things like shoelaces the way Sartre's Roquentin will look at tree roots, he concludes that he, too, is *de trop*, he, too, is absurd: "At the same time as the world, he too was losing all value and all meaning" (p. 140). Then all of humanity appears absurd: "In the vestibule, he came across several faces that he recognized more or less. He admitted their existence, but not their interest; they appeared to him as worthless abstractions" (pp. 140–41).

Around Etienne develops a plot that becomes increasingly complex and farfetched. At the beginning of the novel he is observed by a philo-sophical observer, Pierre le Grand, who is curious about the banality and emptiness of Etienne's life, his closeness to nonbeing. For Etienne at this point, being is merely being perceived, the Berkeleian *esse est percipi*.

Etienne's attractive wife, Alberte, has likewise been the object of the observations of two perpetual girl-watchers, Potice and Narcense. Potice in turn is observed, when run over and killed by a bus, by a sadistic busybody, Mme Cloche, whose brother Dominique happens to own the filthy restaurant that served the unappetizing *bifteck aux pommes* mentioned earlier.

Narcense becomes obsessed by Etienne's wife. He writes her love letters, which she tears up and throws away. But her son Théo pieces them together and writes taunting letters to Narcense. Incensed, Narcense invites Théo to meet him in the woods near Orbonne at midnight, threatening to hang him. Meanwhile, Narcense's concierge, Saturnin, has been reading his mail and is determined to prevent the murder. He tells his widowed sister, a midwife and abortionist, of his plan. This sister happens to be the same Mme Cloche who had witnessed the accident that killed Potice. She also watches at the same place the next evening, hoping to see another accident and does; she sees Etienne grazed by Pierre's taxi. It is thus that Etienne and his observer finally meet as do so many of Queneau's characters: by accident.

Théo does not show up for the encounter with Narcense, who, instead of hanging Théo as he had hoped, is himself found hanging, but still alive, from a tall (and autobiographical) oak. Narcense never explains whether it was an accident or a suicide attempt because, he says, he does not want to bother anyone (including the reader, of course) with matters of "psychology."

Nearly all the characters become involved in observing old man Taupe, a junk dealer. Mme Cloche, misinterpreting some misinformation from her nephew, Clovis, thinks that Taupe is a miserly millionaire and that Etienne, Pierre, and Narcense are international crooks interested in getting to Taupe's treasure before she does. She arranges a marriage between Taupe and the young and "almost pretty" waitress Ernestine, who mysteriously (i.e., the author again does not deign to explain why) dies on her wedding day.

In the seventh and final chapter the plot, which had already mocked realism by its absurd improbabilities, turns literally absurdist. War breaks out between twentieth-century France (but whose inhabitants are now called the Gauls) and the Etruscans, whose queen, Miss Aulini (allusion of course to Mussolini), turns out to be none other than Mme Cloche!

The novel does not end; it begins again. On the last page the characters return to their initial situation, and the last two sentences repeat the first two sentences of the first chapter. Queneau explains the circular structure in the blurb offered originally to the readers of 1933:

> How can all that end? It's very simple, it doesn't end, everything begins again, as lugubrious and ridiculous as on the first page, pretty much. For can one really hope that Mme Cloche will not let herself be deceived again by her power of illusion?[5]

Thus human history, *la bêtise humaine*, repeats itself rather than progresses. France becomes Gaul again, and the national drink is once again mead. The failure of history to produce meaningful evolution is suggested also by the archaic names given to so many of the twentieth-century characters: Clovis, Pierre le Grand, Etienne Marcel, Dagobert, Hector, Hippolyte, Eulalie, Thémistocle. Queneau's attitude toward human history is also expressed unambiguously in a poem:

Stupidity of the 1900s
Stupidity of *la belle époque*
Stupidity of the 1910s
Stupidity of the pant-skirt
Stupidity of the 1920s
Stupidity of the fox-trot
Stupidity of the 1930s
Stupidity of the Stock Exspeculations
Stupidity of the 1940s

Stupidity of the strange war
Stupidity of the 1950s
Stupidity of Left Bank haunts
Stupidity of the 1960s
Stupidity of the 1970s
Stupidity of the 1980s
Stupidity of the 1990s
Stupidity of the 2000s
and all that makes a history
which is deposited on the city
in more or less futile traces
that are deciphered like a wizard's book.

("Un beau siècle" in *Courir les rues*)

*

Etienne and Pierre are not the only characters who meditate about existence. The unemployed saxophonist Narcense has been pondering the pre-Socratic problem of the One and the Many and concludes, against Parmenides, that reality is a "plurality" and admits that he suffers from "becoming." On her deathbed the uneducated waitress Ernestine delivers a Socratic farewell speech, couched in vernacular French, concluding that we are on this earth for no reason and that we leave it for no better world. At the end of chapter 6 Saturnin, the concierge who cannot even spell correctly, delivers a brilliantly funny soliloquy on ontological matters, namely, the dialectics of being and nonbeing. It is a parody of Plato's *Parmenides* and a forerunner of Sartre's *Being and Nothingness*.

> You see, philosophy, it's made two big mistakes; two big oversights; first of all it's forgotten to study the different modes of being, in the first place; and that ain't no little oversight. But that's still nothin'; it's forgotten what's da most importan', the different modes of not being. For example a slab of butter, I'm takin' the first thing that pops into my head, a slab of butter, for instance, that ain't no inn, it ain't a fork or a cliff or an eider-down quilt. And notice that this here mode of not being is precisely its mode of being. I'll come back to that. There's still another mode of not being; for example, the slab of butter that isn't on the table, isn't. That's a stronger degree. Between the two, there's the no-longer-being and the not-yet-having-been. (P. 256).

This meditation on nonbeing goes on for two pages. There is an ambivalent or double irony here; what is being parodied is not only Platonism and modern existentialism (German, not French) but *the author's own obsession* with nonbeing, which runs through the entire novel and throughout the entire opus, even in the comic maxims of *Foutaises:* "Il y a deux sortes d'arbres: les hêtres et les non-hêtres" (There are two kinds of trees: *hêtres* [beeches] and *non-hêtres*—a play on *être et non-être*, h's not being pronounced in French).

At the end of the novel Etienne and Saturnin come to the same philosophical conclusion:

> —Don't you find that nonbeing impregnates being, the latter said to the former, who replied:
> —Doesn't being, rather, conjugate nonbeing? (P. 285)

The primordial reality of nonbeing can be taken to be the novel's major philosophical point since its two leading "philosophers" agree on it, although approaching it here from different angles of vision, and since the main action revolves around a nonexistent treasure that shapes or "conjugates" the lives of most of the characters and apparently ends the lives of two of them. Taupe's death, from grief or murder?—the author once again refuses to explain—soon follows that of his bride of one day. But although Saturnin and Etienne agree, their ideas are expressed not in affirmations but in the form of questions, and the questions themselves are expressed by pretentious metaphorical verbs ("impregnate"; "conjugate") that parody the fuzzy thinking and jargon often encountered in ontological treatises. One thinks, for example, of Rudolph Carnap's classic example of what he considers the nonsensical nature of metaphysics, which he takes from a work that both informs *Le Chiendent* and is parodied by it, Heidegger's *What Is Metaphysics?:* "Nihilation is neither an annihilation of what is, nor does it spring from negation. . . . Nothing annihilates itself."[6]

The novel, then, parodies, ironizes, and partially deconstructs the most overt thesis it propounds.

Queneau's universal irony, hovering over the entire novel and especially the explicitly philosophical passages, points to a radical indeterminacy of meaning and a suspicion of all philosophical systems, *including those to which the author himself is most attracted.* Queneau has made this suspicion quite explicit:

> I have, as they say, a background in philosophy, I'm always concerned with philosophy. . . . But I am not a philosopher, no doubt, for I

distrust systems like the plague—all the systems that real life contradicts
regularly the next day.[7]

*

Le Chiendent is of unquestionable significance in the history of the
French novel. Robbe-Grillet called it the first New Novel, and Georges
Bataille called it the first existentialist novel in France. The kinship with
the *nouveau roman* is obvious: the reaction against psychologism and
against realistic plotting, dialogue, and description; the phenomenological bent; the presentation of a world *not* cozily structured within preestablished meanings; and the implicit interrogation of the very nature
and validity of fiction itself. As an existentialist novel, *Le Chiendent* ante-
dates *La Nausée* by five full years. As a philosophy student, Queneau had
been reading Husserl and Heidegger, among others, during the period
1929–32. In 1931 Sartre, according to Simone de Beauvoir, was reading
Heidegger's *Was ist Metaphysik?* without understanding a word of it.

Etienne's methodical doubt is not only Cartesian but Husserlian; it
reflects the phenomenological reduction, the *Epoché*. And the central
problem of Husserl's *Cartesian Meditations*, that of experiencing and
knowing the mind of others, is reflected in Mme Cloche's misinterpreta-
tions of what she calls "the Others." Etienne's consciousness, characterized mainly by its intentionality, reflects both the pure, rational, and
reflective consciousness of Husserl and the "concrete" consciousness of
Heidegger, a consciousness of things (e.g., rubber ducks, an egg slicer, a
potato peeler, a pair of scissors) viewed in and outside their instrumen-
tality.

> As soon as one looks at things disinterestedly everything
> changes. . . . Not to take into account the purpose of an object, what a
> strange activity! . . .
> —If I neglect the practical side of a manufactured object, said
> Etienne.
> —You are getting into aesthetics, interrupted Pierre. Or magic.
> —But I don't want to get into aesthetics, or magic, protested
> Etienne. Men think they are doing one thing, and then they do another.
> They think they are making a pair of scissors, and it's something else
> they make. Of course, it *is* a pair of scissors, it's made to cut and it does
> cut, but it's something else, too. . . .
> —What would be interesting would be to say what that "something
> else" is. (Pp. 124–26)

At the beginning of *Le Chiendent* Etienne illustrates Heidegger's concept of inauthentic being. He is so absorbed in his daily routine (*métro-boulot-métro-dodo*) that he is oblivious to his own inner being. He has no sense of self; he has lapsed into the "average" or "deficient" mode of "being-in-the-world." He is an anonymous silhouette in an anonymous crowd.

> A man's silhouette stood out; simultaneously, thousands. There were indeed thousands of them. He had just opened his eyes and the teeming streets were agitated, agitated too were the men who worked all day. The silhouette in question moved away from the wall of an immense and unbearable building, an edifice that looked like a suffocation and that was a bank. Detached from the wall, the silhouette wavered, jostled by other forms, with no discernible individual behavior, tormented in varying degrees, less by his own anxieties than by the entirety of the anxieties of his thousands of neighbors. (P. 7)

Etienne recovers his selfhood through two important Heideggerian experiences: boredom and angst. It was boredom that pushed him to really *look* at the rubber ducks for once. And it is boredom that makes him aware of his own existence.

> Then Etienne experienced the power of boredom.... Etienne noted suddenly that he was terribly, totally, irremediably bored. He realized that while tying his shoe laces. (Pp. 128–29)

Angst is one of the novel's major leitmotifs.

> —So, you don't notice anything, Etienne asks again anxiously. (P. 56)

> —Etienne, anxiously, leans forward and looks at those eyes, that mouth. (P. 81)

> —And myself, eh? who am I? ... I have such and such a nature, I experience such and such feelings, I live in such and such a way. Psychologists must be able to analyze me, right? And after that, I still ask who I am! But that's what I am! And in spite of everything, I can persist in asking that everlasting question. It anguishes me; isn't that stupid? (P. 149)

Existential (and existentialist) anguish pushes Etienne toward authentic being. He begins to exercise his freedom and becomes capable of resolute action. He forms a project. Braving the ridicule of his wife and son-in-law, he will visit an unprepossessing restaurant whose sole specialty is the humble French fried potato. But of course, Etienne is all too human. At the end of the novel he will lapse again into inauthenticity. He becomes a silhouette again. However, as Sartre would say, he is *récupérable*.

It is Pierre's existential anguish that makes of him an observer of Etienne and of the Absurd.

> At that moment, he noted with anguish that the silhouette, instead of heading straight for the metro, was going a roundabout way. (P. 11)

> The observer is cooking up something; what, he doesn't know himself. But he is getting ready; either to continue his study of the fellow in his sights, as he calls him, or else to look for some other chance encounter, just as vain, just as useless. After hesitating between various possible ways of occupying himself, he opts for the pernod and the silhouette. . . .

> The observer allows to reach him those vain words that are telling nothing but the truth; he notes with bitterness that those banalities correspond perfectly to reality. (Pp. 15–16)

And Saturnin notices that people in restaurants are eager to have their plates and wine glasses filled to escape their anguish when confronted with nonbeing.

> They have gotten into the habit of eating shoup, and there they are, suddenly obliged to give up this habit so easily acquired. So, they are sad. So, they have the taste of ashes in their mouths. So, they are reduced to despair. They hadn't suspected that the full plate hides an empty plate, just as being hides nonbeing. . . .
>
> But the two waiters borrowed from the Restaurant des Alliés know very well this difficult moment and the way to shorten it: they make the empty plate disappear. Of course another empty plate replaces it; but this one is an expectation, whereas the other was only a disappointment; one is an adumbration, the other a memory. This suppression of emptiness by emptiness, the void by the void, is not enough; the two waiters borrowed from the Restaurant des Alliés complete it by a suppression through the plenum; they fill with wine the glasses which take on the joyous appearance of pharmacists' bottles.
>
> It is thus that one escapes anguish, concluded Saturnin. (Pp. 182–83)

The novel's title, *Le Chiendent* (Crabgrass), is intimately linked to Queneau's personal mythology (the first clue being the presence of *le chien*) and to his obsession with metaphysical anguish. The author has given several of his characters names that are synonymous with *le chiendent:* Agrostis in *Odile,* Gramigni in *Les Enfants du limon,* Miss Weeds in *Un rude hiver.* In *Les derniers jours* General "Faidherbe" (another synonym of "weed") is nicknamed "le Chiendent" because of his pugnacity (*chiendent* is a weed with deep and tenacious roots). In a poem Queneau explicitly links this weed to his obsession with death; while others may imagine their future decomposing corpses pushing up pretty daisies, Queneau sees his pushing up weeds, crabgrass.

> The dice that my molars will become
> the ossicles of my vertebrae
> will be used in childrens' games
> but the soup of my miseries
> and the spasms of my shadows
> will push up the crabgrass to the light of day.
> ("La Mort mobile" in *Le Chien à la Mandoline*)

"Le chiendent" represents not only the fact of death but especially the consciousness and anticipation of death, Heidegger's "being-for-death." Man's glorious distinction from the lower animals resides in his consciousness and self-consciousness, but there's the rub (*voilà le chiendent*): as both Heidegger and Malraux have said, man is an anxious animal, the only animal that knows it is going to die.

> Prince! all that, that's the rub. [c'est le chiendent]
> It's even worse if you think about it
> Death always gets you at the turn of the road
> Winter arrives after autumn.
> ("L'Instant fatal" in *Si tu t'imagines*)

Queneau's anguish, then, is genuine and painful. His resolutely playful treatment of this profound anguish, in *Le Chiendent* as in most of his fictional and poetic work, is part of what makes his irony "romantic."

*

The capricious intricacy of the plot, with its many complications, coincidences, chance encounters, concealments, discoveries, bizarre events, and bizarre people (one of whom has not been mentioned yet: Bébé Toutout, a dwarf and parasite; toutout=chien=Queneau), has made more than one critic speak of the arabesque. Schlegel had conceived of the ironic arabesque in dialectical terms: an interplay of apparent disorder and underlying order, of caprice and constraint. Similarly, Queneau's capricious plotting conceals a rigid underlying structure. The influence of James Joyce is crucial here. Queneau was deeply impressed not only by the boldness with which Joyce handled the vernacular and the parodic switches in prose styles but also by the intricate formal pattern imposed upon the plot of *Ulysses:* eighteen episodes each having its own atmosphere, its special technique and central symbol, its intertextual correspondence to analogous episodes in the *Odyssey*, its representation of a particular hour of the day, and the whole novel covering strictly twenty-four hours of the same day. Queneau was always uncomfortable with the nearly total aesthetic freedom most novelists allow themselves. He felt that the novel should be as carefully structured as a sonnet. In "Techniques du roman" *(Bâtons*, pp. 27–33) and in "Conversation avec Georges Ribemont-Dessaignes" *(Bâtons*, pp. 35–47) he has explained the strict structural constraints he imposed upon *Le Chiendent* in order to invest it with a certain "rhythm." The number of chapters (seven) and subsections (thirteen) was fixed so as to arrive at a predetermined number: ninety-one. This number was chosen because it is the sum of the first thirteen numbers and because of a private symbolism the number had for Queneau at the time.

> . . . 91 being the sum of the first thirteen numbers and its "sum" being 1, it is therefore both the number of the death of beings and that of their return to existence, a return which at that time I conceived of only as the irresolvable perpetuity of hopeless misery. *(Bâtons*, p. 29)

He thought of thirteen as a lucky number because, paradoxically, it was a denial of happiness. The number seven was important for biographical reasons. His first, middle, and last names are each composed of seven letters (three times seven), and he was born on the twenty-first day of the month (three times seven again). The numbers selected seem arbitrary, but as Martin Esslin reminds us, arbitrary numbers are the basis of structure in many types of poems.

Each of the novel's ninety-one sections is a unit. It observes the three unities of time, place, and action and is written within the conventions of a specific genre: narration proper, narration with reported speech, pure dialogue, first-person stream of consciousness, reported monologue, direct monologue, letters, newspaper clippings, dream narratives. A different mode of expression and narrative point of view corresponds to each genre. Every thirteenth section, except the concluding one, is situated "outside" the chapter and represents a pause in the action. The novel is also given what Queneau calls a circular structure but what might more accurately be termed a sudden parabolic loop; as mentioned earlier, the characters at the end of the story suddenly return to their initial situation, and the last two sentences repeat the first two sentences of the initial chapter.

Queneau claims that his characters appear and disappear, situations arise and subside, not by pure chance (and certainly not out of a concern for verisimilitude) but from a concern for rhythm and even "rhyme": "One can make situations or characters rhyme just as one makes words rhyme, one can even settle for alliterations" *(Bâtons,* p. 42). Narcense and Potice, for example, rhyme in several ways. Their names have the same number of syllables; their final syllables, already providing an alliteration, are transpositions one of the other, giving "Narcisse" and "Potence"—narcissism and death by hanging being two of the most important themes in Queneau's work. Narcense and Potice rhyme, too, by their mutual friendship, their mutual interest (in women), and their similar temperaments.

Similarly, Etienne and Saturnin rhyme by their philosophical quest and by their nearly identical philosophies (complete identity is bad rhyming). Pierre le Grand and Etienne rhyme in their observer-observed relationship and in their ontological anguish. The rhyming situations include the following: the hanging of the dog Jupiter (at one point the action is presented from the dog's point of view) announces that of Narcense; Potice's accident rhymes with that of Etienne the following day; the letters unsealed by Saturnin rhyme with those unsealed by Bébé Toutout and Théo.[8] Then there is the symmetry of certain details. For example, the exchange of letters between Théo and Narcense:

1. —Letter from Narcense
2. —Letter from Théo with P.S.
3. —Letter from Narcense
4. —Letter from Théo with 3 P.S.'s
5. —Letter from Narcense
6. —Letter from Théo with P.S.
7. —Letter from Narcense

(From Simonnet, *Queneau déchiffré,* p. 48)

Claude Simonnet has uncovered a ternary rhythm in the sequence of narrative sections, each chapter having three "tetrads" (three times four equals twelve, the thirteenth section being "outside" the chapter). For example, the first four sections of chapter 1 present the silhouette and the observer, the next four present the entrance of Narcense, and the last four that of Mme Cloche.

*

Other aspects of *Le Chiendent* that would have pleased Friedrich von Schlegel are the dialectics of objectivity and subjectivity and of fictional illusion and its deliberate destruction. The epigraph to *Zazie* is germane here: "He who created it razed it to the ground." Vivian Mercier has appropriately entitled an essay "Raymond Queneau: The Creator as Destroyer." Much of *Le Chiendent* reads as straightforward objective narrative, but just as much of it is filled with subjective authorial intrusions and self-conscious ironic devices that destroy the illusion. The novel begins and ends, for instance, with "eloquent objectivity" (Jacques Guicharnaud). And many passages begin objectively enough: "Along the river, it was dark." But the author-narrator immediately deflates his description: "It was dark elsewhere too, but no matter" (p. 208). As Guicharnaud has noted *(Raymond Queneau,* p. 24): "Now it is the fictional objectivity that is called into question, now the contrary."

The circular movement Queneau has given his plot causes the novel, as a temporal structure, to self-destruct. Gerald Prince ("Queneau et l'anti-roman," p. 35) explains:

> To confer a circular form upon a novel is to force the reader to turn back, by moving off at a given moment in a direction opposite to the direction of the narrative; it obliges him to take the opposite view of the facts that he has acquired and to destroy, so to speak, everything he has patiently constructed. That also reverses the most fundamental characteristic of the traditional novel. The latter is a temporal genre par excellence. It requires, as Sartre said, "a continuous duration, a becoming, the manifest presence of time's irreversibility." Now, the circular structure of Queneau's novels eliminates their temporal dimension.

Then the novel flaunts its fictional nature by having characters in the novel *tell* us they are characters in the novel.

> —I am observing a man.
> —Gee. [Are you] a novelist?
> —No. A character. (P. 25)

—It ain't me who made that up, said the queen. It's in the book.
—What book? inquired the two wandering generals.
—Well, this here one. This one right here, the one we're in right now, that repeats what we say as we say it, and that follows us around and tells about us. (P. 294)

The narrator wonders aloud if he has forgotten a significant detail (pp. 21–22), acknowledges that a certain narrative detail is false (p. 119), admits that he is not sure of a character's age (p. 37), and tells us that one of the characters has bought not a novel but a "serious" book. Roland Travy in *Odile* speaks of "an idiotic novel, like all novels." Likewise in *Si tu t'imagines* the poet tells us that "a poem is an insignificant thing." The self-conscious narrator of *Le Chiendent* even invents new punctuation: [¡¡]. These inverted exclamation marks are "indignation marks," we are told. And the author leaves in the text his marginal notes to himself.

> The storm is slow in arriving. . . . Finally, one, two, three drops of water collapse on the asphalt. . . . People worried about their skin raise their nose. Description of a storm in Paris. In the summer. (P. 15)

Another ironic device used for the destruction of illusion is the pseudodescription.

> The sea was beautiful, the sun was beautiful, the land was beautiful, the sky was beautiful, the beach was beautiful, the port was beautiful, the town was beautiful, the countryside was buteeful [*sic*], the atmosphere was beautiful and the air was beautiful. (Pp. 138–39)

The intercalated "dit-il" (said he) of traditional fiction, so despised by novelists like Nathalie Sarraute, is displaced so as to break up normal rhythmic groups, that is, so as to subvert the realistic dialogue.

> Je, commença l'un, ne connais pas. . . .
> I, began the other, don't know. . . .
>
> Ce, commença donc Théo, type qui est venu hier. . . .
> That, began Théo then, guy who came yesterday. . . .
>
> Il, dit Thémistocle, me semble que. . . .
> It, said Themistocles, seems to me. . . .
>
> Je, dit Etienne, crois que. . . .
> I, said Etienne, believe that. . . .

More often the reader is made aware of the fiction's fictionality by the comically and ironically abrupt changes in stylistic register. Queneau has said that he got the idea of his *Exercices de style* about a year or two before its publication in 1947. But *Le Chiendent* is already an *exercice de style* and thereby an exercise in antirealism and the destruction of fictional illusion, as this sampler proves.

EXERCICES DE STYLE	*LE CHIENDENT*

1. Multiple Questions

But there was one of them (or two?) who stood out, I forget exactly how. By his megalomania? By his adiposity? By his melancholy?

Why that one? His greater haste toward the metro? His singularly threadbare jacket? His short chignon, poorly cut? (P. 9)

2. "Négativités"

It was neither a boat, nor a plane, but a means of terrestrial transportation. It was neither morning, nor evening, but noon. It was neither a baby, nor an old man, but a man still quite young.

As for Narcense, he's an artist; neither a painter, nor a poet, nor an architect, nor an actor, nor a sculptor. (P. 181)

3. "Précisions"

At 12:17 on an S-line bus, 10 meters long, 3 wide, 6 high, at 3.6 kilometers from its point of departure, when loaded with 48 people, an individual of the male sex, aged 27 years 3 months 8 days. . . .

57 minutes later, he was 10 meters from the Saint-Lazare station. . . .

A glance at the small classified ads, 5 minutes 12 seconds! He has finished his newspaper. (P. 25)

—His age?
—34.
—Profession?
—Musician.
—Height?
—1 meter 71.
—Weight?

—75 kilos.
—Thoracic perimeter?
—87 centimeters.
[The answers given here
are those of a friend, not a
medical examiner.]

4. "Noble"

At the hour when dawn's
rosy fingers start to get
chapped, I mounted, like a
rapid dart, a cow-eyed bus of
powerful stature.
I was inaugurating a new
hat.

It was the hour when in
the blue-windowed factory
people were manipulating
chloride and sulfuric acid.
(P. 158)
. . . Clovis Belhotel, who is
inaugurating a new suit.
(P. 175)

5. Redundancies

Toward the middle of
the day and at noon, I was
and got on the platform and
rear terrace of a crowded
and almost full bus and public transport vehicle. . . . I
saw and noticed a ridiculous
and quite grotesque young
man and old adolescent. . . .
Two hours afterward
and a hundred and twenty
minutes later I meet and see
him again.

Yes, Ernestine, I am get-
ting you out of financial
trouble, out of financial distress, out of financial hard-
ship. I am getting you out of
poverty, need, indigence.
(P. 109)
This young man is called
and named Théo Marcel.
(P. 142)
The sister-in-law has had
her fill of it. . . . She's sick of
it. She's tired of it. She's fed
up with it. She's had it up to
here. She's had enough of it.
(P. 213)

6. Metaphorical Periphrasis

At the day's center, cast
into the pile of traveling sar-
dines of a coleoptera of
whitish abdomen. . . .

A night in an auto had
advantageously replaced the
usual twelve hours in the
sardine can. (P. 123)

7. "So"

So the bus arrived. So I
got on. So I saw a citizen who

So, they are sad. So, they
have the taste of ashes in

caught my eye. So I saw his
long neck.
  So later I see him
again. . . . So.

their mouths. So, they are
reduced to despair. (P. 182)

8. *"Onomatopées"*

On the platform, pla,
pla, pla, of a bus, teuff, teuff,
teuff, of the S line (pour qui
sont ces serpents qui sifflent
sur), it was about noon, ding,
din, don, ding, din, don. . . .

A car goes coin, coin, the
mailman's bike goes cuicui
and the gardener's wheelbar-
row goes cricri. (P. 225)

9. *Concretization of Abstract
Nouns*

The philosopher who
sometimes gets on the futile
and youtilitarian [*sic*] inexis-
tentiality of an S bus can perceive there with the lucidity
of his pineal eye the fugitive
and faded appearances of a
profane consciousness
afflicted with the long neck
of vanity and the hat braid of
ignorance.

He wraps the serpents of
disdain with the handker-
chief of jealousy. (P. 80)

While thinking about it I
gargle my gullet with the tea
of pride, I rub my skull with
the lotion of vanity, I rub my
sides with the cologne water
of self-satisfaction, I polish
my toes with the brush of
stupidity. (P. 280)

As if these self-conscious stylistic deviations from linguistic and fictional norms were not enough, the novel's narrative is subverted by the
new norms of Neo-French. There are new spellings reflecting authentic
pronunciation (mispronunciation according to purists): *la choupe* (for *la
soupe); l'haricot vert* (for *le haricot vert); au miyeu de* (for *au milieu de); voir
skeu cé* (for *voir ce que c'est*). Other spellings are purely visual in nature,
not "improvements" in phonetic transcription but simply declarations of
orthographical freedom: *banglieue* (for *banlieue); c'était draule* (for *c'était
drôle*). There is a new morphology and syntax:

beaucoup des enfants	for	*beaucoup d'enfants*
son ambition grande	for	*sa grande ambition*
son élimée veste	for	*sa veste élimée*

and *les fourchettes et les couteaux s'artistement rangeaient sur les nappes quasi propres* (for ... *se rangeaient artistiquement* ...). *Très peur,* already a grammatical monstrosity of normal French, becomes *très la trouille.* The occasional *cuirs,* or false liaisons heard in rapid speech, have become generalized:

maizoui	for	*mais oui*
il arriva zinsiza son bouillon	for	*il arriva ainsi à son bouillon*
mal-z-éclairée	for	*mal éclairée*

*

Queneau claims to have been haunted early in life by the world's duality.

> and I was terrified by the mixture
> of ordure and innocence
> that creation presented
>
> *(Chêne et chien)*

And it is true that the opus as a whole ranges between the poles of ordure and innocence. Gaëton Picon and Allen Thiher see intimations of innocence in the festive, carnivalesque atmosphere of the novels. That is to say, the "carnivalesque" is taken in the Bakhtinian sense of legalized licentiousness, of guiltless mockery of officialdom, of prohibitions of every kind, and of normative notions of propriety. (Queneau's humor has, too, what Bakhtin calls the ambivalence of carnival humor: in the sense that it simultaneously derides and extols the bodily functions, in the sense that the laugher knows that he, too, belongs to the world he is laughing at, and in the sense that ordinary life is derided, degraded, and imaginatively "destroyed" so that it may be regenerated.)

Martin Esslin and Anne Clancier see innocence in those heroes, those "wise simpletons" of Queneau who reject the quest for the absolute, for ultimate or even reasonable solutions, and confine themselves to life's simplest pleasures. Many of them drift through life without seeking to understand it; they have developed a detachment from their surroundings that is comic and at the same time stoic. (One thinks of the stoic apathy of Camus's Meursault confronting the Absurd.) They are unambitious and lazy by "Yuppie" standards but have in reality given up the struggle for status, power, prestige, and material goods, realizing, rather vaguely and inarticulately, the vanity of such things and the vanity of most things. They live in "the Sunday of life," beyond all striving and beyond good and evil. Jacques Bens sees some of these innocents not as simpletons but as thinkers. The latter are those who have not lost the sense of wonder and the insatiable curiosity of childhood. They are curious not so much about the good life, the ethical life, or even happiness, so much as life itself. Etienne, like Pierrot of *Pierrot mon ami* an incipient or apprentice hero, says at one point: "It's not happiness I'm concerned with but existence" (p. 93). And as we have seen, Saturnin's most intense moments come when he is pondering, in very funny French, the various modes of being and nonbeing. Though not overly concerned with happiness, such "heroes" are not indifferent toward it. Pierrot, for instance, is content with the minimal, fragile, and ephemeral pleasures that life offers now and then: "Pierrot had a job, at least for the season. In October, he would see. . . . There's enough to be happy and content for someone who permanently knew the days to be uncertain, the weeks improbable and the months very deficient." Queneau's heroes know that happiness is a tenuous thing, that what is really solid in life is misery.

> only misery
> is solid and without shadow
>
> ("Misère de ma vie" in *Si tu t'imagines)*

These heroes are "pure," says Bens, untouched and unconcerned by original sin. Socially, financially, and culturally disadvantaged, vulnerable to mishaps and bad luck in general, they tend to be modest, unassuming, and shy, much like the author himself.

But heroes, even modest and shy ones, incipient heroes, apprentice heroes, and would-be heroes, are by definition exceptional beings. The mass of humanity in Queneau's novels wallows in stupidity and ordure. Queneau presents these characters, however, not with Balzacian condescension or Flaubertian contempt but with amused detachment or even complicitous (Roland Barthes) good humor.

Queneau's ambivalence about human life, then, is seen not only in his literary and extraliterary declarations, but in the very distribution of his dramatis personae. While much of *Le Chiendent* is filled with physical and moral squalor, there are now and then ever so discreet touches of light. For example, several acts of generosity have escaped the notice of most critics because each such act is described in a single sentence.

Etienne gives Dominique, whom he hardly knows, a potato peeler—a humble gift but very appropriate since the specialty of Dominique's greasy restaurant is *pommes frites*. Dominique offers Etienne a drink on the house. Taupe's "treasure" is not a hoard of money hidden behind his blue door but two names, his own and that of his beloved, written on it—a memory of love he has treasured for forty years. Saturnin steals the door and, upon discovering that it is worthless, cuts it up for firewood. But when he sees the names he preserves that part of the door and, in an act of pure kindness, sends it to Taupe. He then gives Narcense his last fifty francs.

But *Le Chiendent* in the final analysis is an extremely pessimistic novel. Its universal satire and world irony seem closer to nihilism than to the more evenly balanced ambivalences of a Diderot or a Stendhal. The author approaches (but never reaches) that "absolute principle of negativity" that Hegel and Kierkegaard thought they saw in Schlegelian irony. There *is* genuine ambivalence in Queneau's work, especially when looked at as a whole, but romantic irony is not the summing up of a career or an opus; its real existence is found in the individual work of art. Existence in *Le Chiendent* is seen mainly (but not entirely) as degeneracy, decay, mental and moral mediocrity. Even Allen Thiher, who stresses the innocence of Queneau's characters, admits *(Raymond Queneau,* pp. 47, 77):

> Queneau is a creator of ironic voices that mimic many points of view, and one reads the presence of the poet as a kind of negative intelligence to whom no single existential stance can be ascribed. . . .
>
> His comedy turns less on a despair about finding "reality" than on a disabused contempt for a reality that is not perhaps worth finding in the first place.

The pessimism is so deep that some critics speak of Queneau's nihilism in *Le Chiendent* and even his entire first manner, up to about 1939, without qualifying the word or the assumption. This has to be an oversimplification given the many ambiguities and ambivalences in *Le Chiendent* and in everything the author has written. We witness, for example, the pursuit of wisdom (Etienne, Saturnin) in *Le Chiendent,* the striving for humility (Jacques l'Aumône) in *Loin de Rueil,* and even the "temptation" of sainthood (Valentin, Ast) in *Le Dimanche de la vie* and *Les Enfants du limon.* Then there is the 'pataphysical law of "the inseparability of opposites," which Queneau has explicitly applied to his own thinking: "Whenever I put forth an assertion, I realize immediately that the opposite assertion is just about as interesting, to the point that it is becoming a superstition with me" *(Entretiens avec Georges Charbonnier,* p. 12). This typically modern tendency to see (and thus to be paralyzed by) the opposing sides of a question was noted by Robert Musil in *The Man Without Qualities,* a supremely ironic novel written at approximately the same time as *Le Chiendent:*

> Today to every thought we also have a counter-thought, and to every tendency an immediate counter-tendency. Today, every act and its opposite are accomplished by the subtlest intellectual arguments, with which one can both defend them and condemn them.

G.-E. Clancier ("Unité poétique," p. 108) has said of Queneau: "Negation, by affirming itself, negates itself." Andrée Bergens *(Queneau,* p. 21) puts it this way: "To doubt, and what is more, to doubt doubt, that is why, deliberately, Queneau will always be a comic skeptic." Gary Handwerk *(Irony and Ethics,* p. 173) has aptly said that "irony adds to skepticism a doubt of one's ability to doubt, because it recognizes the incurable positivity of the mind and language."

I prefer to view the matter thus: *Le Chiendent* and all the other circular, pessimistic novels of Queneau's first manner are saved from their near-nihilism by their romantic irony, which, among other things, is a deconstructive irony protecting a writer from his doubts as well as from his enthusiasms. Queneau's profoundly ironic view of all system and method in philosophic thinking extends to his own tenacious tendency toward systematic and methodical doubt.

10

The Fullness of Chaos:
Beckett's Trilogy

And whether I say this, that or something
else matters little.
(Molloy)

I don't know why I have told this story.
I could just as well have told another.
("L'Expulsé")

HE decaying inhabitants of Samuel Beckett's entropic world have
the feeling that they were born octogenarian, that they were
"born retired." They are often found in supine, horizontal, or
fetal positions; if still vertical, they are often enclosed in jars, cylinders,
or garbage cans, or are buried to the neck in sand or mud. Beckett has
denied the existence of any symbols in his enigmatic work. See "no
symbols where none intended," we are told in *Watt;* the French translation is even more pointed: "honni soit qui symboles y voit." But it is clear
that his decrepit heroes are allegorical figures moving in a world domi-
nated by the fact of death—the death of God and the imminent death of
man—and by the absence of clear meaning and distinct purpose in a
universe as enigmatic as the stories Beckett tells. Both Malone and the
Unnamable divide humanity into two groups: the dead and the dying. It
is a world governed by no consecrated authority. No god, no savior,
walks ahead of man as he crawls from womb to tomb talking to himself
or to strangers in endless circles.

On one level Beckett's work is profoundly tragic. But when one
considers all the possible levels of meaning, including those levels that
seem to deflate man's tragic dignity and even "disfigure" (Lukács) man's

image, as many of Beckett's Christian, Marxist, and humanist critics have complained, and when one considers the curious and comic mélange of literary strategies, structural principles, and stylistic registers employed, his work must be seen as profoundly and essentially ironic. It is informed in fact by romantic irony that, while dealing with serious and tragic matters, is a refusal of the tragic mode and register, a refusal to take itself seriously either as informal philosophy or as formal art.

Molloy is divided into two parts, with two different "heroes," but Moran, who is looking for Molloy, who is looking for his mother, becomes so much like the object of his quest that the two, for our purposes, can be treated collectively as the novel's single hero. Indeed, Molloy can be, and has been, interpreted—notably by Edith Kern—as Moran's repressed, subconscious, and antithetical self, the Jungian shadow side of the self. Molloy can also be interpreted as a progression (even though his story, ironically, precedes Moran's) in Moran's consciousness. As his body withers into that of Molloy, the once-vain Moran succeeds in achieving what he calls "a sharper and clearer sense of my identity," but this means his growing awareness of the poverty of his real self—its invincible impotence, its insuperable ignorance, and its utter solitude.

Molloy is Beckett's best-known and most frequently studied piece of fiction and can serve as a paradigm of the entire canon and of the role of romantic irony within it. The questioning, questing consciousness that unifies the trilogy can be taken as a single narrator, but, again, only for our purposes, since the different proper nouns and personal pronouns with which Beckett has endowed that consciousness point to the multiple selves that can inhabit the same body without any discernible unifying principle connecting these selves in a coherent or meaningful way; they point to the Proustian *moi multiple* or *moi successif* but without the redeeming grace of Proustian memory: "Having been my entire life nothing but a procession or rather a succession of local phenomena."[1] They point to the Heraclitean and Humean flux. The narrative presence is so fragmented in Beckett's work, the attack on the integrity of the speaking subject so radical, that one has to ask, with Gary Handwerk *(Irony and Ethics,* p. 182), how and why one can speak of *a* narrator at all.

I find six principal sources of romantic irony in *Molloy:* the ambivalent deflation of the hero—ambivalent because the deflation is accompanied by a modicum of grudging sympathy, perhaps even admiration, on the part of both implied author and reader; the deflation of the narrator (this term, too, is applied to Molloy and Moran collectively and to the narrators of the other two works of the trilogy, *Malone meurt* and *L'Innomable);* authorial self-parody and self-reflexive irony; the self-deconstruction of the narrative; an explicit recognition by hero, narrator, and implied author of the paradoxical coexistence of contraries of which the human condition is composed; and an intangible ironic spirit hovering over the entire work and aimed not only at God and man but at the work itself and its author—the real author, not just the implied author who often speaks for but just as often masquerades as Samuel Beckett.

Deflation of the hero. In *Watt* and *Murphy* we witness a third-person narrator whose attitude toward the title character is patronizing. In the first-person narrative of *Molloy* we witness, as we so often do in Beckett's fictional and dramatic work, the hero as clown and tramp: a pimply, toothless hero wearing a polka-dot tie around his bare neck and a ludicrous hat tied to his buttonhole or, in Moran's case, his neck. To speak of him simply as an antihero is to put the case mildly; we are dealing with a foul-smelling, urinating, defecating, masturbating hero, a rotting hero, human wreckage, at times, even, a humanoid creature regressing into a larval state. The protagonist, most often engaged in seemingly trivial distractions, Pascalian *divertissements,* is at the (seemingly) farthest remove possible from that highly evolved specimen of homo sapiens traditionally called the Hero. He represents a regression from the *Übermensch* to the *sous-homme.* Molloy-Moran is Humanity writ small.

The Beckettian hero remains largely (but not totally) unheroic, whether he is in one of his frequent befuddled moments or in one of his infrequent moments of lucidity—for example, the maniacal lucidity and precision with which Molloy mentally arranges his "sucking-stones" or of Murphy's exploring the possibilities of eating five crackers in 120 different ways. Except for brief bursts of sadistic energy, he is a passive questor, waiting for something to happen rather than making things happen. He is often a disgusting creature, as when Moran consistently misunderstands and sadistically mistreats his son or when he bashes in the skull of a man who resembles him (probably *because* he resembles him). Molloy steals from an old woman who had helped him and, in a gratuitous fit of pique, tries to beat to death, with his crutch, a stranger who had offered him hospitality. "That calmed him down," says Molloy in a dreadful, Swiftian euphemism. Moments later, noticing that his victim is still breathing, he kicks him in the ribs and leaves him for dead.

Deflation of the narrator. The traditional first-person narrator does not enjoy the omniscience of his third-person counterpart, but the author usually manages to present him as a person of unusual perspicacity endowed with a memory of total recall. In *Molloy* we have a forgetful and imperceptive narrator, one who can't remember the name of his hometown, even though he has lived there most of his life, and who on one occasion has trouble remembering his own name. He frequently forgets why he wants to find his mother. Even when he does remember, the reason given is vague ("to get things straight between us"). The reader is left with the impression that Molloy *never* is sure why he is looking for her. His desire to find his roots and his identity, or to return to the womb, although undoubtedly present, seems unconscious and visceral.

He is an unassertive narrator, punctuating or, rather, puncturing most of his bolder statements with a tentative verb (e.g., "this room *seems* to be mine"), adverb (e.g., "perhaps"), or conjunction (e.g., the concessive "unless" or "but" as in "a little dog was following him, a pomeranian I think, but I don't think so" [M, p. 14]). By his own admission he may be a confused narrator (e.g., M, pp. 18, 208) and asks the reader to correct any lapses he has had. At times he is an inattentive, absentminded narrator, forgetting what he was about to say.

> To tell the truth, let's be frank at least, for quite a while now I don't know what I'm saying. It's because my mind is elsewhere. (INN, p. 73)

> My question, I did have a question, ah yes, whether I had tried everything. . . . My mind is elsewhere. *(Textes pour rien* 7:176)

At one point the narrator of *Textes pour rien* loses his footing, becomes totally confused, and the narrative breaks down.

> When I think, no, that's not it, when those who have known me, indeed still know me, by sight of course, or by odor, when I think about it it's as, as if, what then, I don't know, I don't remember, I shouldn't have started this. (11:203)

Even more disturbing is the fact that he is sometimes a deceitful narrator, admitting that he lied to the reader when he (Moran) said he owned some turkeys. He may even be a totally unreliable narrator. Moran begins his story thus: "It's midnight. The rain is pelting the window panes." But here is the end, which brings us back to the beginning: "So I went back inside the house and I wrote, It's midnight. The rain is pelting the window panes. It wasn't midnight. It wasn't raining." The narrator, who is also a writer, is aware, then, of the artificial and fictional nature of fiction. *All* novelists write things such as "It was midnight. The rain was pelting the window panes," but only romantic ironists create, then deliberately break, the fictional illusion.

The Beckettian narrator-writer is also keenly aware that his professional tool, language, is inadequate. He frequently criticizes the vagueness or inaccuracy of an expression he has just used. This impatience with words reaches one of its many climaxes in the trilogy with the narrator of *Malone meurt,* who claims that he doesn't have time to choose between words, even antonyms: "*Misfortunes, benefit,* I don't have time to choose my words, I'm in a hurry" (MM, p. 60). Similarly the narrator of "Le Calmant" is "too tired" to look for the *mot juste,* the right word.

Authorial self-parody. Since Molloy and Moran are Everyman (more on this later), and since they are to some degree personae of the author, the latter himself is doubly implicated in the ironic debunking and deflation. Self-parody and self-reflexive irony, central and constant ingredients of romantic irony, are implicitly present everywhere in Beckett's fiction. In fact Beckett has made this point quite explicit: "I got to know Molloy and the rest the day I became aware of *my* stupidity."[2]

The Beckettian narrator, who becomes more and more identified with the implied author as the trilogy progresses, constantly confesses that he is a compulsive narrator, that is, a compulsive liar, who has nothing whatsoever of importance to say. And he will admit the gratuitousness of the story he is telling or has just told.

> What was I going to say? Too bad, I'll say something else, it all amounts to the same thing. (INN, p. 57)

> And whether I say this, that or something else matters little. (M, p. 46)

> I don't know why I have told this story. I could just as well have told another. ("L'Expulsé," *Nouvelles,* p. 40)

At one point the narrative voice of *L'Innomable* confesses that all the stories previously told under other names were cowardly and hypocritical disguises used to avoid telling his own story directly and without artifice.

> These Murphys, Molloys and other Malones, I'm not fooled by them. They've made me waste my time, go to a lot of trouble for nothing, by allowing me to talk about them when I should have been talking only about myself, in order to be able to be quiet. (Pp. 32–33)

This admission seems to come directly from the real, not the implied author; that is, this "narrator's confession" seems to be voiced by an author stepping out from behind his surrogate and speaking for himself in a Schlegelian parabasis. Despite the deliberate and rich ambiguity, the author—the real one—seems to be *inviting* the reader to read this as autobiography as well as fiction. The fact that the reader can hear three different speakers here makes the text all the more intriguing—and profound.

Beckett has carried the self-disparagement of romantic irony to new extremes. He has publicly dismissed *Murphy* as "derivative, trivial and without major import"; in the author's view *Watt* is "an unsatisfactory book," *La Fin* is "rubbish," *Textes pour rien* is a "failure," *Comment c'est* is "very bad writing," *Godot* is "a facile attempt to make quick money," *Happy Days* is "another misery." *Mercier et Camier* fills its author with "loathing." Beckett considers his poetry as "the work of a very young man with nothing to say." His essays, he says, are "best forgotten."[3]

Self-deconstruction. The trilogy abounds in metafictional comments on the narrative in progress, which of course short-circuit the narrative and arrest its progress. It is in that sense a work at odds with itself. As early as *Dream of Fair to Middlin' Women* and *More Pricks than Kicks* Beckett had appeared in person in his own fiction as the very visible puppetmaster or, as he puts it in *L'Innomable,* the incompetent ventriloquist. In *Murphy* the intrusive narrator informs the reader ("gentle skimmer") of his various fictional techniques precisely at the moment he employs them.

> Celia's account, expurgated, accelerated, improved and reduced, of how she came to speak of Murphy, gives the following. (P. 12)

> It is most unfortunate, but the point of this story has been reached where a justification of the expression "Murphy's mind" has to be attempted. . . .

> This painful duty having now been discharged, no further bulletins will be issued. (Pp. 107, 112)

And in *Watt* the author, in addition to many other intrusions, places some of his metafictional commentary in paradoxical, self-contradictory footnotes:

> Much valuable space has been saved, in this work, that would otherwise have been lost, by avoidance of the plethoric reflexive pronoun, after *say*. (P. 8)

> Hemophilia is, like enlargement of the prostate, an exclusively male disorder. But not in this work. (P. 102)

And his frequent failure to find the right word is indicated by Sternean blank spaces filled only with a question mark. In *Molloy* the narrator will apologize to the reader for the ambiguity of a certain sentence, for the boredom of a certain passage and even of the whole story; he apologizes for mentioning an unmentionable orifice ("it's my muse who insists on it") and for failing to relate or describe something interesting, saying "that would have made a pretty piece." He admits to the reader that he has left a certain description unfinished, that he lied about a certain detail, that other details were added, not for the sake of truthfulness but for verisimilitude (thus destroying the verisimilitude, of course), and that a certain passage is filled with too much detail. The Unnamable boasts that, as an experienced storyteller, he has learned to distinguish between what is bad in storytelling and . . . what is less bad; and Molloy tells the reader that a skillful narrator must always choose between the things not worth mentioning and those even less so! Our apologetic narrator will also admit that a certain simile just used is inappropriate to the context.

> But at times it seemed to me that I was no longer very far from it, that I was approaching it as the beach is approached by the wave that swells and whitens, a figure of speech that I must say is inappropriate to my situation, which was rather that of shit waiting for the flush. (M, p. 252)

The Swiftian blandness and detachment with which painful, nightmarish, or sadistically cruel episodes are related deconstruct their would-be emotional charge. The first-person narrator seems a stranger to the disquieting events he is telling about his own life, a stranger, even, to his own self-conscious being and his own body. Molloy says that when he looks at his hands they don't seem to belong to him.

The narrative "progression" becomes most often a beating around the bush, a "turning around the pot," partly because of the many digressions, partly because the hero doesn't get anywhere, and partly because there is no apparent causal relationship between successive episodes. What is presented in *Molloy* as a double quest novel becomes a fiction in which the quest, as often as not, is lost sight of. In part one the quest-object itself (the mother) is deflated: "To speak of bicycles and of blowing horns, what repose. Unfortunately it's not a question of that but of the one who gave birth to me, through her asshole if I remember correctly. First shitty situation" (p. 22). The quest is further deflated when we learn that Molloy had actually found his mother on several earlier occasions but without accomplishing anything and merely "hoping to do better next time."

The rambling, seemingly haphazard, and free-associative structure not only deconstructs the quest motif but removes it entirely from stage center, often thrusting it rudely into the wings where it remains invisible for long stretches of narrative. Linear thought processes and linear plot development are constantly short-circuited, as when a sentence ends with a dangling conjunction ("car" [M, p. 13]) or a dangling article ("tous les" [INN, p. 171; *Comment c'est,* p. 90]) or when the narrator admits that he may be confusing two different episodes in his life (M, pp. 18, 208). And the trilogy is studded with anticlimactic disclaimers, as when the narrator tells the reader not to take seriously what has just been narrated.

Throughout the trilogy there is a comic mixture of stylistic registers, from the lofty, intellectual, poetic, or sublime to the slangy, scatological, and obscene. We are dealing, then, with a highly self-conscious artwork and with an author eager to make the reader aware of the artifice, thus inhibiting the reader's willing suspension of disbelief, inhibiting, once again, the very novel in progress.

The narrator of *Malone meurt* is even more self-conscious and intrusive than the two narrators of *Molloy.* Both at the beginning and near the end of the novel, for example, he announces to the reader his "program," that is, his table of contents or game plan.

> I have likewise decided to recall briefly my present situation, before beginning my stories.
> Present situation, three stories, inventory, that's it. (P. 13)

> Here in any case is the program, the end of the program. . . . Here it is. Visit, various remarks, MacMann, repeated references to the death-struggle, MacMann sequence, then mixture of MacMann and death-struggle as long as possible. (P. 180)

Similarly, every third chapter of *Mercier et Camier* is a résumé of the two preceding chapters; and when the narrator is about to start a new paragraph, end a description, or change narrative tenses, he announces the fact: "new paragraph" (p. 136); "end of the descriptive passage" (p. 167); "curious this sudden present tense" (p. 182).

In successive sentences the narrator of *Malone meurt* talks first to the reader and then to himself, criticizing and *erasing* the fictional detail he has just invented.

> Sapo didn't have any friends. No, that won't work. (P. 19)

> In the afternoon he would go off, his books under his arms, under the pretext that he worked better in the open air, no, without explanation. (P. 35)

> For Sapo—no, I can't call him that any more, and I even wonder how I've been able to endure that name up to now. So, because, let's see, MacMann, that's hardly any better but there's no time to lose. (P. 111)

> When my bedpan is full I put it on the table next to the platter. Then I remain twenty-four hours without a bedpan. No, I have two bedpans. (P. 18)

In such passages the reader is led to experience the fact that he is witness both to a story and to the fabrication of the story.

In an aside to himself Malone approves ("That's a pretty piece") or disapproves ("what a bore") of what he has just narrated or, like the narrator of *Jacques le fataliste* ("It's strictly up to me"), proclaims his artistic freedom to invent whatever details please him and linger over them as long or as briefly as he likes: "The little cloud that passes in front of their glorious sun will darken the earth as long as I please" (p. 36).

At several points in *Malone meurt* the text is interrupted, as in *Watt*, by blank spaces indicating the narrator's difficulties with his narration, these difficulties being his increasing physical weakness as death approaches and especially his loathing for what he is writing.

The self-conscious narrator of *L'Innomable* discusses his many literary strategies aloud.

> Say I. Without thinking it. Call that questions, hypotheses. (P. 7)

How to proceed? By pure aporia or else affirmations and negations invalidated as the narrative progresses. (P. 8)

I'm going to have company. To get started. A few puppets. I'll do away with them later. (P. 9)

Enough of these perhapses too. That device is hackneyed. (P. 50)

Let us summarize, after that digression. (P. 207)

Ellipses whenever possible, that saves time. (P. 209)

We are no longer going to fall back into the picaresque genre. (P. 216)

I forgot the apodosis. (P. 237)

The Beckettian narrator is aware of the self-deconstruction he is performing on his narrative: "Everything I say cancels itself," says the narrator of *Les Nouvelles* (p. 43), and Malone admits that his words "have a curious tendency, as I realize at last, to annihilate all they purport to record."[4]

The coexistence of contraries. Another source of romantic irony before, during, and after the trilogy is Beckett's "dialectics of incommensurables." Beckettian man is forever constrained to be "ephectic," to suspend judgments and conclusions since self-evident truths never come to assert themselves with Cartesian clarity, and to be philosophically paralyzed by aporia, "the skepticism arising from awareness of opposed unreconcilable views of a subject."[5] Assertions made by Beckett's narrators are constantly qualified, discredited, challenged, contradicted, or canceled by opposing hypotheses, also presented by the narrator himself. This dialectics of incommensurables reaches its climax in *L'Innomable*.

Here everything is clear. No, everything is not clear. (P. 13)

Everything works out, nothing works out. (P. 190)

They have deceived me . . . they haven't deceived me. (P. 195)

But let's finish our thought, before shitting on it. (P. 104)

How good it feels to know where one is, where one will stay, without being there! (P. 105)

There's only me, I who am not, where I am. (P. 139)

That is a most interesting sign, of what it matters little. (P. 143)

> Confusion must be avoided, while waiting for everything to become confused. (P. 51)

Like Jacques le Fataliste, the Unnamable announces that he will treat the subject of free will—"at the foreordained time"!

*

The ironic "non-dit." Another source of irony, related to German romantic irony, is an intangible spirit hovering over the entire trilogy. It is produced by a disconcerting but intriguing *non-dit,* by what is *not* said, and by a narrative framework that insinuates more than it asserts, thus forcing the reader to make sense of what he is reading by using symbolic, allegorical, or mythological reading codes. The reader is encouraged to do so by the narrator of *Molloy,* who claims that his present tense is the "mythological present." The unlocalized peregrinations and misadventures of Beckett's antiheroes *have* to be read on a higher level than the mimetic and literal, as in some way emblematic of man's (Everyman's) journey as he crawls through life looking for meaning and self-identity in a God-forsaken universe. "All mankind is us," says Vladimir in *Godot,* "whether we like it or not." "In truth the same things happen to us all," says Arsène in *Watt,* "if only we choose to know it."

There are hints everywhere that what the Beckettian hero is really seeking is an answer to the question, "What is man's purpose on this planet?" Molloy and the hero of *La Fin* wonder if they are "on the right planet."

> But what was a hill doing in this barely rolling landscape? And myself, what had I come there for? That's what we are going to try to find out. (M, p. 18)

Read in the allegorical code, the "barely rolling landscape" becomes a synecdoche for the planet Earth seen at a distance and *sub specie ironiae.* In another passage Molloy says that he has never been able to give an adequate answer to the policeman's (and the philosopher's) question, "What are you doing here?" (M, pp. 90–91; *La Fin,* pp. 127, 130).

What does it mean to be human? Our self-taught but nescient narrator, scion of Bouvard and Pécuchet, confesses his ontological ignorance.

> Then it was geology that took up quite a bit of my time. After that anthropology bored me stiff and the other disciplines, such as

psychiatry, that are attached to it, detached from it, and reattached to it again, according to the latest discoveries. What I liked about anthropology was its power of negation, its insistence upon defining man, like God, in terms of what he is not. But on this subject I've never had anything but very confused ideas, not knowing men very well and not knowing exactly what that means, to be. (M, p. 58)

But it is obvious that Molloy has gone to considerable intellectual effort to find answers to his questions. The failure of the *sciences humaines* to provide firm answers to Molloy's questions causes his successor, Malone, to feign indifference: "Besides it hardly matters whether I am or not, whether I have lived or not, whether I am dead or only dying, I shall do as I've always done, in total ignorance of what I am, of who I am, of where I am, and of if I am" (MM, p. 96).

The center of man's being, the very gateway to Being, says Molloy, may very well be, for all he knows, "the asshole."

> I apologize for coming back to this shameful orifice, it's my muse who insists on it. Perhaps one should see in it less the defect that is mentioned than the symbol of those I don't mention, an honor due perhaps to its centrality and of its appearance of being a link between me and the other shit. It is misunderstood, I think, that little hole, people call it the asshole and pretend to scorn it. But might it not be rather the veritable portal of being, whose famous mouth would be only the service entrance? (P. 122)

The "other shit" is the world outside the hole: human life and the entire cosmos, what is called in *La Fin* "la merde universelle."

The apparent meaninglessness of life is suggested by the frequent temptations to commit suicide. If the hero doesn't go through with it, it is because of his premonition of the meaninglessness of death.

> I did not exclude the possibility that [death] was even worse than life, as a state. I thought it normal then not to rush into it and, whenever I forgot myself to the point of making an attempt at it, to catch myself in time. (M, p. 103)

Also typical are the moments when the Beckettian hero yearns not to die immediately but to "rot in peace." Molloy tells us he enjoys reflecting, "in the tranquility of decomposition," on the confused moments that constituted his life, and Moran, like Mr. Rooney of *All That Fall*, yearns for paralysis, deafness, and aphasia.

Everywhere in the trilogy there are intimations that the experimental fable being concocted is an implicit (i.e, ironic) allegory of man's frustrating and thus far fruitless search for self-knowledge and, on the doubtful assumption that such knowledge will be obtained, self-transcendence. Our dubious (and modest) questor places more emphasis on the doubt than the quest. It is typical of the romantic ironist, we recall, to be ambivalently torn between the earnestness of his quest and the simultaneous awareness of the quest's futility.

In his greatest moments of lucidity, Moran tells us, he begins to doubt the existence of his associate, Gaber, then of his boss, Youdi, and in an existentialist insight, "to consider myself solely responsible for my unhappy existence" (p. 166). Then: "And having suppressed Gaber and the boss . . . could I have refused myself the pleasure of——you know what I mean" (M, p. 166). The reader is invited to fill in the blank space with "renouncing God." In another passage Moran speaks of "the silence of which the universe is made" (p. 188), and when he spends time in meditation, it is on "questions of a theological nature." For example, he wonders if the Eucharist would produce the same effect taken on top of beer. (In *Watt* the question is raised as to what happens to a rat who eats a consecrated wafer.) Then, like Joyce's Dedalus, he composes a theological questionnaire.

1. How good is the theory that maintains that Eve came out, not of Adam's rib, but out of a tumor in the calf of the leg (ass?)?
4. How long is the Antichrist going to keep us waiting?
6. What should one think of the oath of the Irish proffered with the right hand on the relics of the saints and the left one on the male organ?
7. Does nature observe the Sabbath?
13. What the hell did God do before the Creation?

These comic questions are typical of Beckett's ironic indirection and the ironic tension he creates between the literal and the allegorical levels of fiction. The slangy verb in "Que foutait Dieu avant la création?" not only deflates the divinity but masks with humor some very disturbing theological questions concerning the existence and nature of God: What can it mean *to be* before the Creation when there was nothing *to do*? What can it mean to be omniscient before the Creation when there was nothing to know? Is an infinitely old physical universe any more unthinkable than an infinitely old God? How did the unmoved Mover get there in the first place?

Beckett gives us other comic signals of allegory, as when we are told that the town of Condom is watered by Fuck (Baïse) and when we learn that Moran is presently residing in a town called not Vanity Fair but Shit. There is, then, a whole network of latent symbols, an unspoken allegory that gives the seemingly pointless narrative its point. Matthew Arnold expressed a similar point, but more explicitly:

> Most men eddy about
> Here and there—eat and drink
> Chatter and love and hate
> Gather and squander, are raised
> Aloft, are hurl'd in the dust
> Striving blindly, achieving
> Nothing; and then they die—
>
> ("Rugby Chapel," Stanza 6, ll. 31–37)

*

There can be no true romantic irony without ambivalence and paradox. If the goal of Beckett's irony were simply to undermine the neutral tonality and thematics of the surface, we would be dealing with the traditional irony of antiphrasis. For Beckett to qualify as a romantic ironist, he must be more than a nihilist. He must be ambivalent about life and death, about mankind, about his chosen representatives of mankind (his heroes), about his major ideas and themes, and about his creative work itself. And he must display this ambivalence not only in extraliterary pronouncements as in memoirs, interviews, or essays commenting after the fact on his own work but during the creative performance itself.

Is Beckett's often alleged nihilism total, or is there a glimmer, a tiny flame, a lonely spark hiding shyly in the ashes? Geneviève Bonnefoi, for one, thinks so: "For within this ridiculous wrapping lives the little flame of the mind, a conscience which, for Christians, makes man similar to God" ("Le tombeau-refuge," p. 133). David Hesla, in a study appropriately entitled *The Shape of Chaos*, has found in each of Beckett's major works "a synthesis of the positive and the negative, the comic and the 'pathetic,' the yes and the no. . . . Optimism and pessimism, hope and despair, comedy and tragedy are counterbalanced by one another; none of them is allowed to become an Absolute" (p. 216). John Fletcher puts the matter this way:

> Underlying the Beckettian man's nihilism is a frustrated hunger for the good and the pure. If Beckett is gloomy about life, he retains a

sort of faith in man . . . a faith that he expresses in his own way, by setting up against the tyrants his heroes, who battle on defiantly against all attempts to subdue them. *(Beckett's Art,* p. 14)

Fletcher may be arguing the case for Beckett's "man" a bit too strongly here, but there is a case to be made for the indisputable presence of a positive dimension in Beckett's largely negative work. Consider the following.

Within the doubting hero-narrator-implied author lies a budding philosopher. As Diderot once proclaimed and Descartes had amply demonstrated, a fruitful first step toward philosophy is methodical doubt.

> Who never doubted never half believed.
> Where doubt, there truth is, —'tis her shadow.

All readers of Beckett have noticed the unembarrassed tendency of his people, like Queneau's, to philosophize. They never succeed in finding answers, but they must be applauded for asking some of the right questions. Heidegger's question for instance: "Why is there something instead of nothing?" Camus's question: "Can I live with the little I know and only that?" Hamlet's question: "To be or not to be?" And the more basic question: "What is Being?"

The Beckettian hero inspires ambivalence in the reader, disgust mainly, but also a grudging admiration for the hero's dogged persistence, his capacity for endurance, his nobility or at least his resilience in adversity, his fidelity to an impossible task. Some critics have spoken of courage. Others have spoken of him as a picaresque saint.

In *Molloy* and throughout the trilogy is expressed the writer's sense of obligation, his obligation to serve not as the conscience of humanity, since there are no absolute or stable values, but as humanity's anguished consciousness. Says Jean Onimus ("Faire parler l'existence," p. 53): "Paradoxically, Beckett's ghostly creatures exist more than the mass of men who live without anxiety. Quite simply because of their questioning, because they *are* a questioning and that is all they are." This sense of duty would be applauded by Immanuel Kant since it must struggle against the author's inclination to do the opposite, to write nothing at all, his inclination to imitate the infinite silence surrounding him. Beckett's expression of this profound and tragic sense of duty is embedded in typically ambivalent statements.

> I have no voice, and I must speak. (INN, p. 40)

> I have to speak, having nothing to say. (INN, p. 58)

In the Duthuit dialogues Beckett says that "there is nothing to express, nothing with which to express, nothing from which to express, together with *the obligation to express.*"[6]

Ambivalence is found not only in the tragicomic tonality that permeates Beckett's entire opus but also in the irony itself, that is, its two-directional movement, the irony on irony. For example, Molloy will tell us that his present tense is "the mythological present," but in the same breath he tells us to disregard it. The irony here does not run simply one way, from positive to negative; it runs both ways: $P \longleftrightarrow N$. We must disregard the notion of the mythological present to some degree since the narrator urges us to do so, but we cannot do so altogether. Nor does the implied author really want us to. Indeed, it is the empirical author, Samuel Beckett, who has deliberately used the term, invented it in fact, as a code signal, as an invitation to read on an allegorical level. The matter can be put another way: Beckett is ironic about his mythological present, but he is also ironic when he discredits it.

This irony on irony parallels Beckett's conception of laughter at laughter, as expressed in *Watt*. The three most important types of laughter, according to his spokesman, Arsène (whose "Haw!" is the guffaw of Democritus for whom "nothing is more real than nothing"), are the bitter, the hollow, and the mirthless, which correspond to successive "excoriations of the understanding" (p. 48). The bitter laugh, or ethical laugh, laughs at that which is not good. The hollow laugh, or intellectual laugh, laughs at what is not true. But the "highest" form of laughter is the mirthless or dianoetic laugh, which laughs at the laughter itself and laughs at what is unhappy. In *Fin de partie* Nell tells Nagg that "nothing is funnier than unhappiness." The tragic farce of the contemporary theater is another avatar of romantic irony; it chooses to laugh not only at what is not good and at what is not true but also at *its own* tragic sense of life *and* at its comic rendition of this tragic sense.

Even the allegorical elements in Beckett's work are self-reflexively ironic. Each allegory is, among other things, a ferocious parody of allegory in general and of itself in particular. As H. Porter Abbot says (*Fiction of Beckett*, p. 68), Beckett's allegory is the reverse of traditional forms since it frustrates the reader's search for meaning, usually leading him down blind alleys. But at the same time it gives the reader a hermeneutic crutch. It helps us discover, partially, what the author is driving at.

It is true that Beckett's heroes yearn for death. Freudian critics see in their frequent "repetition compulsion" a manifestation of the death wish. Besides, the protagonists make no mystery of their yearning for the peace of death and nonbeing. Not nihilism but nihilotropism impels Beckett's people inexorably, yet asymptotically, toward nothingness. They are ambivalent about death. Death will bring an end to their misery, but it will also bring an end to their burning questions, an end to any hope of ever finding even a particle of the truth (cf. Sapo: "Trying desperately all by himself to see a little clearly inside himself, avid for the slightest glimmer" [MM, p. 34]).

It is true that Beckett's heroes despise God, but they also yearn for Him, or at least for "a new and more acceptable version" of Him (Richard Coe, "God and Samuel Beckett," p. 108). They wait for Him as patiently as Vladimir and Estragon wait for Godot. They do not know who or what God is, or if He is. But they wait. And where there is waiting there is hope, hellish hope.

Beckett has spoken of the ambivalence of his worldview: "If there were only darkness, all would be clear. It is because there is not only darkness but also light that our situation becomes inexplicable."[7]

Another way to test for romantic irony is to measure the degree of paradox found in an author's work. Ambivalence is itself a form of paradox since logically incompatible ideas, feelings, or urges are cohabiting the same mind and the same body. And Beckett's dialectics of incommensurables, touched on earlier, is an expression of a worldview at the very center of which lies irreducible paradox.

The Beckettian hero is a creature of paradox. He has been called a GENTLEMAN-VAGABOND. His story is a long enumeration of his many tribulations, but he seems a stranger to those unhappy events, "basically I wasn't there." He is, then, an ABSENT-PRÉSENT, as another critic has labeled him. He will also present himself as a victim of life, of fate, of cosmic irony, of "them," but he is also prone to victimize others when he thinks he can get away with it. He has thus been labeled a BOURREAU-VICTIME. Other critics have spoken of him as a MORT-VIVANT because of his excruciating awareness of that paradox so dear to Christian preachers: "In the midst of life we are in death."

Paradox being an integral part of Beckett's vision, it is not surprising to find it in the stylistic texture of his fiction, not just the deliberate contradictions between two successive sentences or between the beginning and the end of the same sentence (e.g., "I trusted in appearances, all the while believing them vain" [MM, p. 65]) but the maddening non sequiturs, the strange oxymorons, and intriguing *alliances de mots*. Oxymoron is the chief stylistic tic of Beckett's early hero, Belacqua. Molloy will speak of his soul "leaping" to the limit of its "elastic," of his realization that he had to leave his mother's womb for "less compassionate sewers," and of "the only way to progress, to stop." Malone will speak of his "incurious wondering," of himself as an "old fetus," and of the end of life as "vivifying." The Unnamable will speak of Malone's "deadly vivacity," of God as "an instigator of calm," "of a canvas cover impermeable in places," and of his decision to use "abundantly" the principle of "parsimony." And one recalls that the hero of *Watt* had a peculiar way of walking: advancing backward.

Beckett sees his ambition to be a writer as paradoxical; it is the ambition to write a book that can't be written, to name the unnamable ("nothing is namable, nothing is sayable" [*Textes pour rien* 11:203]). He shares with Schlegel the conviction that to be an artist is "to fail as no other dare fail."[8] Like Schlegel, he refers (via Malone) to his storytelling as "play." His philosophical irony, like Schlegel's, points to the infinite fullness of chaos, to the fact that from the nondivine perspective being *is* chaos. Chaos is the key word and major theme of *Murphy*, whose hero arbitrarily chooses "chaos" as the etymology of "gas" ("superficial chaos"), the eventual instrument of his death. A minor character is called a "morsel of chaos," and the beloved Celia is described as an exceptional "figure" emerging from the usually figure-free "ground" of chaos, the "matrix of surds," the "colossal fiasco," the "big blooming buzzing confusion." "The confusion is not my invention," says Beckett. He continues,

> It is all around us and our only chance now is to let it in. The only chance of renovation is to open our eyes and see the mess. . . . There will be new form and . . . this form will be of such a type that it admits the chaos and does not try to say that the chaos is really something else.[9]

The presence of irony is of considerable moment when one attempts to understand and appraise Beckett's art as a whole. It is the romantic irony especially that saves Beckett, "perhaps the last and most ironic Romantic ironist" (Gary Handwerk), from being a nihilist pure and simple. His massive negativism is itself ironic since it springs in reality from positive yearnings. As Nietzsche's Zarathustra says, "I love the great despisers because they are the great adorers, they are arrows of longing for the other shore." The Beckettian hero is not sure there really is another shore, but he never gives up hope of finding it one day, of stumbling onto it in his grotesque gropings. From both a technical and a philosophical point of view, the polar tensions created by ironic ambivalence, contradiction, and paradox hold Beckett's fictional structure together and hold it up. These tensions also provide a brilliant expression of the modern sensibility. In an earlier age, a self-proclaimed Age of Enlightenment, that of Pope and Voltaire, irony could be certain of its many but slyly hidden convictions. In our present age of uncertainty, irony has become uncertain even of itself. To use some of Beckett's words, it is an irony of great formal brilliance but of indeterminate purport.

Appendix

Romantic Irony and the Novel:
Friedrich von Schlegel and Mikhail Bakhtin

Friedrich von Schlegel felt that the novel form was the most suitable vehicle for romantic irony. The novel had already proved to be a flexible genre capable of assimilating other genres in its impressive inclusiveness, and the ideal, romantic *Roman* of the future that Schlegel envisaged could be made so flexible as to include epic, lyric, and dramatic elements. The *Roman* would be the best instrument for expressing the chaos of being as perceived by a finite consciousness ("What is essential in the novel is chaotic form") and for expressing the "eternal mobility" of that consciousness itself.

The novel, he thought, had not reached its perfect, completed form and never would. Indeed romantic literature by definition (Schlegel's) is an art form always in a state of becoming, of continued development and progress. It strives for but can never reach perfection or even fullness of meaning and communication. Romantic irony expresses an exhilarating sense of progress and at the same time a sense of incompleteness and limitation.

Schlegel's view of the novel anticipates that of Mikhail Bakhtin in several ways. The latter's fully articulated view of the novel reveals, better than Schlegel's terse aphorisms, how the novel is indeed the most appropriate genre for the expression of romantic irony. Bakhtin's ideas that are most relevant to romantic irony are found in three essays: "Epic and Novel: Toward a Methodology for the Study of the Novel"; "From the Prehistory of Novelistic Development"; and "Discourse in the Novel." All three essays are collected and brilliantly translated in *The Dialogic Imagination* (1981).

Bakhtin conceives of the novel as a self-conscious genre that dramatizes the gap between what is told and the telling of it. Language in the novel not only represents but is itself an object of representation. A novelist can distance himself from the language of his own work as well as from other aspects. A true novel is always criticizing itself, questioning its own language and form, and always finding them wanting. It is conscious of the impossibility of achieving full meaning and ironically exploits this lack. As Michael Holquist has written, *novel* is the name Bakhtin gives to whatever force is at work within a given literary system to reveal the limits, the artificial constraints of that system. It is fundamentally anticanonical. And just as it was for Schlegel, the novel, for Bakhtin, is not a fully developed, finished, or completed genre; it is a genre-in-the-making. The novelist himself is drawn to everything that is not yet completed.

With its infectious spirit of renovation the novel's novelization of the other genres over which it has become dominant makes them freer and more flexible in form. They become permeated with laughter, irony, humor, and self-parody. Two relevant examples of "novelized" narrative poetry discussed at some length by Bakhtin are Byron's *Don Juan* and Pushkin's *Eugene Onegin*. Even more important is the fact that "the novel inserts into these other genres an indeterminacy, a certain open-endedness, a living contact with unfinished, still-evolving contemporary reality" ("Epic and Novel," p. 6) as opposed to "epic distance," which radically separates the epic world from contemporary reality. It is precisely the novel's contact with the inconclusive present that keeps the genre from congealing.

This indeterminacy (cf. Stuart Sperry's "Toward a Definition of Romantic Irony") is fostered also by the novel's essence: it is an action seen from various points of view (cf. Sartre) and expressed in various languages (heteroglossia). No single language or viewpoint can be taken as the author's; each is relativized as just one of many rejoinders in a lively dialogue that is both intra- and intertextual, that uses languages and citations (direct, indirect, and disguised) from both literary and extraliterary sources. Schlegel, who not only perceived but preached heteroglossia, referred to this complex design as an "arabesque." The relationship of the author to a language conceived as "the common view" is never static; it is always found in a state of movement and oscillation. This eternal mobility is reminiscent of the Schlegelian conception of romantic irony. Bakhtin observes on several occasions that pseudo-objective (i.e., ironic) motivation is characteristic of novel style.

Schlegel had urged the romantic ironist to distance himself from his own enthusiasms. Similarly Bakhtin sees polyglossia and heteroglossia as freeing artistic consciousness from the tyranny of its own consciousness. The novel is a hybrid genre held together and even defined by its internal tensions, the dialectical or, in Bakhtinian terms, the "dialogical" interaction between the diverse languages and points of view it orchestrates to express, in refracted form, its own. Being a diversity of individual voices, viewpoints, and stratified languages, it lends itself to—in fact cannot avoid—presenting that diversity of moods and stylistic registers so typical of romantic irony. Instead of establishing a canonical language, the novel often fights for the renovation of an antiquated literary language. That tendency reaches one of its apexes with Queneau.

Finally, the novel, by its nature and origins, lends itself to many of the ambivalences of romantic irony. It has its deepest roots, according to Bakhtin, in folkloric humor, the ambivalent laughter of the carnivalesque, at once "cheerful and annihilating." Folk humor's "laughter of uncrowning" destroys epic distance. Three other sources of ambivalence in the novel stem from its roots in the Socratic dialogues with (1) their ambivalent irony of wise ignorance, (2) their mixture of humor and earnestness, and (3) the tension between the urge to arrive at final truths and, on the other hand, the inconclusiveness of the Socratic dialectic. Socrates spent much more time debunking false views than in constructing a canonical one.

Notes

Chapter 1

1. Sylvan Barnet et al., *A Dictionary of Literary Terms* (Boston: Little, Brown and Co., 1960), p. 52. Page references to secondary sources will be placed in the text itself with a shortened title. For full publication information consult the Bibliography.

2. Friedrich von Schlegel, *Ideen*, no. 69 (1800), in *Kritische Friedrich Schlegel Ausgabe*, ed. Hans Eichner, vol. 2 (Paderborn: Schöningh, 1967), p. 263; hereafter abbreviated as KA. Since most of the titles of works cited from Schlegel are relatively short, the only other abbreviated references will be as follows:

AMW = *The Aesthetic and Miscellaneous Works*, trans. E. S. Millington (London: H. G. Bohn, 1849).

LF = *Lucinde and the Fragments*, trans. Peter Firchow (Minneapolis: Univ. of Minnesota Press, 1971).

Translations from KA are mine. Translations from the *Lycaeum* and the *Athenaeum* are from *Dialogue on Poetry and Literary Aphorisms*, trans. Ernest Behler and Roman Struc (University Park: Pennsylvania State Univ. Press, 1968).

3. See Paul de Man, "The Rhetoric of Temporality," in *Interpretation: Theory and Practice*, ed. Charles Singleton (Baltimore: Johns Hopkins Univ. Press, 1969), pp. 201–2.

4. For Schlegel's view of irony as an endless series of mirrors, see *Athenaeum*, 116. Cf. also Martin Walser, *Selbstbewusstsein und Ironie* (Frankfurt: Suhrkamp, 1981), who discusses the romantic ironists' destruction of illusion: "Das Bewusstsein des Bewusstseins. . . . Beim Dichten immer dazudichten, das man dichte" (The consciousness of consciousness. . . . In the act of writing always to write that one is writing [pp. 51–52]). Schlegel's favorite formula for this play of mirrors is that of a poetry that would be at the same time a "poetry of poetry." In dramatic works it is revealed both by parabasis and by the play-within-and-reflecting-the-play.

As Hegel was the first to note, the dialectical rhythm animating Schlegel's conception of irony was an offshoot of Fichtean idealism. Fichte's goal was to obtain genuine knowledge through pure contemplation of self, through a consciousness of consciousness. See Ernst Behler (1972, pp. 57–59) for a succinct and judicious appraisal of Fichte's influence on Schlegel.

See also Friedrich Gundolf, "Friedrich Schlegels romantische Schriften," in *Ironie als literarisches Phänomen*, ed. Hans-Egon Hass and Gustav-Adolf Mohrlüder (Cologne: Kiepenheuer & Witsch, 1973), p. 144: "Ironie ist das Relativnehmen alles endlichen

Chiffern, und Ironie ist das spielerische Ernstnehmen der relativen Chiffern, aber Ironie ist auch Relativnehmen des Relativnehmens und so ins Unendliche" (Irony is the relativizing of all finite signs, and irony is the playful-earnest treatment of the relative signs, but irony is also the relativizing of the relativizing and so on ad infinitum; my translation).

5. See Percy Matenko, *Tieck and Solger* (New York: Westermann, 1933), p. 60.

6. Quoted by D. C. Muecke, *Irony* (London: Methuen, 1970), p. 18.

7. See Paul de Man, "Rhetoric of Temporality," p. 200.

8. Friedrich Schlegel, *Philosophische Lehrjahre,* quoted by Bernhard Heimrich, *Fiktion und Fiktionsironie in Theorie und Dichtung der deutschen Romantik* (Tübingen: Niemeyer, 1968), p. 63. My translation.

9. Jonathan Culler, *Flaubert: The Uses of Uncertainty* (Ithaca: Cornell Univ. Press, 1974), p. 202.

10. Certain literary critics, historians, and aestheticians, those who claimed to find only "objectivity" in romantic irony, insisted that the reference to the *buffo* was purely figurative or metaphorical. But as Ingrid Strohschneider-Kohrs has argued at some length *(Die romantische Ironie in Theorie und Gestaltung,* 2d rev. ed. [Tübingen: Niemeyer, 1977], pp. 18–20), the reference to the *buffo* was meant "in the full and concrete sense" (p. 20).

11. See Alfred Edwin Lussky, *Tieck's Romantic Irony* (Chapel Hill: Univ. of North Carolina Press, 1932), pp. 68–69.

12. Quoted by René Bourgeois, *L'Ironie romantique* (Grenoble: Presses Univ. de Grenoble, 1974), p. 20. See also Strohschneider-Kohrs, *Die romantische Ironie,* p. 95. All translations from the French, throughout the book, are mine.

13. Beda Allemann, *Ironie und Dichtung,* 2d rev. ed. (Pfullingen: Neske, 1969), pp. 22, 99–100. See also Lilian Furst, *Fictions of Romantic Irony* (Cambridge: Harvard Univ. Press, 1984), p. 29.

14. On the more melancholy bent of French romantic irony see D. C. Muecke, *The Compass of Irony* (London: Methuen, 1969), p. 231.

Mikhail Bakhtin *(Rabelais and His World* [Cambridge: M.I.T. Press, 1968]) relates Schlegel's concept of the arabesque to the romantic grotesque, with its modern emphasis on melancholy, isolation, alienation, distrust, and fear of the world. But for Schlegel, as Bakhtin admits, the arabesque expressed positive values: fantasy, playfulness, total aesthetic freedom ("caprice"), and especially the world's rich, fertile, and dynamic heterogeneity.

15. Quoted by Morton Gurewitch, "European Romantic Irony" (Ph.D. diss., Columbia University, 1957), p. 61.

16. Valentine Brunet, *Le Lyrisme d'Alfred de Musset dans ses poésies* (Toulouse: Imprimerie Régionale, 1932), p. 349. She is commenting on the French romantic period.

17. Quoted by Léon Séché, *Alfred de Musset* (Paris: Mercure de France, 1907), 1:109; emphasis added.

18. The traces of romantic irony that can be found in Mérimée and in minor romantics such as Jules Janin, Pétrus Borel, and Charles Lassailly are fleeting and largely inconsequential. See René Bourgeois, *L'Ironie romantique,* pp. 55–84. See Bourgeois also for lengthy discussions of romantic irony in Nerval and Nodier.

19. See Pierre Fortassier, "L'expression indirecte du réel et sa théorie chez Valéry, La Fontaine, Musset," *L'Information littéraire* 20, 15–16.

20. Lilian Furst, *Fictions of Romantic Irony*, p. 37. See also Hans Eichner, "The Rise of Modern Science and the Genesis of Romanticism," *PMLA* 97 (Jan. 1982):8–30.

21. René Bourgeois, *L'Ironie romantique*, p. 27.

Chapter 2

1. Denis Diderot, *Jacques le fataliste et son maître*, in *OEuvres* (Paris: Gallimard, 1951), p. 475. All page references are to this edition and will subsequently be placed in the text.

2. From the *Réfutation d'Helvétius*, quoted by Otis Fellows, *Diderot* (Boston: Twayne, 1977), p. 143.

3. Quoted by J. Robert Loy, *Diderot's Determined Fatalist* (New York: King's Crown Press, 1950), p. 128.

4. Letter of October 7, 1762, in *Correspondance*, ed. Georges Roth (Paris: Editions de Minuit, 1958), 4:189.

5. Ibid., p. 172.

6. Bergen Evans, introduction to *The Life and Opinions of Tristram Shandy* (New York: Modern Library, 1950), p. xiv.

7. Quoted by Leo Spitzer, "The Style of Diderot," in *Linguistics and Literary History: Essays in Stylistics* (Princeton: Princeton Univ. Press, 1948), p. 155.

8. Quoted by David Berry, "The Technique of Literary Digression in the Fiction of Diderot," *Studies on Voltaire and the Eighteenth Century* 118 (1974):232.

9. See Lester Crocker, *Diderot's Chaotic Order* (Princeton: Princeton Univ. Press, 1974), p. 6.

10. Ibid., pp. 10–11.

11. The *OEuvres philosophiques* (Paris: Garnier, 1961) will henceforth be abbreviated in the text as OPH.

12. Quoted by Aram Vartanian, "*Jacques le fataliste:* A Journey into the Ramifications of a Dilemma," in *Essays on Diderot and the Enlightenment in Honor of Otis Fellows*, ed. John Pappas (Geneva: Droz, 1974), p. 330.

13. *Garrick ou les Acteurs anglais*, quoted by Philippe Garcin, "Diderot et la philosophie du style," *Critique* 142 (1959):199.

14. *Salon de 1767*, quoted by Garcin, ibid.

15. *Le Rêve de d'Alembert*, quoted by Garcin, ibid.

Chapter 3

1. *Poésies complètes*, ed. Maurice Allem (Paris: Gallimard, 1957). All quotations of Musset's poetry are taken from this edition. More specific references (i.e., canto and stanza numbers) will be given only for the main work under consideration, *Namouna*.

2. For a discussion of the romantic hero as *puer senex* see my book, *The Romantic Hero and His Heirs in French Literature* (Bern & New York: Peter Lang, 1984), pp. 13–15.

3. Lord Byron, fragment on the back of the poet's manuscript for the first canto of *Don Juan*.

4. As Hubert Juin has said, insofar as the hero, as hero, is deconstructed, the poem, as a linear narrative continuum, is likewise deconstructed. See Hubert Juin, "le poème d'Alfred de Musset," *Europe* 55, nos. 583–84 (Nov.-Dec. 1977):150.

5. See Maurice Allem, n. 37 in Musset's *Poésies complètes*, pp. 705–6.

6. Quoted by Margaret Rees, *Alfred de Musset* (New York: Twayne, 1971), p. 31.

7. Quoted by Emile Henriot, *Alfred de Musset* (Paris: Hachette, 1928), p. 103.

8. Sainte-Beuve, quoted by Gauthier-Ferrières, *Alfred de Musset: Vie et oeuvre* (Paris: Larousse, 1909), p. 99.

9. See Hermine B. Riffaterre, *Orphisme dans la poésie romantique* (Paris: Nizet, 1970), pp. 125–26, for a discussion of this type of imagery in Musset.

10. See Michael Herschensohn, "Imagery in the Works of Alfred de Musset" (Ph.D. diss., University of Pennsylvania, 1971), p. 66.

11. For a good discussion of the organic philosophy of the romantics, see Hans Eichner, "The Rise of Modern Science and the Genesis of Romanticism," *PMLA* 97 (Jan. 1982):8–30.

Chapter 4

1. Abeel's discussion is nevertheless an improvement on that of Grahame Jones. She adds that the irony in *Le Rouge* is "complicated and enriched by the fact that sometimes the implied author himself may hold conflicting views of a character" (p. 22) and that "often there is no bedrock of simple truth, no definitive view: once we tease out Stendhal's voice we have still to contend with his ambivalence, with equivocations" (p. 34).

2. Jones analyzes Stendhal's ambivalence toward Julien in terms of identification versus a sense of superiority, Brombert in terms of a paradoxical mixture of vengeance and compensation (for his own disappointments) on the one hand and self-punishment (since he is identifying with his autobiographical hero) on the other.

3. Morton Gurewitch, "European Romantic Irony" (Ph.D. diss., Columbia University, 1957), pp. 188ff. For Gurewitch, innocence is the heroic imperative, and the susceptibility to wonder. Experience is Julien's "cunning care for his future" and revenge for imagined contempt. One could just as easily place these last two impulses under the heading of inexperience, but at least Gurewitch has defined his terms.

4. Stendhal, *Romans et nouvelles,* ed. Henri Martineau (Paris: Gallimard, 1952), 1:257. All page references to the novels of Stendhal are to this edition. Subsequent references to *Le Rouge* appear in the text. For a more detailed analysis of Julien as "comic lover" and as comic hero in general, see Sandye Jean McIntyre, "The Comic Hero in Stendhal's *Le Rouge et le Noir*" (Ph.D. diss., Case Western Reserve University, 1974). McIntyre does not claim, any more than I do, that Julien is fundamentally a comic hero, but this dissertation is the first attempt to study this aspect of Stendhal's hero in detail and in depth.

5. For a discussion of objective, subjective, and naive irony, see p. 11.

6. On those rare occasions when Julien can concentrate on the beauty of Mme de Rênal the demonstrative does not convey a sense of distance, e.g., "pressant cette main qui lui plaisait comme parfaitement jolie" (p. 279) and "ces bras si beaux" (p. 282).

7. See p. 611 for the "jeune philosophe" passage. Octave is also called "notre philosophe" (p. 75), precisely during a moment—rare for him—of intellectual frailty.

8. Stendhal, *Romans et nouvelles* 2:124.

9. I have studied the use of romantic irony as foreshadowing in the *Gilles* novels of Drieu la Rochelle. See Lloyd Bishop, *In Search of Style* (Charlottesville: Univ. Press of Virginia, 1982), Appendix C, pp. 165–68.

10. Stendhal, "Projet d'article sur *Le Rouge et le Noir*," *Romans et nouvelles* 1:703.

11. Martin Turnell, *The Novel in France* (New York: Vintage Books, 1958), p. 110. I am also indebted to Robert Nelson and Neal Oxenhandler *(Aspects of French Literature* [New York: Appleton-Century-Crofts, 1961], p. 33) for their lucid discussion of the baroque.

12. Quoted by Turnell, *Novel in France*, p. 110.

13. See John Nist, "The Art of Chaucer: Pathedy," *Tennessee Studies in Literature* 11 (1966):2.

14. Alvin Eustis, introduction to *Le Rouge et le Noir* (New York: Dell, 1963), pp. 17–18.

Chapter 5

1. Gautier, *Histoire du romantisme* (Paris: Flammarion, 1929), p. 2.

2. Quoted by Johanna Richardson, *Théophile Gautier: His Life and Times* (New York: Coward-McCann, 1958), pp. 132–33.

3. Gautier, preface to *Les Grotesques*, ix; quoted by P. E. Tennant, *Théophile Gautier* (London: Athlone Press, 1975), p. 11.

4. Gautier, preface to *Le Baroque;* quoted by Tennant, ibid.

5. Gautier, *Histoire du romantisme*, p. 305. Marcel Voisin *(Le Soleil et la nuit* [Brussels: Editions de l'Univ. de Bruxelles, 1981]) sums up Gautier's aesthetic as "la dialectique des contraires" (p. 313) and "l'esthétique de l'arabesque" (p. 324).

6. Quoted by Richard B. Grant, *Théophile Gautier* (Boston: Twayne, 1975), pp. 118–19.

7. Gautier, *Mademoiselle de Maupin* (Paris: Garnier, 1966), p. 43. All subsequent references are to this edition.

8. Gautier, *Poésies complètes de Théophile Gautier,* ed. René Jasinski (Paris: Nizet, 1970), 1:157. Subsequent references are to this edition and indicate stanza numbers.

9. P. E. Tennant, *Théophile Gautier,* p. 45.

10. The critic is Johanna Richardson and is quoted by Tennant, ibid., p. 46.

11. See Richard B. Grant, *Gautier,* p. 35.

12. Vladimir Jankélévitch, *L'ironie ou la bonne conscience,* 2d ed. (Paris: Presses Univ. de France, 1950), pp. 22–23.

Chapter 6

1. Charles Baudelaire, *Mon coeur mis à nu,* in *OEuvres complètes,* ed. Claude Pichois (Paris: Gallimard [Pléiade], 1975), 1:682–83. Unless otherwise indicated, all references to works of Baudelaire are based on volume 1 of this edition, which will be abbreviated as OC. Page numbers for prose works will be given only for *La Fanfarlo,* except occasionally, as in n. 2, when accompanying OC.

2. OC, p. 703.

3. Letter dated April 7, 1855, *Correspondance générale*, ed. Jacques Crépet, 6 vols. (Paris: Conard, 1947–53), 1:331.

4. See Henri Peyre, *Connaissance de Baudelaire* (Paris: Corti, 1951), p. 170.

5. Bernard Howells has seen the romantic irony of *La Fanfarlo:* "In Baudelaire's own view irony, that is, Romantic irony, is a fundamental aspect of modernism in literature; although not in 1846 as *vorace* as it will later become, it is already, in *La Fanfarlo,* a form of duality which cannot be recuperated within the 'system of nature' since it emphasizes the division of consciousness *from* nature and renders impossible any identification with a 'vue synthétique'—that is, with a stable system or a stable view of self" ("Baudelaire: A Portrait of the Artist in 1846," *French Studies* 37, no. 4 [Oct. 1983]:426).

See also Francis S. Hick, "Baudelaire's *La Fanfarlo:* An Example of Romantic Irony," *The French Review* 49, no. 3 (Feb. 1976):328–36.

For Baudelaire's ties with German romanticism, see Albert Béguin, *L'Ame romantique et le rêve* (Paris: Corti, 1939), pp. 400–401; Roger Bauer, "Baudelaire und die deutsche Romantik," *Euphorion* 75, no. 4 (1981):430–43; and René Galand, *Baudelaire: Poétique et poésie* (Paris: Nizet, 1965), p. 529.

6. This is Henri Peyre's list.

7. See Martin Turnell, *Baudelaire: A Study of His Poetry* (New York: New Directions, 1953), p. 37.

8. See Auerbach, "The Aesthetic Dignity of the *Fleurs du mal,*" in *Baudelaire: A Collection of Critical Essays,* ed. Henri Peyre (Englewood Cliffs: Prentice-Hall, 1962), pp. 153–68.

9. For a detailed stylistic analysis of "Au Lecteur" see Nathaniel Wing, "The Stylistic Function of Rhetoric in Baudelaire's *Au Lecteur,*" *Kentucky Romance Quarterly* 19 (1972):447–60.

10. See J. B. Ratermanis, *Etude sur le style de Baudelaire* (Baden-Baden: Editions Art et Science, 1949), pp. 131–374, for an almost exhaustive and certainly exhausting list of such couplings of the concrete and the abstract. Baudelaire was conscious of such couplings as being an important aspect of his style: "Tragic sky. Epithet of an abstract nature offered to a material being" *(Fusées).*

Chapter 7

1. Flaubert, *Un Coeur simple,* in *OEuvres de Flaubert,* ed. A. Thibaudet and R. Dumesnil, vol. 2 (Paris: Gallimard, 1952), p. 595.

2. Flaubert, *Madame Bovary* (Paris: Gallimard, 1972), pp. 308–9. All references to *Madame Bovary* are from this edition.

3. B. F. Bart, "Art, Energy and Aesthetic Distance," in *Madame Bovary and the Critics,* ed. B. F. Bart (New York: New York Univ. Press, 1966), p. 89. This essay combines two essays published separately: "Balzac and Flaubert: Energy versus Art," *Romanic Review* 42 (1951):198–204, and "Aesthetic Distance in *Madame Bovary,*" *PMLA* 59 (1954):1112–26.

4. For a detailed discussion of the connection between Flaubert's use of the *style indirect libre* and his romantic irony, see Vaheed Ramazani, *The Free Indirect Mode: Flaubert and the*

Poetics of Irony (Charlottesville: Univ. Press of Virginia, 1988). For the role of irony in general in the *style indirect libre*, see especially Claude Perruchot, "Le style indirect libre et la question du sujet dans *Madame Bovary*," in *La production du sens chez Flaubert*, ed. Claudine Gothot-Mersche (Paris: Union Générale d'Edition, 1975), pp. 278–89; Henry H. Weinberg, "Irony and 'Style Indirect Libre' in *Madame Bovary*," *Canadian Review of Comparative Literature* 8, no. 1 (Winter 1981):1–9; and Ranier Warning, "Irony and the 'Order of Discourse' in Flaubert," *New Literary History* 13, no. 2 (Winter 1982):253–86.

    5. Jonathan Culler, *Flaubert: The Uses of Uncertainty* (Ithaca: Cornell Univ. Press, 1974), p. 232. See also Victor Brombert, "Flaubert and the Status of the Subject," in *Madame Bovary and the Critics*, pp. 100–113.

    6. For Flaubert's tendency toward self-mockery, see Murray Sachs, "Flaubert's Laughter," *Nineteenth-Century French Studies* 3, nos. 1–2 (Fall-Winter 1974–75):112–23.

    7. See Culler, *Flaubert: The Uses of Uncertainty*, p. 192.

Chapter 8

    1. *OEuvres complètes* (Pléiade, 1970). The first number refers to canto, the second to strophe.

    2. For an interesting commentary on this particular passage see Patricia M. Lawlor, "Figuring (Out) Maldoror: 'Nous ne sommes plus dans la narration.' Rhetoric and Narration in the *Chants de Maldoror*," *Nineteenth-Century French Studies* 16 (Spring-Summer 1988):372–78.

    3. *OEuvres complètes* (Pléiade, 1970), p. 138.

    4. Ibid. (Cros and Corbière are combined in this edition), pp. 710–12.

    5. Ibid., p. 742.

    6. Quoted by Geoffrey Brereton, *An Introduction to the French Poets* (London: Methuen, 1956), p. 233.

    7. The two critics are Michael Collie and J. M. L'Heureux, in their edition of Laforgue's *Derniers Vers* (Toronto: Univ. of Toronto Press, 1965), p. 85.

    8. "Plume voyage," in *Plume, précédé de Lointain intérieur* (Paris: Gallimard, 1963), p. 143. All translations from *Plume* are mine. The original title of the work was *Un certain Plume*. Other works of Michaux used in this study are as follows:

Qui je fus (Paris: Gallimard, 1927)

Face aux verroux (1954; reprint, Paris: Gallimard, 1967)

Connaissance par les gouffres (Paris: Gallimard, 1967)

La Vie dans les plis (1949; reprint, Paris: Gallimard, 1972)

L'Espace du dedans (Paris: Gallimard, 1966)

Emergences-Résurgences (Geneva: Skira, 1972)

L'Espace du dedans collects important works of Michaux written between 1927 and 1959. It will be used often in this study, abbreviated as ED.

    9. Quoted by C. A. Hackett, "Michaux and Plume," *French Studies* 17 (1963):45.

    10. Quoted by Hackett, ibid., p. 40.

    11. T. S. Eliot, "The Love Song of J. Alfred Prufrock," *Collected Poems 1909–1962* (New York: Harcourt, Brace & World, 1963), p. 137.

12. For a more detailed stylistic analysis of "Clown," see my article, "Michaux's 'Clown,' " *The French Review* 36 (Dec. 1962):152–57.

13. Preface to the 1943 edition of *Plume*.

14. "Quelques renseignements sur cinquante-neuf années d'existence," *Cahiers de l'Herne* 8 (1966):14.

15. For the importance of movement and mutation in Michaux's work see, in addition to Edson, the following three articles in the special issue on Michaux published by the *Cahiers de l'Herne* 8 (1966): René Micha, "Plume et les anges," pp. 143–58; Jean Roudaut, "Notes à propos du titre d'un livre d'Henri Michaux: *L'Espace du dedans*," pp. 205–13; Gilbert Lascaut, "Les monstres et l'Unheimliche," pp. 214–26. See also Virginia A. La Charité, *Henri Michaux* (Boston: Twayne, 1977), pp. 92–106.

16. See Laurie Edson, *Henri Michaux and the Poetics of Movement*, pp. 4, 95.

Chapter 9

1. Raymond Queneau, *Chêne et chien* (Paris: Gallimard, 1952).

2. Quoted by Jacques Bens, *Queneau* (Paris: Gallimard, 1962), pp. 215–16.

3. See Allen Thiher, *Raymond Queneau* (Boston: Twayne, 1985), p. 11, and especially Claude Simonnet, *Queneau déchiffré* (Paris: Julliard, 1962), chapter 7.

4. Raymond Queneau, *Le Chiendent* (Paris: Gallimard, 1933), p. 55. All subsequent references are to this edition.

5. Quoted by Jean Queval, "Queneau explorateur," *Critique* 45 (Dec. 1984):1007.

6. Quoted by John Passmore, *A Hundred Years of Philosophy* (Baltimore: Penguin, 1968), p. 477.

7. Quoted by Jacques Bens, *Queneau*, p. 113.

8. These examples are taken from Simonnet, *Queneau déchiffré*, pp. 47ff.

Chapter 10

1. Samuel Beckett, *Malone meurt* (Paris: Editions de Minuit, 1951), p. 112. References to the novels of the trilogy will be abbreviated as follows:

Molloy (Paris: Editions de Minuit, 1951)= M

Malone meurt = MM

L'Innomable (Paris: Editions de Minuit, 1956) = INN

Other primary sources cited more than once include the following:

Watt (New York: Grove Press, 1959)

Murphy (New York: Grove Press, 1957)

Nouvelles et textes pour rien (Paris: Editions de Minuit, 1958)

Comment c'est (Paris: Editions de Minuit, 1961)

Mercier et Camier (Paris: Editions de Minuit, 1970)

2. Interview with Gabriel d'Aubarède, in "Waiting for Beckett," *Trace* 42 (Summer 1961):158.

3. See Rubin Rabinovitz, *The Development of Samuel Beckett's Fiction* (Urbana: Univ. of Illinois Press, 1984), p. 1.

4. MM, p. 162. English translation in *Beckett: Three Novels* (New York: Grove Press, 1965).

5. J. D. O'Hara, "About Structure in *Malone Dies*," in *Twentieth Century Interpretations of Molloy, Malone Dies, The Unnamable,* ed. J. D. O'Hara (Englewood Cliffs: Prentice-Hall, 1970), p. 67.

6. "Three Dialogues with Georges Duthuit," *Cahiers de l'Herne* 31 (1976):73.

7. Interview with Tom Driver, in Tom Driver, "Beckett by the Madeleine," *Columbia University Forum* 4, no. 3 (Summer 1961):23.

8. "Three Dialogues with Georges Duthuit," p. 74.

9. Interview with Tom Driver, pp. 22–23.

Bibliography

Abbot, H. Porter. *The Fiction of Samuel Beckett: Form and Effect.* Berkeley: Univ. of California Press, 1973.

Abeel, Erica. "The Multiple Authors in Stendhal's Ironic Interventions." *The French Review* 50, no. 1 (Oct. 1976):21–34.

Allem, Maurice. *Alfred de Musset.* Paris: Arthaud, 1947.

Allemann, Beda. *Ironie und Dichtung.* 2d rev. ed. Pfullingen: Neske, 1969.

———. "Ironie als literarisches Prinzip." In *Ironie und Dichtung,* edited by Albrecht Schaefer, pp. 11–33. Munich: Beck, 1970. Translated into French as "De l'ironie en tant que principe littéraire," *Poétique* 36 (1978):385–98.

Arnold, Matthew. *The Poems of Matthew Arnold.* Edited by Miriam Alliot. 2d ed. London: Longman, 1965.

Aron, Thomas. "Le roman comme représentation de langage: ou Raymond Queneau à la lumière de Bakhtine." *Europe* 61, nos. 650–51 (June-July 1983):46–58.

Attuel, Josiam. "Le style de Stendhal, une union des contraires." *Stendhal Club* 24, no. 93 (1981):1–22.

Auerbach, Erich. "The Aesthetic Dignity of the *Fleurs du mal.*" In *Baudelaire: A Collection of Critical Essays,* edited by Henri Peyre, pp. 153–68. Englewood Cliffs: Prentice-Hall, 1962.

Babbitt, Irving. *Rousseau and Romanticism.* Boston: Houghton Mifflin, 1919.

Bakhtin, Mikhail. *Rabelais and His World.* Cambridge: M.I.T. Press, 1968.

———. *The Dialogic Imagination.* Translated by Caryl Emerson and Michael Holquist. Austin: Univ. of Texas Press, 1981.

Baligand, Renée. "Raymond Queneau or Le Chien à la mandoline." *Language and Style* 11 (Summer 1978):168–72.

Barnard, G. C. *Samuel Beckett: A New Approach.* New York: Dodd, Mead, 1970.

Barnet, Sylvan et al. *A Dictionary of Literary Terms.* Boston: Little, Brown and Co., 1960.

Barry, David A. "Beckett: l'entropie du langage et de l'homme." *The French Review* 51, no. 6 (May 1978):853–63.

Bart, Benjamin F. "Art, Energy and Aesthetic Distance." In *Madame Bovary and the Critics,* edited by B. F. Bart, pp. 73–105. New York: New York Univ. Press, 1966.

———. *Flaubert.* Syracuse: Syracuse Univ. Press, 1967.

———. "Hypercreativity in Stendhal and Balzac." *Nineteenth-Century French Studies* 3, nos. 1–2 (Fall-Winter 1974–75):18–39.

Barthelme, May B. "A View of Julien Sorel with Reference to Soren Kierkegaard's *The Concept of Irony.*" *Kierkegaardiana* 10 (1977):246–52.

Barthes, Roland. "Zazie et la littérature." In *Essais critiques,* pp. 125–31. Paris: Seuil, 1964.

———. *S/Z.* Paris: Seuil, 1970.

Baudelaire, Charles. "De l'essence du rire." In *OEuvres complètes de Charles Baudelaire,* edited by Jacques Crépet. Vol. 2. Paris: Conrad, 1923.

———. *Correspondance générale.* Edited by Jacques Crépet. Vol. 1. Paris: Conrad, 1947–53.

———. *OEuvres complètes.* Edited by Claude Pichois. Vol. 1. Paris: Gallimard (Pléiade), 1975.

———. "La Fanfarlo." In *OEuvres complètes,* edited by Claude Pichois. Vol. 1. Paris: Gallimard (Pléiade), 1975.

Bauer, Roger. "Baudelaire und die deutsche Romantik." *Euphorion* 75, no. 4 (1981):430–43.

Beaujour, Michel. "Sens et Nonsense: Glu et Gli et le grand combat." *Cahiers de l'Herne* 8 (1966):133–42.

Beckett, Samuel. *Molloy.* Paris: Editions de Minuit, 1951.

———. *Malone meurt.* Paris: Editions de Minuit, 1951.

———. *L'Innomable.* Paris: Editions de Minuit, 1956.

———. *Murphy.* New York: Grove Press, 1957.

———. *Nouvelles et textes pour rien.* Paris: Editions de Minuit, 1958.

———. *Watt.* New York: Grove Press, 1959.

———. *Mercier et Camier.* Paris: Editions de Minuit, 1970.

———. "Three Dialogues with Georges Duthuit." *Cahiers de l'Herne* 31 (1976): 72–77.

———. *Comment c'est.* Paris: Editions de Minuit, 1961.

Beguelin, Marianne. *Henri Michaux, esclave et demiurge.* Lausanne: L'Age d'Homme, 1973.

Béguin, Albert. *L'Ame romantique et le rêve.* Paris: Corti, 1939.

Behler, Ernst. *Klassische Ironie, Romantische Ironie, Tragische Ironie.* Darmstadt: Wissenschaftliche Buchgesellschaft, 1972.

Bellour, Raymond. *Henri Michaux ou une mesure de l'être.* Paris: Gallimard, 1965.

———. "La Passion de Narcisse." *Cahiers de l'Herne* 8 (1966):49–79.

Benjamin, Walter. "Der Begriff der Kunstkritik in der deutsche Romantik." In *Ironie als literarisches Phänomen,* edited by Hans-Egon Hass and Gustav-Adolf Mohrlüder, pp. 145–48. Cologne: Kiepenheuer & Witsch, 1973.

Bens, Jacques. *Queneau.* Paris: Gallimard, 1962.

Bense, Max. "Esthétique et métaphysique d'une prose." *Cahiers de l'Herne* 8 (1966):241–55.

Bergens, Andrée. *Raymond Queneau.* Geneva: Droz, 1963.

———. "Apparences et réalités." *Cahiers de l'Herne* 29 (1975):9–11.

Bernal, Olga. *Langage et fiction dans le roman de Beckett.* Paris: Gallimard, 1969.

———. "Le glissement hors du langage." *Cahiers de l'Herne* 31 (1976):219–25.

Bernstein, J. M. "Transcendental Dialectic: Irony as Form." In *The Philosophy of the Novel: Lukács, Marxism and The Dialectics of Form,* pp. 185–227. Minneapolis: Univ. of Minnesota Press, 1984.

Berry, David. "The Technique of Literary Digression in the Fiction of Diderot." *Studies on Voltaire and the Eighteenth Century* 118 (1974):215–72.

Bertelé, René. *Henri Michaux.* Paris: Seghers, 1957.

Beswick, U. J. "Le Chiendent: Roman Surréaliste?" *Essays in French Literature* 18 (Nov. 1981):72–85.

Bishop, Lloyd. "Michaux's 'Clown.' " The French Review 36 (Dec. 1962):152–57.

———. "Romantic Irony in Musset's *Namouna.*" *Nineteenth-Century French Studies* 7 (Spring-Summer 1979):181–91.

———. "Romantic Irony in *Le Rouge et le Noir:* Julien as Lover and Thinker." In *In Search of Style: Essays in French Literary Stylistics,* pp. 46–63. Charlottesville: Univ. Press of Virginia, 1982.

Blin, Georges. *Stendhal et les problèmes du roman.* Paris: Corti, 1953.

Bonnefoi, Geneviève. "Le tombeau-refuge." In *Les Critiques de notre temps et Beckett,* edited by Dominique Nores, pp. 132–36. Paris: Garnier, 1971.

Booth, Wayne C. *A Rhetoric of Irony.* Chicago: Univ. of Chicago Press, 1974.

Boucher, Maurice. "L'ironie romantique." *Cahier du Sud,* num. spécial, 16 (1937):29–32.

Bourgeois, René. *L'Ironie romantique.* Grenoble: Presses Univ. de Grenoble, 1974.

———. "L'ironie romantique chez les écrivains du Groupe de Coppet." In *Le Groupe de Coppet,* edited by Simone Bolayé, pp. 185–94. Geneva: Slatkine, 1977.

Bourget, Paul. *Sociologie et littérature.* Paris: Plon, 1906.

Bové, Paul A. "Beckett's Dreadful Postmodern: The Deconstruction of Form in *Molloy.*" In *De-Structuring the Novel: Essays in Applied Postmodern Hermeneutics,* edited by Leonard Orr, pp. 185–218. Troy, NY: Whitson, 1982.

Bowie, Malcolm. *Henri Michaux: A Study of His Literary Works.* Oxford: Clarendon Press, 1973.

Bréchon, Robert. *Michaux.* Paris: Gallimard, 1959.

Brée, Germaine, and Margaret Guiton. *An Age of Fiction.* New Brunswick: Rutgers Univ. Press, 1957.

Brereton, Geoffrey. *An Introduction to the French Poets.* London: Methuen, 1956.

Breton, André. *Anthologie de l'humour noir.* Paris: Pauvert, 1966.

Brombert, Victor H. "Stendhal: Le romancier des interventions." *Aurea Parma,*
    fasc. 2 (July-Dec. 1950):1–13.
———. *Stendhal et la voie oblique.* New Haven: Yale Univ. Press, 1954.
———. "Flaubert and the Status of the Subject." In *Madame Bovary and the Critics,*
    edited by B. F. Bart, pp. 100–113. New York: New York Univ. Press, 1966.
Brook, Peter. "Dire oui à la boue." *Cahiers de l'Herne* 31 (1976):232–35.
Brooks, Cleanth. *The Well Wrought Urn.* New York: Harcourt, Brace & World,
    1947.
———. "Irony as a Principle of Structure." In *Literary Opinion in America,* edited
    by Morton D. Zabel, pp. 729–41. 2d rev. ed. New York: Harper, 1951.
Brunet, Valentine. *Le Lyrisme d'Alfred de Musset dans ses poésies.* Toulouse: Im-
    primerie Régionale, 1932.
Byron, Lord. *Don Juan.* In *The Poetical Works of Byron,* edited by Robert F. Gleck-
    ner. Boston: Houghton Mifflin, 1975.
Butler, R. "Flaubert's Exploitation of the 'Style indirect libre': Ambiguities
    and Perspectives in *Madame Bovary.*" *Modern Languages* 62, no. 4 (Dec.
    1981):190–96.
Capra, Fritjof. *The Tao of Physics.* 2d ed. New York: Bantam, 1983.
Carter, A. E. *Charles Baudelaire.* Boston: Twayne, 1977.
Christensen, Inger. *The Meaning of Metafiction: A Critical Study of Selected Novels by
    Sterne, Nabokov, Barth and Beckett.* Bergen: Universitetsforlaget, 1981.
Clancier, Anne. "A la recherche d'une ascèse: Esquisse d'une philosophie de
    Raymond Queneau." *Cahiers de l'Herne* 29 (1975):148–53.
Clancier, Georges-Emmanuel. "Unité poétique et méthodique de l'oeuvre de
    Raymond Queneau." *Cahiers de l'Herne* 29 (1975):98–114.
Clough, W. O. "Irony: A French Approach." *Sewanee Review* 47, no. 2 (April-
    June 1939):175–83.
Coe, Richard N. *Samuel Beckett.* New York: Grove Press, 1964.
———. "God and Samuel Beckett." In *Twentieth Century Interpretations of Molloy,
    Malone Dies, The Unnamable,* edited by J. D. O'Hara, pp. 91–111. Englewood
    Cliffs: Prentice-Hall, 1970.
Cohn, Ruby. *The Comic Gamut.* New Brunswick: Rutgers Univ. Press, 1962.
———. *Back to Beckett.* Princeton: Princeton Univ. Press, 1973.
———. "*Watt* à la lumiere du *Château.*" *Cahiers de l'Herne* 31 (1976):306–17.
Collie, Michael, and J. M. L'Heureux. Introduction to *Laforgue: Derniers Vers.*
    Toronto: Univ. of Toronto Press, 1965.
Conard, Peter. *Shandyism: The Character of Romantic Irony.* Oxford: Blackwell,
    1978.
Cook, Albert. "Stendhal and the Discovery of the Ironic Interplay." *Novel* 9, no. 1
    (Fall 1975):40–54.
Creech, James. *Diderot: Thresholds of Representation.* Columbus: Ohio State Univ.
    Press, 1986.

Crocker, Lester. *Diderot's Chaotic Order.* Princeton: Princeton Univ. Press, 1974.

Cros, Charles, and Tristan Corbière. *OEuvres complètes,* edited by Louis Forestier and Pierre-Olivier Walzer. Paris: Gallimard, 1970.

Culler, Jonathan. *Flaubert: The Uses of Uncertainty.* Ithaca: Cornell Univ. Press, 1974.

Danan, Joseph. "Etude d'un mot 'poétique' dans *Le Chiendent.*" *Cahiers de l'Herne* 29 (1975):171–77.

Diderot, Denis. *Jacques le fataliste et son maître.* In *OEuvres.* Paris: Gallimard, 1951.

———. *Correspondance.* Edited by Georges Roth. Vols. 1 and 4. Paris: Editions de Minuit, 1955.

———. *OEuvres philosophiques.* Paris: Garnier, 1961.

———. *Diderot's Letters to Sophie Volland.* Translated by Peter France. London: Oxford Univ. Press, 1972.

———. "Chaos." In *Encyclopédie,* pp. 358–64. Vol. 2. Paris: Hermann, 1976.

Didier, Béatrice. "Contribution à une poétique du leurre: 'lecteur' et narrataires dans *Jacques le fataliste.*" *Littérature* 31 (1978):3–21.

———. " 'Je' et subversion du texte: le narrateur dans *Jacques le fataliste.*" *Littérature* 48 (1982):92–105.

Dieckmann, Herbert. "Diderot et le lecteur." *Mercure de France* 319 (1957):620–48.

Dolder, C. *Le thème de l'être et le paraître dans l'itinéraire spirituel de Musset.* Zurich: Juris-Verlag, 1968.

Dranch, Sherry A. "Flaubert: portraits d'un ironiste." *Nineteenth-Century French Studies* 11, nos. 1–2 (Fall-Winter 1982–83):106–16.

Driver, Tom. "Beckett by the Madeleine." *Columbia University Forum* 4, no. 3 (Summer 1961):21–25.

Drouart-Fiske, Michèle E. "Romantic Irony and Théophile Gautier." Ph.D. diss., Indiana, 1986.

Dyson, A. E. *The Crazy Fabric: Essays on Irony.* London: Macmillan, 1965.

Edson, Laurie. "Henri Michaux: Artist and Writer of Movement." *Modern Language Review* 78, no. 1 (Jan. 1983):46–60.

———. *Henri Michaux and the Poetics of Movement.* Saratoga: Anma, 1985.

Eichner, Hans. "Friedrich Schlegel's Theory of Romantic Poetry." *PMLA* 72 (1956):1018–41.

———. *Friedrich Schlegel.* New York: Twayne, 1970.

———. "The Rise of Modern Science and the Genesis of Romanticism." *PMLA* 97 (Jan. 1982):8–30.

Ellmann, Richard. "The Ductile Universe of Henri Michaux." *Kenyon Review* (Spring 1949):187–98.

Engstrom, Alfred G. "Flaubert's Letters and Ironic and Symbolic Structure in *Madame Bovary.*" *Studies in Philology* 46 (1949):480–95.

Esslin, Martin. "Raymond Queneau." In *The Novelist as Philosopher,* edited by John Cruickshank, pp. 79–101. London: Oxford Univ. Press, 1962.

Eustis, Alvin. Introduction to *Le Rouge et le Noir,* by Stendhal. New York: Dell, 1963.

Evans, Bergen. Introduction to *The Life and Opinions of Tristram Shandy,* by Laurence Sterne. New York: Modern Library, 1950.

Federman, Raymond. "Le Paradoxe du menteur." *Cahiers de l'Herne* 31 (1976):183–92.

Fellows, Otis. *Diderot.* Boston: Twayne, 1977.

Flaubert, Gustave. *OEuvres de Flaubert.* Edited by A. Thibaudet and R. Dumesnil. Paris: Gallimard, 1951.

———. *Madame Bovary.* Paris: Gallimard, 1972.

———. *Correspondance.* Edited by Jean Bruneau. Paris: Gallimard, 1973.

Fletcher, John. "Samuel Beckett et Jonathan Swift: vers une étude comparée." *Littératures* (Toulouse) 10 (1962):81–117.

———. *The Novels of Samuel Beckett.* London: Chatto & Windus, 1964.

———. *Samuel Beckett's Art.* London: Chatto & Windus, 1967.

Fornassier, Nori. "Pulsions et fonctions de l'idéal dans les contes fantastiques de Gautier." *Bulletin de la Société Théophile Gautier* 6 (1984):67–72.

Fortassier, Pierre. "L'expression indirecte du réel et sa théorie chez Valéry, LaFontaine, Musset." *L'Information littéraire* 20, 15–16.

Fredman, Alice G. *Diderot and Sterne.* New York: Octagon Books, 1973.

Friedemann, Käte. "Die romantische Ironie." *Zeitschrift fur Ästhetik und allgemeine Kunstwissenschaft* 13 (1919):270–82.

Furst, Lilian. *Fictions of Romantic Irony.* Cambridge: Harvard Univ. Press, 1984.

Galand, René. *Baudelaire: Poétique et poésie.* Paris: Nizet, 1965.

Garcin, Philippe. "Diderot et la philosophie du style." *Critique* 142 (1959):195–213.

Gastinel, Pierre. *Le Romantisme d'Alfred de Musset.* Paris: Hachette, 1933.

Gauthier-Ferrières. *Alfred de Musset: Vie et oeuvre.* Paris: Larousse, 1909.

Gautier, Théophile. *Histoire du romantisme.* Paris: Flammarion, 1929.

———. *Mademoiselle de Maupin.* Paris: Garnier, 1966.

———. *Poésies complètes de Théophile Gautier.* Edited by René Jasinski. Vols. 1 and 3. Paris: Nizet, 1970.

Gayot, Paul. *Raymond Queneau.* Paris: Editions Univ., 1967.

Glicksberg, C. I. *The Ironic Vision in Modern Literature.* The Hague: Nijhoff, 1969.

Gontarske, S. E. "The Intent of Undoing in Samuel Beckett's Art." *Modern Fiction Studies* 29, no. 1 (Spring 1983):5–23.

Gothot-Mersch, Claudine. "Sur le narrateur de Flaubert." *Nineteenth-Century French Studies* 12, no. 3 (Spring 1984):344–65.

Grant, Richard. *Théophile Gautier.* Boston: Twayne, 1975.

Gray, Stanley E. "Beckett and Queneau as Formalists." *James Joyce Quarterly* 8 (1971):392–404.

Grimsley, Ronald. "L'ambiguité dans l'oeuvre romanesque de Diderot." *Cahiers de l'Association Internationale des Etudes Françaises* 13 (1961):223–37.

Guicharnaud, Jacques. "Raymond Queneau's Universe." *Yale French Studies* 8 (1951):38–47.

———. *Raymond Queneau.* New York: Columbia Univ. Press, 1965.

Gundolf, Friedrich. "Friedrich Schlegels romantische Schriften." In *Ironie als literarisches Phänomen,* edited by Hans-Egon Hass and Gustav-Adolf Mohrlüder, pp. 143–44. Cologne: Kiepenheuer & Witsch, 1973.

Gurewitch, Morton. "European Romantic Irony." Ph.D. diss., Columbia University, 1957.

Hackett, C. A. *Anthology of Modern French Poetry.* New York: Macmillan, 1956.

———. "Michaux and Plume." *French Studies* 17 (1963):40–49.

Handwerk, Gary J. *Irony and Ethics in Narrative: From Schlegel to Lacan.* New Haven: Yale Univ. Press, 1985.

Harrington, John P. "Pynchon, Beckett, and Entropy: Uses of Metaphor." *The Missouri Review* 5, no. 3 (Summer 1982):129–38.

Hayward, Susan. "Two Anti-Novels: *Molloy* and *Jacques le fataliste.*" In *Studies in Eighteenth-Century French Literature,* edited by J. H. Fox, M. H. Waddicor, and D. A. Watts, pp. 97–107. Exeter: Univ. of Exeter Press, 1975.

Hegel, G. W. F. "Irony." In *Aesthetics,* translated by T. M. Knox, pp. 64–69. Vol. 1. Oxford: Clarendon Press, 1975.

Heimrich, Bernhard. *Fiktion und Fiktionsironie in Theorie und Dichtung der deutschen Romantik.* Tübingen: Niemeyer, 1968.

Hélein-Koss, Suzanne. "Discours ironique et ironie romantique dans *Salammbô* de Gustave Flaubert." *Symposium* 40, no. 1 (Spring 1986):16–40.

Henriot, Emile. *Alfred de Musset.* Paris: Hachette, 1928.

Herschensohn, Michael. "Imagery in the Works of Alfred de Musset." Ph.D. diss., University of Pennsylvania, 1971.

Hesla, David. *The Shape of Chaos: An Interpretation of the Art of Samuel Beckett.* Minneapolis: Univ. of Minnesota Press, 1971.

Hewitt James R. "The Tropes of Self in the Poetry of Alfred de Musset." Ph.D. diss., New York University, 1973.

Hick, Francis S. "Baudelaire's *La Fanfarlo:* An Example of Romantic Irony." *French Review* 49, no. 3 (Feb. 1976):328–38.

———. "'La Beauté': Enigma of Irony." *Nineteenth-Century French Studies* 10, nos. 1–2 (Fall-Winter 1981–82):85–95.

Highnam, David. "*Jacques le fataliste:* Narrative Structure and New Physics." *Man and Nature* 2 (1984):15–26.

Hillen, Wolfgang. *Raymond Queneau: Bibliographie des études sur l'homme et son oeuvre.* Cologne: Edition Gemini, 1981.

Hokenson, Jan. "Three Novels in Large Black Pauses." In *Samuel Beckett: A Collection of Criticism,* edited by Ruby Cohn, pp. 73–84. New York: McGraw-Hill, 1975.

Houdebine, Jean-Louis. "Description d'un portrait." *Promesse,* num. spécial sur Michaux (Fall-Winter 1967):8–36.

Houston, John P. *Fictional Technique in France: 1802–1927.* Baton Rouge: Louisiana State Univ. Press, 1972.

Howe, Elizabeth A. "Irony in Michaux's *Plume.*" *The French Review* 56, no. 1 (May 1983):896–903.

Howells, Bernard. "Baudelaire: A Portrait of the Artist in 1846." *French Studies* 37, no. 4 (Oct. 1983):426–39.

Immerwahr, Raymond. "The Subjectivity or Objectivity of Friedrich Schlegel's Poetic Irony." *The Germanic Review* 26 (1951):173–91.

———. "Romantic Irony and Romantic Arabesque prior to Romanticism." *The German Quarterly* 42 (1969):665–84.

Ionesco, Eugène. "A propos de Beckett." *Cahiers de l'Herne* 31 (1976):149–51.

Jankélévitch, Vladimir. *L'ironie ou la bonne conscience.* 2d ed. Paris: Presses Univ. de France, 1950.

———. *L'Ironie.* Paris: Flammarion, 1964.

Janvier, Ludovic. *Pour Samuel Beckett.* Paris: Editions de Minuit, 1966.

Jasinski, René. *Les années romantiques de Th. Gautier.* Paris: Vuibert, 1929.

Jeune, Simon. "Aspects de la narration dans les premières poésies d'Alfred de Musset." *Revue d'Histoire Littéraire de la France* 76, no. 2 (March-April 1976):179–91.

Jones, Grahame C. *L'Ironie dans les romans de Stendhal.* Lausanne: Editions du Grand Chêne, 1966.

Juin, Hubert. "Le poème d'Alfred de Musset." *Europe* 55, nos. 583–84 (Nov.-Dec. 1977):147–54.

Kabelac, Sharon L. "Irony as a Metaphysics in *Le Neveu de Rameau.*" *Diderot Studies* 14 (1971):97–112.

Kahn, Gustave. "L'Ironie dans le roman français." *La Nouvelle Revue* 24 (1903):528–34.

Kavanaugh, Thomas. "*Jacques le fataliste:* An Encyclopedia of the Novel." In *Diderot: Digression and Dispersion,* edited by Jack Undank and Herbert Josephs, pp. 150–65. Lexington: French Forum, 1984.

Keffer, Charles. "Rencontre avec Raymond Queneau." *Romance Notes* 16 (1974):33–37.

Kenner, Hugh. *Samuel Beckett: A Critical Study.* Berkeley: Univ. of California Press, 1968.

Kern, Edith. "Moran-Molloy: The Hero as Author." In *Twentieth Century Interpretations of Molloy, Malone Dies, The Unnamable,* edited by J. D. O'Hara, pp. 35–45. Englewood Cliffs: Prentice-Hall, 1970.

———. *Existential Thought and Fictional Technique.* New Haven: Yale Univ. Press, 1970.

———. "Ironic Structure in Beckett's Fiction." *L'Esprit créateur* 11, no. 3 (Fall 1971):3–13.

Kierkegaard, Soren. *The Concept of Irony.* Bloomington: Indiana Univ. Press, 1965.

Knapp, Bettina. "Raymond Queneau." In *French Novelists Speak Out,* edited by Bettina Knapp, pp. 42–46. Troy, NY: Whitson, 1976.

Kusher, Eva. "L'Humour de Michaux." *The French Review* 40 (1967):495–504.

La Charité, Virginia A. *Henri Michaux.* Boston: Twayne, 1977.

Lacoste, Claudine. "L'ironie ludique chez Gautier." *French Literature Series* 14 (1987):83–95.

Laforgue, Jules. *Poésies complètes.* Edited by Pascal Pia. Vol. 1. Paris: Gallimard, 1970.

Lascaut, Gilbert. "Les monstres et l'Unheimliche." *Cahiers de l'Herne* 8 (1966):214–26.

Laudi, Jean. "Voyages." *Cahiers de l'Herne* 8 (1966):159–65.

Lautréamont, and Germain Nouveau. *OEuvres complètes.* Edited by Pierre-Olivier Walzer. Paris: Gallimard (Pléiade), 1970.

Lawlor, Patricia M. "Figuring (Out) Maldoror: 'Nous ne sommes plus dans la narration.' Rhetoric and Narration in the *Chants de Maldoror.*" *Nineteenth-Century French Studies* 16 (Spring-Summer 1988):372–78.

Lips, Marguerite. *Le Style indirect libre.* Paris: Payot, 1926.

Loy, J. Robert. *Diderot's Determined Fatalist.* New York: King's Crown Press, 1950.

———. "Jacques Reconsidered: Digression as Form and Theme." In *Diderot: Digression and Dispersion,* edited by Jack Undank and Herbert Josephs, pp. 166–79. Lexington: French Forum, 1984.

———. "A Select Bibliography of Critical Studies on *Jacques le fataliste,* 1936–1982." In *Diderot: Digression and Dispersion,* edited by Jack Undank and Herbert Josephs, pp. 278–82. Lexington: French Forum, 1984.

Lukács, Georg. *The Theory of the Novel.* Translated by Anna Bostock. Cambridge: M.I.T. Press, 1971.

Lussky, Alfred Edwin. *Tieck's Romantic Irony.* Chapel Hill: Univ. of North Carolina Press, 1932.

McHale, Brian. "Free Indirect Discourse: A Survey of Recent Accounts." *PTL* 3 (1978):249–87.

McIntyre, Sandye Jean. "The Comic Hero in Stendhal's *Le Rouge et le Noir.*" Ph.D. diss., Case Western Reserve University, 1974.

McKenna, Andrew J. "After Bakhtin: On the Future of Laughter." *University of Ottawa Quarterly* 53, no. 1 (Jan.-March 1983):67–82.

Madou, Jean-Pol. "Ironie socratique, ironie romanesque, ironie poétique." *French Literature Series* 14 (1987):62–73.

Magny, Claude-Edmonde. "L'Univers d'Henri Michaux et de Kafka." *Revue Internationale* 6 (Oct. 1946):240–44.

Man, Paul de. "The Rhetoric of Temporality." In *Interpretation: Theory and Practice,* edited by Charles S. Singleton. Baltimore: Johns Hopkins Univ. Press, 1969.

Marisell, André. *Beckett.* Paris: Classiques du XXe Siècle, 1963.

Matenko, Percy. *Tieck and Solger.* New York: Westermann, 1933.

Maurras, Charles. "Ironie et poésie." In *Barbarie et Poésie.* Paris: Nouvelle Librarie Nationale (Champion), 1925.

Mautner, Stephen. "The Story of the Compromised Author: Parabasis in Friedrich Schlegel and Denis Diderot." *Comparative Literature Studies* 16, no. 1 (March 1979):21–32.

Mellor, Anne K. *English Romantic Irony.* Cambridge: Harvard Univ. Press, 1980.

Mercier, Vivian. *The New Novel from Queneau to Pinget.* New York: Farrar, Strauss & Giroux, 1966.

———. *Beckett/Beckett.* New York: Oxford Univ. Press, 1977.

Micha, René. "Plume et les anges." *Cahiers de l'Herne* 8 (1966):143–58.

Michaux, Henri. *Qui je fus.* Paris: Gallimard, 1927.

———. *Passages.* Paris: Gallimard, 1963.

———. *Plume, précédé de Lointain intérieur.* Paris: Gallimard, 1963.

———. *L'Espace du dedans.* Paris: Gallimard, 1966.

———. "Quelques renseignements sur cinquante-neuf années d'existence." *Cahiers de l'Herne* 8 (1966):14–17.

———. *Connaissance par les gouffres.* Paris: Gallimard, 1967.

———. *Face aux verroux.* Paris: Gallimard, 1967.

———. *Emergences-Résurgences.* Geneva: Skira, 1972.

———. *La Vie dans les plis.* Paris: Gallimard, 1972.

Moreau, Pierre. "L'ironie de Musset." *Revue des Sciences Humaines,* num. spécial, no. 108 (Oct.-Dec. 1962):501–14.

Morier, Henri. "Ironie." In *Dictionnaire de poétique et de rhétorique,* pp. 555–95. 2d ed. Paris: Presses Univ. de France, 1975.

Muecke, Douglas. *The Compass of Irony.* London: Methuen, 1969.

———. *Irony.* London: Methuen, 1970.

———. "Analyses de l'ironie." *Poétique* 36 (Nov. 1978):478–94.

———. "Images of Irony." *Poetics Today* 4 (1983):399–413.

Mundhenk, Michael. "Samuel Beckett: The Dialectics of Hope and Despair." *College Literature* 8, no. 3 (Fall 1981):227–48.

Murat, N. *Michaux.* Paris: Editions Universitaires, 1967.

Musset, Alfred de. *Correspondance d'Alfred de Musset.* Edited by Leon Séché. Paris: Mercure de France, 1907.

———. *Poésies complètes.* Edited by Maurice Allem. Paris: Gallimard, 1957.

———. *OEuvres complètes.* Edited by Philippe Van Tieghem. Paris: Seuil, 1963.

Musset, Paul de. *Biographie d'Alfred de Musset.* In *Musset: Oeuvres complètes,* edited by Philippe Van Tieghem. Paris: Seuil, 1963.

Neptune, Patricia Mae. "Raymond Queneau's *Le Chiendent:* Parody as Réécriture carnavalesque." Ph.D. diss., University of Berkeley, 1986.

Neumann, Gui. "Diderot précurseur de Beckett: La modernité dans *Jacques le fataliste.*" *New Zealand Journal of French Studies* 4, no. 1 (May 1983):43–58.

Nist, John. "The Art of Chaucer: Pathedy." *Tennessee Studies in Literature* 11 (1966):44–57.

Odoul, Pierre. *Le Drame intime d'Alfred de Musset.* Paris: Pensée Universelle, 1974.

O'Hara, J. D. "About Structure in *Malone Dies.*" In *Twentieth Century Interpretations of Molloy, Malone Dies, The Unnamable,* edited by J. D. O'Hara, pp. 6–18. Englewood Cliffs: Prentice-Hall, 1970.

———, ed. *Twentieth Century Interpretations of Molloy, Malone Dies, The Unnamable.* Englewood Cliffs: Prentice-Hall, 1970.

Onimus, Jean. "Faire parler l'existence." In *Les Critiques de notre temps et Beckett,* edited by Dominique Nores, pp. 52–53. Paris: Garnier, 1971.

Ostrovsky, Erik. "Black Humor and the Modern Sensibility." *Modern Language Studies* 2 (1972):13–16.

Palante, Georges. "L'Ironie: étude psychologique." *Revue philosophique de la France et de l'étranger* 61 (Feb. 1906):147–63.

Panaitescu, Val. "Le Jeu des antimonies dans l'humour de Queneau." *Cahiers de l'Herne* 29 (1975):139–47.

Pascal, Roy. *The Dual Voice: Free Indirect Speech and its Functioning in the Nineteenth-Century European Novel.* Manchester: Manchester Univ. Press, 1977.

Passmore, John. *A Hundred Years of Philosophy.* Baltimore: Penguin, 1968.

Perruchot, Claude. "Le style indirect libre et la question du sujet dans *Madame Bovary.*" In *La Production du sens chez Flaubert,* edited by Claudine Gothot-Mersche, pp. 278–89. Paris: Union Générale d'Edition, 1975.

Peyre, Henri. *Connaissance de Baudelaire.* Paris: Corti, 1951.

———. "Baudelaire, Romantic and Classical." In *Baudelaire: A Collection of Critical Essays,* edited by Henri Peyre, pp. 19–27. Englewood Cliffs: Prentice-Hall, 1962.

———. *Literature and Sincerity.* New Haven: Yale Univ. Press, 1963.

———. "Laforgue among the Symbolists." In *Jules Laforgue: Essays on a Poet's Life and Work,* edited by Warren Ramsey, pp. 39–51. Carbondale: Southern Illinois Univ. Press, 1969.

Picon, Gaëton. *Panorama de la nouvelle littérature française.* Paris: Gallimard, 1960.

————. "Queneau plutôt à part." *Cahiers de l'Herne* 29 (1975):69–73.

Pierre-Sylvestre. "La fête quenienne: innocence et folie." *Cahiers de l'Herne* 29 (1975):154–62.

Pilling, John. *Samuel Beckett.* London: Routledge & Kegan Paul, 1976.

Pommier, Jean. *Alfred de Musset.* Oxford: Clarendon Press, 1957.

Porter, Dennis. "Flaubert and the Difficulty of Reading." *Nineteenth-Century French Studies* 12, no. 3 (Spring 1984):366–78.

Poulet, Georges. *Etudes sur le temps humain.* Edinburgh: Edinburgh Univ. Press, 1949.

————. "Henri Michaux et le supplice des faibles." *Cahiers de l'Herne* 8 (1966): 166–71.

————. *La Poésie éclatée.* Paris: Presses Univ. de France, 1980.

Prang, Helmut. *Die romantische Ironie.* Darmstadt: Wissenschaftliche Buchgesellschaft, 1980.

Priestley, J. B. *Literature and Western Man.* New York: Harper, 1960.

Prince, Gerald. "Noms équivoques dans l'oeuvre romanesque de Queneau." *Romance Notes* 11, no. 1 (Autumn 1969):1–3.

————. "Queneau et l'anti-roman." *Neophilologus* 55 (1971):33–40.

Prokop, Jan. "Raymond Queneau ou la présence au monde." *Kwartalnik Neofilologiczny* 18 (1971):11–24.

Queneau, Raymond. *Le Chiendent.* Paris: Gallimard, 1933.

————. *Les derniers jours.* Paris: Gallimard, 1936.

————. *Pierrot mon ami.* Paris: Gallimard, 1942.

————. *Exercices de style.* Paris: Gallimard, 1947.

————. *Chêne et chien.* Paris: Gallimard, 1952.

————. *Entretiens avec Georges Charbonnier.* Paris: Gallimard, 1952.

————. *Bâtons, chiffres et lettres.* Paris: Gallimard, 1965.

————. *Le Chien à la Mandoline.* Paris: Gallimard, 1965.

————. *Courir les rues.* Paris: Gallimard, 1967.

————. *Battre la campagne.* Paris: Gallimard, 1968.

————. *Si tu t'imagines.* Paris: Gallimard, 1968.

————. *Chêne et chien suivi de Petite cosmogonie portative.* Paris: Gallimard, 1969.

Queval, Jean. "Queneau explorateur." *Critique* 45 (Dec. 1984):1006–13.

————. *Raymond Queneau: Portrait d'un poète.* Paris: Veyrier, 1984.

Rabinovitz, Rubin. *The Development of Samuel Beckett's Fiction.* Urbana: Univ. of Illinois Press, 1984.

Raboin, Claudine, ed. *Les Critiques de notre temps et Kafka.* Paris: Garnier, 1973.

Ramazani, Vaheed. "Emma Bovary and the Free Indirect Si(g)ns of Romance." *Nineteenth-Century French Studies* 15, no. 13 (Spring 1987):274–84.

————. *The Free Indirect Mode: Flaubert and the Poetics of Irony.* Charlottesville: Univ. Press of Virginia, 1988.

Ramsey, W. J. *Jules Laforgue and the Ironic Inheritance.* New York; Oxford Univ. Press, 1953.

Ratermanis, J. B. *Etude sur le style de Baudelaire.* Baden-Baden: Editions Art et Science, 1949.

Ray, William. "A Writer of Our Times" [Diderot]. *L'Esprit créateur* 24, no. 1 (1984): 76–84.

Rees, Margaret. *Alfred de Musset.* New York: Twayne, 1971.

Richard, Jean-Pierre. *Etudes sur le romantisme.* Paris: Seuil, 1970.

Richards, I. A. *Principles of Literary Criticism.* 4th ed. New York: Harcourt Brace, 1930.

Richardson, Johanna. *Théophile Gautier: His Life and Times.* New York: Coward-McCann, 1958.

Riffaterre, Hermine B. *Orphisme dans la poésie romantique.* Paris: Nizet, 1970.

Riffaterre, Michael. "Rêve et réalité dans *l'Italia* de Théophile Gautier." *L'Esprit créateur* 3, no. 1 (Spring 1963):18–25.

———. "Flaubert's Presuppositions." *Diacritics* 11, no. 4 (Winter 1981):2–11.

Rincé, Dominique. *Baudelaire et la modernité poétique.* Paris: Presses Univ. de France, 1984.

Rongieras, E. "La tragi-comédie beckettienne." *Revue d'Histoire du Théâtre* 36, no. 1 (Jan.-March 1984):27–29.

Roudaut, Jean. "Notes à propos du titre d'un livre d'Henri Michaux: *L'Espace du dedans." Cahiers de l'Herne* 8 (1966):205–13.

Royère, Jean. *Poèmes d'amour de Baudelaire.* Paris: Albin Michel, 1927.

Roza, Robert. "A Freedom Beyond Dignity: Two Pataphysical Novels." *American Society of the Legion of Honor Magazine* 44 (1973):139–49.

Ruff, M. A. *Baudelaire.* Translated by Agnes Kertesz. New York: New York Univ. Press, 1966.

Sachs, Murray. "Flaubert's Laughter." *Nineteenth-Century French Studies* 3, nos. 1–2 (Fall-Winter 1974–75):112–23.

Sainte-Beuve, Charles Augustin. *Causeries du lundi.* Vol. 13. Paris: Garniers Frères, 1883.

Sareil, Jean. "Sur le comique de Queneau." *Cahiers de l'Herne* 29 (1975): 115–24.

Sartre, Jean-Paul. *L'Idiot de la famille.* Vol. 2. Paris: Gallimard, 1971.

Savater, Fernando. "Fatalité et liberté chez Diderot." In *Interpréter Diderot Aujourd'hui,* edited by Elizabeth Fontenay and Jacques Proust, pp. 233–46. Paris: Sycamore, 1984.

Schick, Constance G. "Irony as Auto-Deconstruction: A Look at Charles Cros' *Le Coffet de santal." French Literature Series* 14 (1987):116–23.

Schlegel, Friedrich von. *The Aesthetic and Miscellaneous Works.* Translated by E. S. Millington. London: H. G. Bohn, 1849.

———. *Literary Notebooks (1797–1801)*. Edited by Hans Eichner. Toronto: Univ. of Toronto Press, 1957.

———. *Kritische Friedrich Schlegel Ausgabe*. Vol. 2, edited by Hans Eichner, 1967; vol. 18, edited by Ernst Behler, 1963. Paderborn: Schöningh, 1967.

———. *Dialogue on Poetry and Literary Aphorisms*. Translated by Ernst Behler and Roman Struc. University Park: Pennsylvania State Univ. Press, 1968.

———. *Lucinde and the Fragments*. Translated by Peter Firchow. Minneapolis: Univ. of Minnesota Press, 1971.

Schnack, Arne. "Surface et profondeur dans *Mademoiselle de Maupin*." *Orbis Litterarum* 36, no. 1 (1981):28–36.

Schneider, Pierre. "Baudelaire, poète de la fragmentation." *Critique* 7, nos. 51–52 (Aug.-Sept. 1951):675–85.

Schor, Naomi, and Henry F. Majewskii, eds. *Flaubert and Postmodernism*. Lincoln: Univ. of Nebraska Press, 1984.

Séché, Leon. *Alfred de Musset*. Paris: Mercure de France, 1907.

Shattuck, Roger. "Superliminal Note [On 'Pataphysics]." *Evergreen Review* 4, no. 13 (May-June 1960):24–28.

Sheringham, Michael. *Beckett: Molloy*. London: Grant & Cutler, 1985.

Sherzer, Dina. *Structure de la trilogie de Beckett*. Paris: Mouton, 1976.

Shorley, Christopher. *Queneau's Fiction: An Introductory Study*. Cambridge: Cambridge Univ. Press, 1985.

Simon, Alfred. *Beckett*. Paris: Belfond, 1983.

Simon, John Kenneth. "Plume, sa vision." *Cahiers de l'Herne* 8 (1966):283–86.

Simonnet, Claude. *Queneau déchiffré*. Paris: Julliard, 1962.

———. "Note sur la genèse du *Chiendent*." *Europe* 61, nos. 650–51 (June-July 1983):44–46.

Smith, Albert B. *Ideal and Reality*. Gainesville: Univ. of Florida Press, 1969.

———. *Théophile Gautier and the Fantastic*. University, Miss.: Romance Monographs, 1977.

———. "Romantic Irony in Théophile Gautier's *Une larme du diable*." *French Literature Series* 14 (1987):74–82.

Smith, James. "Gautier, Man of Paradox." *L'Esprit créateur* 3, no. 1 (Spring 1963):34–39.

Sonnenfeld, Albert. "Romantisme (ou ironie): les épigraphes de 'Rouge et Noir.'" *Stendhal Club* 20 (1978):143–54.

Sperber, Dan, and Deirdre Wilson. "Les ironies comme mentions." *Poétique* 36 (Nov. 1978):399–412.

Sperry, Stuart M. "Toward a Definition of Romantic Irony in English Literature." In *Romantic and Modern: Revaluations of Literary Tradition*, edited by George Bornstein, pp. 3–28. Pittsburgh: Pittsburgh Univ. Press, 1977.

Spitzer, Leo. "The Style of Diderot." In *Linguistics and Literary History: Essays in Stylistics*, pp. 135–91. Princeton: Princeton Univ. Press, 1948.

———. *Etudes de style*. Paris: Gallimard, 1970.

Starobinski, Jean. *L'Oeil vivant*. Vol. 2. Paris: Gallimard, 1961.

Steinmetz, Jean-Luc. "La Poésie d'Henri Michaux." *Promesse*, num. spécial sur Michaux (Fall-Winter 1967):80–96.

Stendhal. *Romans et nouvelles*. Edited by Henri Martineau. Paris: Gallimard, 1952.

Sterne, Laurence. *The Life and Opinions of Tristram Shandy, Gentleman*. New York: Modern Library, 1950.

Strohschneider-Kohrs, Ingrid. "Zur Poetik der deutschen Romantik: Die romantische Ironie." In *Die Deutsche Romantik, Poetik, Formen und Motive*, edited by Hans Steffen, pp. 75–97. Göttingen: Vandenhoeck & Ruprecht, 1976.

———. *Die romantische Ironie in Theorie und Gestaltung*. 2d rev. ed. Tübingen: Niemeyer, 1977.

Szondi, Peter. "Friedrich Schlegel und die romantische Ironie." *Euphorion* 48 (1954):397–411.

Tartar, Maria M. "E. T. A. Hoffmann's 'Der Sandmann': Reflection and Romantic Irony." *Modern Language Notes* 95, no. 3 (1980): 585–608.

Tennant, P. E. *Théophile Gautier*. London: Athlone Press, 1975.

Thiher, Allen. *Raymond Queneau*. Boston: Twayne, 1985.

Thompson, A. R. *The Dry Mock: A Study of Irony in Drama*. Berkeley: Univ. of California Press, 1948.

Toesca, Maurice. *Alfred de Musset ou l'amour de la mort*. Paris: Hachette, 1970.

Trefil, James S. *From Atoms to Quarks*. New York: Scribners, 1980.

Turnell, Martin. *Baudelaire: A Study of His Poetry*. New York: New Directions, 1953.

———. *The Novel in France*. New York: Vintage Books, 1958.

———. "Madame Bovary." In *Madame Bovary and the Critics*, edited by B. F. Bart, pp. 144–68. New York: New York Univ. Press, 1966.

Undank, Jack. *Diderot: Inside, Outside, and In-Between*. Madison: Coda Press, 1979.

Van Tieghem, Philippe. *Musset*. Paris: Hatier, 1969.

Van Tooren, Marjolein. "Aspects métadiscursifs de l'ironie dans *Le Rouge et le Noir*." In *La Littérature des doubles*, edited by Leo H. Hoeck, pp. 110–26. Groningen: Instit. voor Romaanse Talen, 1985.

Vartanian, Aram. "*Jacques le fataliste*: A Journey into the Ramifications of a Dilemma." In *Essays on Diderot and the Enlightenment in Honor of Otis Fellows*, edited by John Pappas, pp. 325–47. Geneva: Droz, 1974.

———. "Diderot's Rhetoric of Paradox, or, The Conscious Automaton Observed." *Eighteenth-Century Studies* 14, no. 4 (1981):379–405.

———. "Diderot, or, The Dualist in Spite of Himself." In *Diderot: Digression and*

Dispersion, edited by Jack Undank and Herbert Josephs, pp. 250–68. Lexington: French Forum, 1984.

Verlaine, Paul. *OEuvres posthumes.* Paris: Messein, 1926.

Vesely J. "Denis Diderot et la mise en question du genre narratif du 18e siècle." *Philologia Pragensia* 24, no. 4 (1984):210–18.

Vivier, Robert. *L'Originalité de Baudelaire.* Brussels: Palais des Académies, 1952.

Voisin, Marcel. *Le Soleil et la nuit.* Brussels: Editions de l'Univ. de Bruxelles, 1981.

———. "Introduction à l'humour narratif de Gautier." *Bulletin de la Société Théophile Gautier* 6 (1984):21–41.

Walser, Martin. *Selbstbewusstsein und Ironie.* Frankfurt: Suhrkamp, 1981.

Ward, Hoover. "Irony and Absurdity in the Avant-Garde Theater." *The Kenyon Review* (Summer 1960):436–54.

Warning, Ranier. "Irony and the 'Order of Discourse' in Flaubert." *New Literary History* 13, no. 2 (Winter 1982):253–86.

———. "Reading Irony in Flaubert." *Style* 19, no. 3 (Fall 1985):304–16.

Warren, Robert Penn. "Pure and Impure Poetry." *The Kenyon Review* (Spring 1943):228–54.

Weinberg, Henry H. "Irony and 'Style Indirect Libre' in *Madame Bovary.*" *Canadian Review of Comparative Literature* 8, no. 1 (Winter 1981):1–9.

———. "Centers of Consciousness Reconsidered." *Poetics Today* 5 (1984):767–73.

Wellek, René. *A History of Modern Criticism (1750–1950).* Vol. 2. New Haven: Yale Univ. Press, 1955.

Wellershoff, Dieter. "Toujours moins, presque rien." *Cahiers de l'Herne* 31 (1976):169–82.

Werner, Stephen. *Diderot's Great Scroll: Narrative Art in Jacques le fataliste.* Banbury: Voltaire Foundation, 1975.

Wheeler, Kathleen M., ed. *German Aesthetic and Literary Criticism: The Romantic Ironists and Goethe.* Cambridge: Cambridge Univ. Press, 1984.

Wilde, Alan. *Horizons of Assent: Modernism, Postmodernism and the Ironic Imagination.* Baltimore: Johns Hopkins Univ. Press, 1981.

Wing, Nathaniel. "The Stylistic Function of Rhetoric in Baudelaire's *Au Lecteur.*" *Kentucky Romance Quarterly* 19 (1972):447–60.

———. "The Poetics of Irony in Baudelaire's *La Fanfarlo.*" *Neophilologus* 59 (1975):165–89.

Wolf, Fred A. *Taking the Quantum Leap.* New York: Harper & Row, 1981.

Wright, Andrew H. "Irony and Fiction." *Journal of Aesthetics and Art Criticism* 12 (Sept. 1953):111–18.

Ziegler, Heide. "Postromantic Irony in Postromantic Times." In *Representation and Performance in Postmodern Fiction,* edited by Maurice Couturier, pp. 85–98. Nice: Proceedings of the Nice Conference on Postmodern Fiction, 1982.

Zukav, Gary. *The Dancing Wu Li Masters.* New York: Bantam, 1979.

Index of Names